Bills of Lading Incorporating Charterparties

Melis Özdel

• H A R T •
PUBLISHING
OXFORD AND PORTLAND, OREGON
2017

Hart Publishing
An imprint of Bloomsbury Publishing Plc

Hart Publishing Ltd
Kemp House
Chawley Park
Cumnor Hill
Oxford OX2 9PH
UK

Bloomsbury Publishing Plc
50 Bedford Square
London
WC1B 3DP
UK

www.hartpub.co.uk
www.bloomsbury.com

Published in North America (US and Canada) by
Hart Publishing
c/o International Specialized Book Services
920 NE 58th Avenue, Suite 300
Portland, OR 97213-3786
USA

www.isbs.com

First published in hardback, 2015
Paperback edition, 2017

British Library Cataloguing-in-Publication Data
A catalogue record for this book is available from the British Library.

ISBN: PB: 978-1-50991-377-0
HB: 978-1-84946-679-0

Typeset by Compuscript Ltd, Shannon
Printed and bound in Great Britain by
Lightning Source UK Ltd

BILLS OF LADING INCORPORATING CHARTERPARTIES

Vessels very frequently serve under a long chain of charterparties and sub-charterparties. When this is the case, the legal issues are more convoluted than they might at first seem. Incorporation clauses are commonplace in bills of lading used in the tramp trade due to the desire to make this web of contracts back-to-back. The extent to which the terms of the charterparty referred to can be carried across to the bill of lading has, over the centuries, been hotly disputed in many jurisdictions. Entirely dedicated to the topic of the incorporation of charterparty terms into bills of lading, this book discusses and analyses the legal and practical issues surrounding this topic under English and US law. Through discussions on the incorporation of a wide range of different charterparty terms, the book combines the peculiar and sophisticated rules of incorporation with the legal and practical issues concerning shipping, international trade, arbitration and conflict of laws and jurisdiction.

To Professor Charles Debattista

PREFACE

This book is the product of my doctoral research in a territory that cuts across the boundaries of various areas of maritime law. It gives a detailed account of the English and US rules of incorporation through the examination of the essential links between the rules and the fundamentals of shipping, international trade and maritime conflict of laws and jurisdiction. An earlier version of this work was submitted as a PhD thesis in late 2010. Since then, the English and US rules of incorporation have attracted further judicial refinement. Also, recent years have seen an increasing interaction between the rules of incorporation and the enforcement of forum selection clauses in bills of lading. In this book, I have tried to chart these developments, while also discussing some additional points of interest based on the issues that await further judicial scrutiny.

These issues include the decision of Males J in *The Channel Ranger* [2014] 1 Lloyd's Rep 337. The decision introduces a relaxation of the description test, which was established more than a century ago with the leading House of Lords decision in *Thomas & Co v Portsea Steamship Ltd* [1912] AC 1. As the decision in *The Channel Ranger* has been appealed, it is now for the Court of Appeal to tell if this is the way forward. Further judicial developments also remain to be seen across the Atlantic in the wake of *Maroc Fruit Board SA v M/V Vinson* 2012 WL 2989195 (D Mass 2012)—the first US federal decision to distinguish the famous US Supreme Court decision in *The Sky Reefer* 515 US 528 (1998). It will be interesting to see the extent to which the former decision will affect the pro-arbitration policy primarily reflected by *The Sky Reefer* in the bill of lading context. No doubt the coming years will also show how far the Brussels I Revised Regulation will succeed in enhancing the enforcement of arbitration clauses incorporated into bills of lading. All these, and many other, recent developments have thrown up issues that have important links with the incorporation of charterparty clauses into bills of lading. This has necessitated extensive rewriting of all the chapters of my original thesis.

This book aims to offer a rigorous analysis of the rules of incorporation, with an eye to offering a practical and analytical framework for their current and future developments. I hope the book will be enlightening to practitioners and scholars alike.

I owe a great debt of gratitude to the many people who have assisted and encouraged me in the completion of this book. My deepest gratitude goes first to my PhD supervisor, Professor Charles Debattista of Stone Chambers, formerly Professor of Law at the University of Southampton, for his continuous guidance, support and encouragement, without which this book would not have been possible. It was a true privilege to have him as my supervisor, to work with him and to learn from him. Thank you so much for having faith in me.

I am grateful to the examiners of my PhD thesis, Professor Yvonne Baatz of the University of Southampton and Professor Andrew Tettenborn of Swansea University, for their insightful comments on my thesis during my viva voce examination. I am indebted also to Deborah Renshaw and Carolyn Fox for their invaluable assistance in the latter stages of preparation, especially for their careful reading of the manuscript. I would like to extend my thanks to Richard Hart and Rachel Turner, both of Hart Publishing, for their wonderful support and assistance.

My deepest debt is to my family. I am immensely grateful to my mother and father for their endless support and encouragement. Last, but not least, I want to thank my fiancé, for being a constant source of wisdom, joy and support.

The law is stated as of 1 June 2014.

Melis Özdel
8 June 2014
London

CONTENTS

TABLE OF CASES

United Kingdom

European Union Court of Justice

Alphabetical listing

Numerical listing

Singapore

United States of America

TABLE OF LEGISLATION

United Kingdom

Indonesia

United States of America

TABLE OF INTERNATIONAL CONVENTIONS, RULES ETC

Introduction

Vessels carry vast quantities of goods by virtue of the contracts of carriage evidenced under bills of lading. Frequently, the international sale of the goods is performed with reliance on these contracts, which usually pass through the hands of numerous traders. While the way international trade is conducted does not allow the holders to negotiate the bill of lading provisions with their respective carriers, incorporation clauses frequently stipulated thereunder also leave them wondering about the actual conditions of the carriage. The reason for this is that it has proved difficult for these parties to ascertain their rights and obligations under bills of lading, since they are seldom provided with copies of the charterparties to which bills of lading refer. Not surprisingly, this position has prompted a long array of disputes as to whether merely directing the holders to a charterparty is sufficient to bind them to the terms of this contract.

In the face of these difficulties and disputes, referring to a charterparty in order to make its provisions a part of bills of lading has been used as a contract drafting technique for a long time. Above all, it is no longer unexpected that the holders may be bound by a number of unseen charterparty provisions, so long as the bills of lading and the relevant charterparty overcome a set of hurdles, which are popularly known as the rules of incorporation. It is evident that the rules of incorporation have a large scale impact, not only on the contractual position of carriers and cargo interests, but also on relations between sellers and buyers. Equally evident is that the rules lead to a considerable number of discussions as to whether they are workable in the ongoing and fast-changing shipping and international trade practice. In particular, these rules raise various questions about the protection they afford to cargo interests, their contribution to the attainment of certainty in international trade and finally about their eventual implications.

In this book, the English and United States rules of incorporation are compared and examined mainly by reference to case law, statute and international Conventions. The English and US approaches towards the issues are usually explained conjunctively so as to convey to the reader a comparative evaluation of these jurisdictions in a more effective and simple manner. With a view to avoiding repetition, this method is employed particularly in cases where the courts of England and the United States provide similar answers to the questions posed. However, where there are considerable differences between English law and US law relating to a particular issue, the two approaches are considered separately.

A number of significant factors shape the suggestions raised in this study. To begin with, due consideration is given to the fact that the rules of incorporation need to be commercially workable, fair, simple, certain and consistent with each other. Priority is given to certainty and consistency by reason of the heavy reliance on the bills of lading as transferable instruments. Notably, whilst evaluating the issues, the sharp differences in the legal methods adopted in English law and US law are also highlighted. In this respect, specific account is given to the fact that US law takes the position of every subsequent holder as a basis when determining the incorporation issue, while English law rejects a resolution of the issue upon such variable grounds. In light of this observation, the central premise of the book is that neither the actual position of the bill of lading holders, nor their actual or constructive knowledge of the charterparty referred to, should be relevant in resolving the issues of incorporation. The justification for this is made on the grounds that a safer international trade environment can only be achieved upon the satisfaction of two conditions: the bill of lading needs to provide invariable terms of carriage to its every endorsee, and the intention of the original parties to bills of lading which can objectively be ascertained from the wording of the incorporation clause must always be regarded as 'paramount' in resolving the incorporation question. In order to reach the latter objective, this book goes on to suggest that charterparty clauses should not be decisive on incorporation.

The latest international attempt to unify the rules governing bills of lading, embodied in the United Nations Convention on Contracts for the International Carriage of Goods Wholly or Partly by Sea ('the Rotterdam Rules'), has shown a tendency to protect cargo interests against forum selection clauses. As a response to this, this book raises the suggestion that these movements should have been in the direction of limiting the incorporation and enforceability of the charterparty clauses the application of which results in the imposition of disproportionate and unforeseeable liabilities on the holders. With the Recast Regulation,[1] a more liberal approach to the enforcement of forum selection clauses has been taken. One incident during the carriage of goods by sea may affect several cargo interests holding bills of lading as their contract of carriage. Common sense dictates that, in such cases, all the claims of these cargo interests should be dealt with in one forum pursuant to one legal system provided in the bills of lading. If this cannot be achieved, there is no doubt that much expense will be wasted on litigation in a number of different jurisdictions, with the obvious risk of irreconcilable judgments over the same incident. Viewed particularly against this background, the Recast Regulation is applauded for enhancing the effectiveness of forum selection clauses in bills of lading.

As the underpinning of these findings, this book presents a detailed analysis of the rules of incorporation under five main chapters. The first chapter examines the methods by which the law governing the question of incorporation are determined. The second chapter analyses the formal requirements of incorporation, discussing the main question of what forms of charterparty and bill of lading are appropriate for incorporation. Leaving aside the formalities, the third chapter

[1] Regulation (EU) No 1215/2012 of the European Parliament and of the Council of 12 December 2012 on jurisdiction and the recognition and enforcement of judgments in civil and commercial matters (recast).

moves on to the construction of the incorporation wording in bills of lading. In so doing, it provides a guideline of the extent to which the charterparty provisions can be carried across to the bill of lading through the words of incorporation. At this stage the reader's attention is also drawn to how US and English courts read the incorporated charterparty provisions in the context of bills of lading. In light of these observations, the fourth chapter examines whether the charterparty provisions, or those in bills of lading, determine the scope of incorporation. Finally, the fifth chapter goes on to discuss how English and US courts resolve the inconsistencies between the express bill of lading provisions and those incorporated charterparty clauses.

1

The Law Governing the Incorporation Issue

The issue of governing law usually presents itself as a preliminary issue for the resolution of disputes arising from carriage of goods by sea. Usually connected to more than one state, such disputes routinely leave the courts and arbitrators with the task of determining which legal system should be selected as the law governing the dispute in question. English and US courts determine the governing law by reference to the conflict of laws rules of the forum.[1] When considered in an arbitration that has its seat in one of these jurisdictions,[2] this issue is not necessarily determined pursuant to the conflict of laws rules in the seat of the arbitration.

Under section 46(3) of the English Arbitration Act 1996 ('the 1996 Act'), arbitral tribunals have discretion to select the conflict of laws rules that they consider applicable to the dispute.[3] The 1996 Act does not, however, vest arbitral tribunals

[1] For US law, Restatement (Second) on Conflict of Laws, §§4(1), 6(1); *Klaxon Co v Stentor Electric Mfg Co* 313 US 487, 61 SCt. 1020, 1022 (US 1941). Federal courts sitting in admiralty apply 'federal maritime choice-of-law principles', which emanate from the US Supreme Court decision in *Lauritzen v Larsen* 345 US 571 (US 1953) and its progeny, see *Triton Marine Fuels Ltd SA v M/V Pacific Chukotka* 575 F 3d 409, 413 (4th Cir 2009); *Trans-Tec Asia v M/V Harmony Container* 518 F 3d 1120, 1124 (9th Cir 2008), *cert denied*, 129 SCt 628, 172 L Ed 2d 639 (US 2008), quoting *Gulf Trading & Transportation Co v Vessel Hoegh Shield* 658 F 2d 363, 366–67 (5th Cir 1981). For English law, see *The Star Texas* [1993] 2 Lloyd's Rep 445, 450 per Lord Steyn (CA); *Compagnie Tunisienne de Navigation SA v D'Armement Maritime SA* [1970] 2 Lloyd's Rep 99, 117 (HL); *Trafigura Beheer BV v Kookmin Bank Co* [2006] 1 CLC 1049, 1064 and 1069.

[2] Part I of the English Arbitration Act 1996 ('the 1996 Act'), which is entitled 'Arbitration pursuant to an arbitration agreement', only applies in its entirety to an arbitration that has its seat in England, Wales or Northern Ireland, see s 2(1) of the 1996 Act.

[3] Section 46 of the 1996 Act applies to arbitral tribunals sitting in England, Wales or Northern Ireland, see n 2. When exercising the discretion under s 46, the tribunal is not permitted to choose a legal system without resorting to any set of conflict of laws rules. See DAC (Departmental Advisory Committee) Report on Arbitration Law, paras 222–25; L Collins, *Dicey, Morris & Collins on the Conflict of Laws*, 15th edn (London, Sweet & Maxwell, 2012) paras 16-055 *et seq*. Nonetheless, this rule can be displaced by the parties, for s 46 of the 1996 Act is not mandatory. See Schedule I to the Act. See, as an example, Art 21(2) of the ICC Rules of Arbitration. The article rules out the necessity of resorting to a set of conflict of laws rules.

with such discretion in the case of an express or implied[4] choice of law[5] by the parties.[6] The same is also true in cases where the parties have agreed to make the resolution of their disputes subject to 'such other considerations agreed by them or determined by the tribunal'.[7] In these circumstances, the arbitral tribunal is required, by virtue of section 46(1) of the 1996 Act, to determine the dispute in accordance with such choice or agreement by the parties. In the absence of such choice or agreement, maritime arbitrators sitting in London generally resort to the English conflict of laws rules to determine the governing law.[8]

On the other side of the Atlantic, as with federal courts sitting in admiralty, maritime arbitrators sitting in New York usually apply 'federal maritime choice-of-law rules'.[9] A choice-of-law clause in a maritime contract is enforceable except in cases where the enforcement of the clause would be unreasonable and unjust or where the clause is invalid due to reasons such as fraud or public policy.[10] In the absence of a choice-of-law clause, the law governing the dispute is determined through the evaluation of the connecting factors established by the Supreme Court decision in *Lauritzen v Larsen* and its progeny.[11]

[4] For implied choice of law, see the decision in *Compagnie Tunisienne de Navigation SA v Compagnie d'Armement Maritime SA* [1970] 2 Lloyd's Rep 99 (HL), where their Lordships took the view that forum selection clauses were persuasive in determining the law applicable to the contract. This approach survives the Convention on the law applicable to contractual obligations 1980 ('the Rome Convention') and Regulation on the law applicable to contractual obligations 2008 ('Rome I'). See *Egon Oldendorff v Libera Corporation* [1996] 1 Lloyd's Rep 380, where an arbitration clause providing for arbitration in London was taken as an implied choice of English law, in the absence of any 'compelling indications to the contrary in the other terms of the contract or the surrounding circumstances of the transaction'.

[5] This is usually taken to refer to the laws of a country. See C Ambrose et al, *London Maritime Arbitration*, 3rd edn (London, Informa Law, 2009) ch 5, n 10.

[6] Section 46(1)(a) of the 1996 Act.

[7] Section 46(1)(b) of the 1996 Act. The parties can thus invite the tribunal to resolve their dispute *ex aequo et bono* or as *amiable compositeur*.

[8] See Ambrose et al (n 5) ch 5, n 10.

[9] *The M/V Reliant*, Society of Maritime Arbitrators ('SMA') Award No 3077, 12 May 1994. For federal maritime choice-of-law rules, see n 1.

[10] See *Chan v Expeditions Inc* 123 F 3d 1287, 1297 (9th Cir 1997). There, it is also stated that federal common law follows the approach taken in Restatement (Second) On Conflict of Laws. Under Restatement (Second) On Conflict of Laws §187(1) courts must honour the parties' choice of law where the issue is 'one which the parties could have resolved by an explicit provision in their agreement directed to that issue'. Where the issue is not one which can be resolved by an explicit provision, the courts must still honour the parties' choice of law unless 'the chosen state has no substantial relationship to the parties or the transaction and there is no other reasonable basis for the parties' choice or application of the law of the chosen state would be contrary to a fundamental policy of a state which has a materially greater interest than the chosen state in the determination of the particular issue', see ibid, at §187(2).

[11] See n 1. Similar considerations arise also in the context of the Rome Convention and Rome I. See, in general, Arts 4 and 5 of Rome I and Art 4 of the Rome Convention. For contracts of carriage see Art 5 of Rome I and Art 4(4) of the Rome Convention. Rome I is the shorthand form of Regulation (EC) No 593/2008 of the European Parliament and of the Council of 17 June 2008 on the law applicable to contractual obligations. Rome I has been the successor to the Convention on the law applicable to contractual obligations ('the Rome Convention'). There is no complete succession in that the Rome Convention is still applicable to contracts concluded before 17 December 2009. See Art 28 of Rome I. It must be noted that for present purposes, the rules do not contain any substantial differences.

It is clear from these observations that, in most cases, an implied or express choice of law puts the question of governing law to rest, with the arbitral tribunals and courts usually honouring the parties' choice of law. In the absence of a choice of law, a dispute arising from a contract would be governed by the law that is 'sufficiently' connected to the contract.[12] However theoretically straightforward these rules may be, they are somewhat unhelpful in determining the law governing the incorporation of charterparty provisions into bills of lading. What law is applied to this issue is of great importance to both carriers and bill of lading holders, given the drastic differences between US law and English law with respect to the rules of incorporation. As will be discussed in this chapter, the English and US approaches to determining the law governing the incorporation issue are also significantly different from each other.

I. Choosing the Law Governing the Incorporation Issue

In determining the applicable law of contracts, English courts draw guidance mainly from Rome I,[13] which has been the successor to the Rome Convention.[14] The conflict of laws rules at common law can, however, find room for application where a dispute comes within the purview of the exceptions envisaged in Rome I. Included in the exceptions are arbitration and choice-of court-agreements.[15] The courts can also resort to the common law rules in cases where they are mandatorily applicable or where their avoidance runs counter to public policy.[16]

[12] In determining the law which is sufficiently connected to the relevant contract, English courts are guided by Rome I and the Rome Convention, see n 11, whilst US courts apply a somewhat different test for this purpose, see n 1.

[13] See n 11.

[14] ibid.

[15] See Art 1(2)(e) of Rome I. See also Art 1(2)(c) thereof, which excludes 'obligations arising under bills of exchange, cheques and promissory notes and other negotiable instruments to the extent that the obligations under such other negotiable instruments arise out of their negotiable character'. So far as English law is concerned, this exclusion does not apply to bills of lading, for they are not treated as negotiable instruments. Although Art 1(2)(d) of Rome I contains the same exception, Recital 9 of Rome I clarifies that the exclusion applies to bills of lading only 'to the extent that the obligations under the bill of lading arise out of its negotiable character'.

[16] See Art 7(2) of the Rome Convention and Arts 9(1) and 9(2) of Rome I, both of which talk of overriding mandatory provisions of the law of the forum. *The Hollandia* [1983] 1 Lloyd's Rep 1 (HL), where the House of Lords struck down the choice-of-law clause in a bill of lading providing for Dutch law on the basis of Art III/8 of the Hague-Visby Rules, which prohibited carriers from contracting out or lessening their liabilities otherwise than as provided therein. For more discussions on this decision see Chapter 5. See also Art 9(3) of Rome I, which gives the courts the discretion to apply the overriding mandatory provisions of the country where the contract is or has been performed to the extent that 'those overriding mandatory provisions render the performance of the contract unlawful'.

As with other contractual disputes arising from bills of lading, the issues as to the validity and scope of an incorporation clause in a bill of lading are decided pursuant to the law applicable to the bill of lading. Under English law, this proposition draws support from Article 12 of Rome I, which provides that the law applicable to a contract governs, inter alia, the interpretation and performance of the contract.[17] In US law, the main underpinning is section 186 of the Restatement (Second) on Conflict of Laws, whereby all contractual issues are resolved in accordance with the applicable law of the contract in question.[18]

When determining the applicable law, English courts give a much greater weight to party autonomy: whilst US federal courts sitting in admiralty do not enforce a choice of law clause which they consider unreasonable and unjust,[19] English courts do not take specific account of the reasonableness of choice-of-law clauses. Nor do English courts set aside a choice-of-law clause on the basis of inequality of bargaining power between the parties. In principle, the law chosen by the parties need not even have any connection with the parties or their contract.[20] English courts to date have been inclined to uphold the parties' choice of law to the extent that doing so is not contrary to the English mandatory rules and public policy.[21] Party autonomy has its roots in English common law,[22] although it is now mainly based on Article 3(1) of Rome I, which sets out the freedom of choosing the applicable law on similar grounds.

The choice of law can be either express or implied.[23] In US law, the incorporation of the Hague Rules into the bill of lading may indicate an implied choice of US law.[24] Arbitration clauses in a bill of lading may also give rise to an inference that the law of the seat of the arbitration is intended to be the applicable law of the contract contained in or evidenced by the bill of lading.[25] English courts have also drawn such an inference from arbitration clauses both before and after the adoption of the Rome Convention.[26] In general terms, English courts have long acknowledged that tacit agreements of the parties on the choice of law are enforceable provided that the choice is reasonably certain.[27] In the wake of

17 See n 11.

18 See n 10.

19 See n 10.

20 See *Vita Food Products Inc v Unus Shipping Co Ltd* [1939] 63 Ll L Rep 21, 28.

21 ibid. See also *Bas Capital Funding Corporation v Medfinco Ltd* [2004] 1 Lloyd's Rep 652, 678.

22 See n 20.

23 For US law, see Restatement (Second) On Conflict of Laws §187, comment a. For English law, see Art 3(1) of Rome I.

24 See *Duferco Steel Inc v M/V Kalisti*, 121 F 3d 312, 325 (7th Cir 1997). See also M Davies and R Force, 'Forum Selection Clauses in International Maritime Contracts' in M Davies (ed), *Jurisdiction and Forum Selection in International Maritime Law: Essays in Honour of Robert Force* (The Hague, Kluwer Law International, 2005) 36.

25 See *Splosna Plovba v Agrelak S.S. Corp* 381 F Supp 1368, 1975 AMC 146, 148 (SDNY 1974).

26 See n 4.

27 See n 4. In *Amin Rasheed Shipping Corporation v Kuwait Insurance Co*, the House of Lords inferred from the parties' use of the Lloyd's Standard Marine policy that the parties had intended English law to govern their contract, see [1983] 2 Lloyd's Rep 365, 369 (HL). In some other cases, English courts have also drawn an inference that interrelated contracts are intended to be governed

Rome I, the English position on implied choice of law is still the same, for there is no substantial difference between the Rome Convention and its successor, Rome I, on this matter. For this reason, forum selection clauses still usually tip the balance in favour of the law of the chosen forum. In the absence of an implied or express choice of law, the applicable law of the bill of lading is the law with which the bill of lading and the parties are 'sufficiently' connected, although the English courts' consideration of 'connecting factors' will be somewhat different from that of US courts.[28]

When the applicable law of the bill of lading can be decided with any of the identified methods, there are no formidable obstacles in addressing the incorporation issue: the law chosen or, in its absence, the law that is sufficiently connected to the parties and the bill of lading, should govern all the issues arising from bills of lading, including the incorporation issue.[29] The solution based on the applicable law of the bill of lading might at first seem straightforward. However, where a bill of lading that is silent as to its governing law refers to a charterparty which contains an implied or express choice of law, can the applicable law of the bill of lading be ascertained with reasonable certainty?

With almost all charterparties containing either an express or implied choice of law, the applicable law of the bill of lading, in most cases, depends on whether the charterparty is incorporated. When this is the case, the solution based on the applicable law of the bill of lading is inevitably unhelpful, for it does no more than raise a circular argument: what should come first 'the decision on incorporation' or 'the decision on the applicable law'? To solve this conundrum, English law and US law set diametrically opposed presumptions on the applicable law of the bill of lading in such cases. In both jurisdictions, the courts have been inclined to avoid

by the same applicable law, see *The Njegos* [1936] P 90, 100; *The Elli 2* [1985] 1 Lloyd's Rep 107 (CA); *Egon Oldendorff v Libera Corporation* [1996] 1 Lloyd's Rep 380 (QBD); *The SLS Everest* [1981] 2 Lloyd's Rep 389, 392 (CA).

[28] For English law, see Art 5 of Rome I. The 'connecting factors' are also used at English common law when determining the governing law, see *Bonython v Commonwealth of Australia* [1951] AC 201, 219; *Whitworth Street Estates (Manchester) Ltd v James Miller Partners Ltd* [1970] AC 583 (HL). See also n 11. For US law, see Restatement (Second) On Conflict of Laws §188. In this respect, US courts are also guided by the connecting factors established in *Lauritzen v Larsen* 345 US 571 (US 1953). See also *Trans-Tec Asia v M/V Harmony Container* 2008 AMC 684, 518 F 3d 1120, 1124–25 (9th Cir 2008). For US law, see also n 1.

[29] For US law, see *Liverpool and London SS Protection and Indemnity Association Ltd v Queen of Leman MV* 296 F 3d 350, 353–54 (5th Cir 2002). There, the court applied US law to the issue of whether maritime lien existed, despite the English law being chosen as the applicable law. The reasoning of the court was that the choice of law clause contained an exception which gave the insurers the right to assert lien in 'any jurisdiction in accordance with the local law'. English law was, therefore, not applied to that particular issue in order not to render the lien provisions 'meaningless'. Under English law, the parties have the right to choose more than one legal system to govern different issues in their contracts, see Art 3(1) of Rome I. This right is also recognised at English common law, *Hamlyn v Talisker Distillery* [1894] AC 202, 207 (HL). In both jurisdictions, where the choice of law clauses stipulate only one system of law, the courts are inclined to give a wider scope to these choices. For US law, see *Bominflot Inc v The M/V Henrich S* 465 F 3d 144, 148–50 (4th Cir 2006) and *Sembawang Shipyard Ltd v Charger Inc* 955 F 2d 983, 986 (5th Cir 1992). For English law, see *Egon Oldendorff v Libera Corp* [1996] 1 Lloyd's Rep 380, 387. See also Art 12 of Rome I.

the application of the law of the forum to the question of incorporation. The justification for this has been the well-accepted view that every contract should be governed by its own applicable law.[30]

II. Presumptive Solutions in Ascertaining the Applicable Law: the English Approach

A. The Use of Putativity

Under English law, the hostility towards the application of *lex fori* to the question of incorporation has its main justification under Article 10(1) of Rome I. The Article provides that the material validity of a contract, or of any term of a contract, is to be decided pursuant to the law that would govern it if the contract or the term therein were valid. Under Article 10(2), there is an exception to the application of this putative thinking: the application of the putative applicable law can be set aside when it is established that (1) it is unreasonable to apply the putative applicable law to the issue of contract formation and (2) the parties have not consented to be bound by such a contract or term.[31]

Article 10(2) of Rome I raises one question: could bill of lading holders make use of this provision in order to avoid the putative applicable law that supposedly governs the bill of lading by reason of an implied or express choice of law in the charterparty? The holders may view it as a compelling argument to assert that being subject to the choice of law made under the charterparty is unreasonable, particularly since they seldom have the chance and the right[32] to see the charterparty referred to. The prospects for the success of such an argument are, however, illusory in the wake of *The Epsilon Rosa*.[33] There, the holders unsuccessfully relied on this provision to prevent the incorporation of the charterparty arbitration clause providing for arbitration in London.[34] The arbitration clause carried with

[30] For English law, see *Amin Rasheed Shipping Corp v Kuwait Insurance Co* [1984] AC 50, 64 (CA) quoted in A Briggs, 'Wider Still and Wider: The Bounds of Australian Exorbitant Jurisdiction' [1989] *LMCLQ* 216, 219. For US law, see Restatement (Second) On Conflict of Laws §186.

[31] The opposing parties need to establish *consensus ad idem* in light of the legal system of their habitual residence. Article 10(2) of Rome I, and *Mackender v Feldia* [1972] 2 QB 590 (CA).

[32] *Finska Cellulosaforeningen v Westfield Paper Co Ltd* [1940] 2 All ER 473, where it was held that the seller was not obliged to tender a copy of the charterparty referred to in the bill of lading to the buyer. However, see the views of Donaldson J in *SIAT di dal Ferro v Tradax Overseas SA* [1978] 2 Lloyd's Rep 470 at 492, which suggest that the buyer will be entitled to sight of the relevant charterparty where the incorporated charterparty terms affect the rights of the buyer. See also C Debattista, *Bills of Lading in Export Trade*, 3rd edn (Haywards Heath, Tottel Publishing, 2008) para 8.34; M Bridge, *Benjamin's Sale of Goods*, 8th edn (London, Sweet & Maxwell, 2010) para 19-041.

[33] *The Epsilon Rosa* [2002] 2 Lloyd's Rep 701.

[34] ibid.

it an implied choice of English law, and therefore the putative proper law of the bill of lading was English law. Steel J took the view that applying the putative proper law of the bill of lading, namely English law, to the question of incorporation was not unreasonable, although the holders did not even have a chance to see the terms of the charterparty referred to. In support of this, Steel J also held that the arbitration clause was not, contrary to the holders' submission, unreasonable, given the wide use of arbitration clauses in charterparties. To support the application of the putative proper law to the question of incorporation, Steel J relied on Article 8(1) of the Rome Convention, which now has its counterpart in Article 10(1) of Rome I.[35]

Steel J did not err in applying the putative 'proper law'[36] of the bill of lading, although his reliance on the Rome Convention was, with respect, at odds with the fact that arbitration and choice-of-court agreements were excluded from the scope of the Rome Convention.[37] English common law rules should be applied to the question of incorporation of an arbitration clause or a jurisdiction clause. In *The Epsilon Rosa* guidance should thus have been drawn from the English common law rules, which would also entail the application of English law as the putative proper law of the bill of lading. Had Rome I been in force then, Steel J's reliance on Article 10(1) of Rome I would have attracted the same argument by reason of Article 1(2)(e) thereof.

At English common law, the initial step in resolving contractual disputes is also to rely on the proper law of the contract.[38] Where the proper law of the bill of lading cannot be ascertained due to an implied or express choice of law in the charterparty referred to in the bill of lading, the common law rules also dictate the application of the putative proper law of the bill of lading—the law that would govern the bill of lading if the charterparty were incorporated. There is a trio of judicial decisions, namely *The Parouth*, *The Atlantic Emperor* and *The Heidberg*, that supports the putative thinking. The foundations of this putative thinking were laid in *The Parouth*.[39] There, the dispute was whether leave for service of the claim form out of the jurisdiction should be granted on the basis that there was arguably a binding charterparty governed by English law.[40] The order to serve the claim form out of the jurisdiction was granted on the grounds that if the dispute as to the validity of the charterparty were brought before an English court, it would apply English law as the putative proper law of the charterparty. The charterparty contained an arbitration clause providing for London arbitration,

[35] ibid, at 704.

[36] In the context of Rome I and the Rome Convention, the law governing the contractual obligations is referred to as the 'applicable law' of the contract, whilst at common law it is generally referred to as the 'proper law' of the contract. For the purposes of this chapter, the proper law and applicable law will be used interchangeably.

[37] See Art 1(2)(d) of the Rome Convention.

[38] Collins (n 3) para 32-008.

[39] *The Parouth* [1982] 2 Lloyd's Rep 351 (CA).

[40] See CPR r 6.36 and CPR PD 6B 3.1(6)(c), which was formerly RSC, Ord 11, r 1(1)(f).

and this had 'the important result of making the proper law of this dispute probably ... English law'.[41]

The facts of *The Atlantic Emperor*[42] were different from those of *The Parouth.* Here, the key issue before the Court was not whether there was a binding contract with an arbitration clause: it was whether there was a valid arbitration clause in a binding contract of sale. This issue was also addressed pursuant to the putative proper law of the contract, namely English law, which would be the law governing the entire contract if the arbitration clause were valid.[43]

HHJ Diamond QC in *The Heidberg* followed the reasoning of the Courts in *The Parouth* and *The Atlantic Emperor* when determining the law governing the question of whether a charterparty arbitration clause was incorporated into the bill of lading.[44] Thus, he took the view, *obiter*, that the question of incorporation should be decided according to the putative proper law of the bill of lading—ie on the assumption that the arbitration clause was part of the bill of lading.[45] However, he could not apply this putative reasoning to the question of incorporation. In *The Heidberg* there were two charterparties that could potentially be incorporated into the bill of lading and each of these charterparties contained an arbitration clause pointing to different proper laws. For this reason, HHJ Diamond QC was left with two alternative methods: application of the 'putative objective proper law', which would be the law governing the bill of lading if the possible incorporation were ignored,[46] or of the law of the forum (*lex fori*). HHJ Diamond QC preferred the latter method and applied English law as *lex fori*, taking specific account of the potential effects of incorporation on the governing law of the bill of lading.[47] He took this stance also because there were insufficient legal grounds justifying the application of a legal system other than English law.[48]

[41] See [1982] 2 Lloyd's Rep 351 (CA), Ackner LJ at 353.

[42] *The Atlantic Emperor* [1989] 1 Lloyd's Rep 548 (CA).

[43] ibid.

[44] *The Heidberg* [1994] 2 Lloyd's Rep 287.

[45] ibid, at 304.

[46] This would be French law, which has the 'closest and most real connection with the bill of lading', see ibid.

[47] It is possible that HHJ Diamond QC took this stance also because arbitration and jurisdiction agreements are not viewed as neutral factors. See n 39.

[48] Having decided that the ruling of the French court on the question of incorporation was binding, the views of HHJ Diamond QC on incorporation were in fact *obiter*. See also *The Wadi Sudr* [2009] 1 Lloyd's Rep 666, where Gloster J held that the Spanish court's preliminary decision on incorporation was not binding and that the bill of lading incorporated the charterparty arbitration clause providing for arbitration in London. The Court of Appeal overturned the judgment, holding that the preliminary ruling of the Spanish court on incorporation fell within the scope of Council Regulation (EC) No 44/2001 of 22 December 2000 on jurisdiction and the recognition and enforcement of judgments in civil and commercial matters ('the Brussels I Regulation'). See [2009] EWCA Civ 1397. One of the main foundations for this decision was the opinion of the Advocate General in *The Front Comor.* There, the Advocate General took the view that a preliminary ruling in relation to the applicability of an arbitration clause was to be categorised as within the Brussels I Regulation where the merits of the dispute fell within the scope of the Brussels I Regulation. See Case C-185/07 *The Front Comor* [2009] 1 AC 1138. Recently, the Brussels I Regulation has been subject to reform, and its reformed version, Regulation (EU) No 1215/2012 of the European Parliament and of the Council of 12 December 2012

Recently, Gloster J in *The Wadi Sudr* followed this presumptive reasoning, although there were in fact two charterparties that could potentially be incorporated: the head time charterparty and the voyage charterparty.[49] Unlike the position in *The Heidberg*, here English law governed both charterparties by implication: both charterparties contained a London arbitration clause. Thus, there was no basis for the application of *lex fori* or 'putative objective proper law'. Applying English law to the question of incorporation, Gloster J held that the arbitration clause in the sub-charterparty was incorporated into the bill of lading,[50] despite the decision of the Spanish court—as the court first seised[51]—that no arbitration clause was incorporated. Although the judgment was later overturned by the Court of Appeal on the grounds that the Spanish court's decision on incorporation was binding upon English courts,[52] the views expressed on incorporation were in line with *The Parouth* and its progeny.

On the whole, one can easily see that the presumptive thinking adopted by English courts creates circularity:[53] it initially permits incorporation of the charterparty referred to in order to decide what law governs the bill of lading, and later it throws back the question of incorporation with a view to deciding whether the charterparty is actually incorporated into the bill of lading. This presumptive thinking produces effective and pragmatic results[54] in 'one-contract-cases', where the question of incorporation arises from contracts made between the same parties, or where the dispute is merely concerned with the incorporation of standard rules accessible to both parties.[55] The same is also true of disputes concerned with the existence and validity of a single contract. In all these cases, not only does this hypothetical thinking help the parties achieve what they have sought to attain with their flawed contracts, it also prevents them from avoiding the contractual obligations that they have undertaken.[56]

on Jurisdiction and the recognition and enforcement of judgments in civil and commercial matters ('the Brussels I Recast') will apply from 10 January 2015. The Brussels I Recast removes the effects of *The Wadi Sudr* by expressly providing that the courts of a Member State will not be bound by the decision of the court of another Member State on the validity and scope of an arbitration agreement. See Recital 12 of the Brussels I Recast.

[49] In this case, the *Wadi Sudr* was in fact subject to three charterparties. The vessel had successively been time chartered, sub-time chartered and voyage chartered. There, neither party raised the suggestion that the sub-time charter was relevant. See para 111 of the judgment.

[50] See Chapter 2.

[51] See Chapter 2.

[52] [2009] EWCA Civ 1397.

[53] For a similar view, see McKeown J in *Trans-Tec Asia v M/V Harmony Container* 518 F 3d 1120, 1124 (9th Cir 2008).

[54] See EB Crawford, 'The Uses of Putativity and Negativity in the Conflict of Laws' (2005) 54(4) *ICLQ* 829.

[55] See *Habas Sinai ve Tibbi Gazlar Isthisal Endustri AS v Sometal SAL* [2010] EWHC (Comm) 29, para 13, where the rules of an organisation of which both parties are members, or those standard terms which are relevant in a particular area of business, were treated as standard terms. See also *The Athena (No 2)* [2006] EWHC 2530 (Comm).

[56] See n 54.

This presumptive thinking does not, however, yield such welcome results in 'two-contract-cases', where a contract seeks to incorporate another contract to which either only one or none of the parties is a party. The incorporation of charterparties into bills of lading comes under this type of case. Almost invariably, bills of lading refer to a charterparty which has been entered into either between one of the parties to the bill of lading and a third party or between two other parties.[57] Here the main cause for concern is evident: given that bill of lading holders hardly ever have the chance and the right to see the charterparty provisions referred to, the use of putative proper law is a stumbling block for the holders to foresee what law is applicable to the question of incorporation—the answer to which greatly affects their rights and obligations in the bill of lading. Furthermore, this line of presumptive thinking runs counter to the well-settled rule established by the Court of Appeal in *The Varenna:* the bill of lading is the primary document to be considered when deciding the issue of incorporation.[58] Since the inquiry as to the incorporation, in essence, needs to start and end with the terms of the bill of lading,[59] it is hard to justify the operation of the putative proper law, which is based on the supposedly incorporated charterparty.[60]

B. An Alternative Method to the Use of Putativity

Following the leading judgment in *The Njegos*,[61] earlier decisions adopted a different method when choosing the legal system to apply to the question of incorporation.[62] Where the charterparty referred to in a bill of lading contained an express or implied choice of English law, English courts in these decisions raised an inference that the shipper and the carrier also intended English law to govern the bill

[57] It is important to note that where the parties to a charterparty are the same as those of the bill of lading, as between these parties, the contract of carriage is, in principle, the charterparty. In such cases, the bill of lading merely operates as a receipt of the goods shipped. For English law see *Rodocanachi v Milburn* (1886) 18 QBD 67 (CA). For US law, see *The Fri* 154 F 333, 337 (2d Cir 1907); *Associated Metals & Minerals Corp v S/S Jasmine* 983 F 2d 410, 413 (2d Cir 1993), quoting *Nichimen Co v MV Farland* 462 F 2d 319, 328 (2d Cir 1972). Under English law, when a charterer buys goods covered by a bill of lading while using the vessel as a 'general ship', the carriage of the goods will, however, be governed by the bill of lading, see *Calcutta Company Limited v Andrew Weir & Co* [1910] 1 KB 759, quoted in Debattista (n 32) paras 8.7–8.12.

[58] *The Varenna* [1983] QB 599 (CA).

[59] As will be seen elsewhere in this book, the question of whether a charterparty provision incorporated into the bill of lading is binding upon the holder may depend, to some extent, on the charterparty provision. Thus, the courts may need to turn to the charterparty in order to determine whether a specific provision therein falls within the general and/or special words of incorporation in the bill of lading. See Chapters 3 and 4.

[60] See *The Varenna* [1983] QB 599 (CA) at 616.

[61] (1935) 53 Ll L Rep 286.

[62] For the cases that followed the approach taken in *The Njegos*, see *The Elli 2* [1985] 1 Lloyd's Rep 107 (CA); *The Freights Queen* [1977] 2 Lloyd's Rep 140; *The San Nicholas* [1976] 1 Lloyd's Rep 8 (CA).

of lading.[63] The courts accepted that such an inference could only be drawn in the absence of an expressed intention in the bill of lading.

One can see the rationale for this inference by looking at the reason for the use of incorporation clauses in bills of lading: to ensure that the shipowner who is also the carrier under a bill of lading could turn to and face bill of lading holders on the same terms as under its charterparty. To put it simply, this inference was drawn in order to give business efficacy to the incorporation clauses in bills of lading, particularly in cases where the charterparty is governed by English law expressly or by implication. Lurking behind this method was also the view that the bill of lading and the charterparty to which it referred were closely connected to each other.

In terms of the result it creates, this method is not in fact distinct from the use of putative proper law of the bill of lading, for it also yields equally unwelcome consequences to bill of lading holders. Furthermore, this method attracts criticism due to the almost mechanical inference that the shipper and carrier intended that the proper law of the bill of lading would be the same as that of the charterparty referred to. The view that there is a 'close connection' between these contracts is also hard to justify. The content and the form of a bill of lading could in many cases suggest a different applicable law from that of the charterparty referred to.[64] This is particularly so because, in most cases, the parties to the bill of lading are not even the same as those of the charterparty.[65] Furthermore, it is clear from the rules of incorporation that irrespective of the intention of the parties to the relevant charterparty, the bill of lading may simply fail to incorporate the charterparty.[66] As will be explained later in this book, what the parties to the relevant charterparty intended as to the incorporation of the charterparty into the bill of lading cannot be taken into account when deciding the question of incorporation.[67] When this is accepted, there is no room for the argument that these two contracts are 'closely connected' to justify such a mechanical inference as suggested by *The Njegos*.

There is a further difficulty with the mechanical inference adopted in *The Njegos*. It violates the principle that a bill of lading holder who is not also the shipper should only be bound by those provisions that are expressed or incorporated into the bill of lading. Hence, the intention of the shipper and the carrier as to governing law should not be binding upon the holder who is not also the shipper, unless the intention can objectively be ascertained from the bill of lading provisions. The inference that the shipper and carrier intended that the proper law of the bill of lading would be the same as that of the charterparty referred

63 Where a bill of lading is transferred to a consignee or an endorsee, an expressed intention in the bill of lading as to choice of law should also be binding upon such a party. See *The Channel Ranger* [2014] 1 Lloyd's Rep 337 at para 33.

64 *The Metamorfosis* [1953] 1 Lloyd's Rep 196.

65 See n 57.

66 See Chapter 4.

67 ibid.

to is therefore not a sound justification for the application of English law to the question of incorporation.

The High Court of Singapore in *The Dolphina* has recently followed this unattractive mechanical inference when holding that English law was the proper law of the bill of lading. There, the bill of lading was silent as to its governing law, while English law governed the charterparty by implication due to the London arbitration clause contained therein. The decision that English law governed the bill of lading was alternatively supported by the general words of incorporation, which were held to be apt to incorporate the implied choice of English law in the relevant charterparty.[68]

Recently, Males J in *The Channel Ranger* also considered the question of whether a bill of lading was governed by English law.[69] This question arose as a result of the carriers' application for service of the claim form on the bill of lading holders out of the jurisdiction. In support of this application, the carriers relied on the two jurisdictional gateways in paragraph 3.1(6) of Civil Procedure Rules Practice Direction (CPR PD) 6B. In specific terms, they submitted that (a) the carriers' claim against the bill of lading holders was made in respect of a contract contained in the bill of lading which was governed by English law, and that (b) the bill of lading contained an exclusive jurisdiction clause in favour of English courts. Both submissions depended on the question of incorporation of the charterparty into the bill of lading: the charterparty referred to in the bill of lading contained an express choice of English law, as well as an exclusive jurisdiction clause designating English courts.

When holding that the carriers had an 'extremely' strong case that the bill of lading was subject to an express choice of English law, Males J did not adopt the mechanical inference suggested in *The Njegos*. To put it simply, instead of adopting the mechanical inference that the parties to the bill of lading intended the proper law of the charterparty to govern the bill of lading—which was the case in *The Njegos*—he correctly took specific account of the expressed intention in the bill of lading: there were two express and specific references in the bill of lading to the governing law clause of the charterparty to which it referred. With respect, there was, however, a logical leap in the solution offered: nowhere in the judgment was there any discussion on the law governing the question of incorporation. Without any reference to the putative proper law of the bill of lading, English law was assumed to be the law governing this question. Since the decision has been referred to the Court of Appeal, the way in which the Court of Appeal will determine the law governing the incorporation issue remains to be seen.

[68] For the description test see Chapter 3.

[69] *The Channel Ranger* [2014] 1 Lloyd's Rep 337.

III. Presumptive Solutions in Ascertaining the Applicable Law: the US Approach

In stark contrast to the previous and current English law positions, US courts to date have ascertained the law governing the question of incorporation without paying attention to the probable effects of incorporation on bills of lading. Hence, the courts apply the law that would govern the bill of lading as if the probable effects of the purported incorporation were completely ignored—ie the 'putative objective proper law' in the words of HHJ Diamond QC in the English case of *The Heidberg.*[70]

In *Duferco Steel Inc v M/V Kalisti* the Court adopted this putative thinking when addressing the incorporation issue pursuant to the law that would govern the bill of lading if the incorporation of the charterparty referred to therein were completely ignored.[71] In *Trans-Tec Asia v M/V Harmony Container* the US Court of Appeals for the Ninth Circuit also adopted the same line of reasoning.[72] There, the Court was concerned with the question of whether a bunker agreement incorporated a choice-of-law clause providing for US law. The Court refused to apply US law to this question. The view of the Court was that before taking the anterior step of determining its incorporation, the choice-of-law clause providing for US law could not be considered as part of the bunker agreement. Hence, there was no room for application of US law to the question of incorporation, with the Court taking the view that applying US law to this question would 'put the tug before the barge'.[73] Consequently, the incorporation issue was resolved by reference to Malaysian law, which had 'the most significant relationship' with the bunker agreement, since both the flag of the vessel and the nationality of her owner were Malaysian.

From a practical standpoint, bill of lading holders are better positioned when the US putative thinking is adopted. With the holders seldom having any means of knowing the provisions of the charterparty referred to, the US approach has, in fact, much to commend it. When compared with its counterpart under English law, the US putative thinking enables the holders to anticipate what legal system will govern the question of incorporation and whether the bill of lading is apt to bring in the provisions of the charterparty to which it refers. It is also in line with the widely accepted 'bill-centric' view that the inquiry as to the incorporation should start and end with the provisions of the bill of lading.[74]

[70] [1994] 2 Lloyd's Rep 287, 304.

[71] *Duferco Steel Inc v M/V Kalisti* 121 F 3d 321, 324–25 (7th Cir 1997).

[72] *Trans-Tec Asia v M/V Harmony Container* 583 F 3d 1120 (9th Cir 2008).

[73] ibid, at 1124.

[74] Similar to the legal position under English law, this so called 'bill-centric' approach also dominates the US legal position, see *Keytrade US Inc v Ain Temouchent M/V* 2005 AMC 948 (5th Cir 2005). However, in certain circumstances, this inquiry embraces construction of both the charterparty and bill of lading, *Cia Platamon v Empresa Colombiana* 1980 AMC 538, 539 (SDNY 1979). For English

On the surface, there seems to be no difficulty in applying the US approach. The reason for this is that the bill of lading can have its own proper law when functioning as a contract of carriage, without the need for incorporation of an express or implied choice of law clause from a charterparty.[75] Thus, there would appear to be no reason for relying on the implied or express choice-of-law clause in the charterparty referred to when addressing the incorporation issue. However, on closer examination, it would appear that this approach creates yet another logical shortcoming: it loses sight of the fact that an implied or express choice-of-law clause in a charterparty referred to in a bill of lading has the probable effect of being the main determinant of the proper law of the bill of lading. When compared with its counterpart under English law, the US putative reasoning goes in the opposite direction, although it gives rise to similar circular arguments.

IV. Conclusion: Should the Putative Proper Law Lead the Way?

Despite the circular arguments they create, these two methods show that where the proper law of the bill of lading depends on the incorporation of an implied or express choice of law clause in a charterparty, there are actually two different putative proper laws: the one that would govern the bill of lading, if the incorporation were ignored, and the other that supposedly becomes the governing law of the bill of lading when the charterparty is assumed to have been incorporated. In a case where each of the two different putative proper laws points to a different legal system, is it possible to say that the putative proper law can be ascertained with reasonable certainty?

This perplexing problem does not usually arise in 'one-contract cases', where the parties seek to incorporate either a contract that they have previously made or a set of standard terms accessible to both parties.[76] As is clear from *The Parouth* and *The Atlantic Emperor*, the same is also true of cases relating to the material validity of a contract or of a term contained therein: in all these cases, there is potentially one proper or putative proper law of the contract to resolve the question of incorporation or of material validity.[77]

law, see *The Varenna* [1983] 1 Lloyd's Rep 416, 419 (CA). For further discussions on this issue, see Chapter 4.

[75] See *Amin Rasheed Shipping Corp v Kuwait Insurance Co* [1984] AC 50, 64 (HL), which supports the proposition that every contract must be governed by its proper law.

[76] See n 55.

[77] See n 55 and the 'Report on the Convention on the law applicable to contractual obligations' by Mario Guiliano, Professor, University of Milan, and Paul Lagarde, Professor, University of Paris I, OJ C282, 31/10/1980 P. 0001-0050 ('Guiliano-Lagarde Report'), para 3 under the heading 'Article 3 Freedom of Choice'.

As will be recalled, the English decisions in *The Heidberg* and *The Wadi Sudr* suggest that the application of the putative reasoning be extended to the cases of the incorporation of charterparties into bills of lading, which are, in essence, 'two-contract cases'. In light of the observations, one should pause to consider whether this extended application of the putative reasoning gives rise to more problems than it solves: with bill of lading holders seldom having the chance and the right to see the provisions of the charterparty referred to, the English putative reasoning creates a stumbling block for the holders in foreseeing what law is applicable to the question of incorporation. No such problems arise in cases where the bill of lading contains an express or implied choice-of-law clause. It is likely that English courts in such cases will apply the law chosen in the bill of lading to the question of incorporation, irrespective of an implied or express choice of law in the charterparty referred to.

Whether or not the bill of lading contains an express or implied choice of law, US courts in any case ascertain the law governing the question of incorporation without taking into account the charterparty referred to and its terms. The US approach thus leaves no such stumbling block in the way of the holders to anticipate whether a charterparty can be part of the bill of lading to govern their legal relations with their respective carriers. However, one might argue that this approach is also not immune from criticism, for it places too much emphasis on the position of the holders, while giving too little regard to incorporation clauses in bills of lading.

At this point, a question arises as to whether the application of the *lex fori* to the question of incorporation is the way forward. Given that the application of the *lex fori* does no more than provide fortuitous solutions to the incorporation issue,[78] US and English courts have so far shown a preference for the putative proper law. However, where the putative proper law of the contract cannot be ascertained with reasonable certainty, no law other than the *lex fori* can apply to this question.

This chapter examined briefly the English and US conflict-of-law rules on the law applicable to the question of incorporation. In the following chapters, the significance of this issue will be seen more clearly with a detailed examination of the issues surrounding the incorporation of charterparty clauses into bills of lading.

[78] As was also raised by HHJ Diamond QC in *The Heidberg* [1994] 2 Lloyd's Rep 287, 303.

2

Choosing the Charterparty to be Incorporated

Where a vessel is subject to at least one charterparty, it is likely that the carriage of goods by sea will be subject to at least two separate contracts: the charterparty and the contract of carriage contained in or evidenced by a bill of lading.[1] There is nothing unusual or surprising about the existence of two separate contracts in such cases, given that bills of lading seldom remain in the hands of charterers. A shipowner who is also the carrier in the bill of lading habitually seeks to link these two contracts by inserting an incorporation clause into the bill of lading. Making these contracts back-to-back means that the shipowner can turn to and face bill of lading holders on the same terms as their respective charterparties. In practical terms, the upshot of this is that where the shipowner cannot collect the sums due under the charterparty from the charterer due to either legal[2] and/or practical reasons, the shipowner can instead recover these sums against the bill of lading holder. Alternatively, the shipowner can have recourse against the shipper—if different from the charterer and the holder—who was the original party to the bill of lading.[3]

At this juncture, one may take the view that the incorporation of charterparty provisions into the bill of lading will not be a matter of concern to the holder unless a shipowner looks to the bill of lading holder for the collection of these sums. However, concerns over the terms of carriage, coupled with the incorporation issue, will arise also in cases where the goods covered by the bill of lading are short-delivered or delivered in damaged condition. In a cargo claim against the

[1] It is possible that such a contract of carriage can instead be contained in or evidenced by another type of transport document, such as a seawaybill, ship's delivery order or electronic transport document. For the purposes of our discussion reference is made to bills of lading. By and large, the rules of incorporation can equally apply to incorporation clauses contained in these types of transport document.

[2] See Chapter 5 on cesser clauses.

[3] See s 3(3) of the Carriage of Goods by Sea Act ('COGSA') 1992. It must be noted that the bill of lading in such cases operates only as evidence of contract of carriage. The upshot of this is that the shipper's liability towards the carrier will not exclusively be subject to the terms of the bill of lading and those of the charterparty to which it refers. Where the shipper is the charterer, his/her contract of carriage will in most cases be the charterparty. When this is the case, such a shipper is not treated as an original party to the bill of lading, particularly since the bill of lading in his/her hands merely operates as a receipt. See Chapter 1, n 57.

carrier under a bill of lading, the holder would naturally wish to know what terms govern his/her legal relation with the carrier. Where the bill of lading contains an incorporation clause, as it inevitably does in tramp trade, the holder will not be able to see the terms of carriage in their entirety. Such a bill of lading does not set out all the charterparty provisions referred to *in extenso*. It does no more than direct the holder to a separate contract, a charterparty, with a view to incorporating its provisions. The holder's position is made worse by the fact that a copy of the charterparty referred to hardly ever travels with the bill of lading.[4]

In search of the overall contractual picture, the holder may also find that the incorporation clause is of no assistance as to which charterparty the bill of lading actually refers to: whatever effect this may have on the holder, incorporation clauses may not contain any charterparty details. Where the bill of lading is silent as to which charterparty it seeks to incorporate, the initial question for the holder is: can a bill of lading with such an incorporation clause incorporate any charterparty? To put it another way, is there a condition to identify the charterparty for its incorporation into the bill of lading? If this question is answered in the affirmative pursuant to the law governing the incorporation issue,[5] the holder of such a bill of lading should no longer be concerned about incorporation, since no charterparty will be incorporated in such cases. If the answer to this question is 'no', then the holder will need to move on to the second question: where the vessel is subject to more than one charterparty, which charterparty should be incorporated?

Undoubtedly, the rules of incorporation relating to this question are essential for the holder, as well as for the carrier, both of whom would wish to be certain about their respective legal positions. From the perspective of a shipowner who is also the carrier under a bill of lading, this issue is of particular importance: it would be in his/her best interest to know if the rules of incorporation facilitate the incorporation of his/her charterparty, which is the head charterparty, as opposed to others in the picture. If the rules do not assist the shipowner in achieving the incorporation of the head charterparty, he/she will need to make sure that the details of the head charterparty are provided in the incorporation clause. To make this happen, an astute shipowner would stipulate in the head charterparty that the charterer must present for signature bills of lading that contain an incorporation clause with the details of the head charterparty.

It is very common for charterparties to be concluded by means of a fixture recap that refers to a charterparty previously made by the parties or to a standard form charterparty. Equally common is that an informal fixture is concluded over the telephone, and that this oral contract subsequently is set out in a formal charterparty signed by the parties. Where the rules of incorporation point to a charterparty that is not reduced to writing or not signed by the parties, is such a charterparty capable of being incorporated into a bill of lading? Leaving aside the considerations as to the form of the charterparty, can a charterparty which

[4] See n 8 below.
[5] See Chapter 1.

has been rescinded, rectified, amended, or that has become null and void be incorporated? Are the incorporation clauses construed in such a way that these charterparties can be incorporated?

It is clear that the answer to the first question radically affects the chances of the holder obtaining a copy of the charterparty referred to. In practical terms, it is unlikely that a holder will be provided with the terms of such a charterparty contained in a recap telex, while this will be impossible where the charterparty referred to has not even been reduced to writing. As regards the second question, it also has a profound effect on the legal position of the holder vis-à-vis the carrier. This is particularly the case where a charterparty has been amended after the bill of lading was issued and transferred to the holder. To accept that such a charterparty is capable of being incorporated with its amendments would undoubtedly cause difficulties for the holder when deciding whether to demand delivery of the goods and/or to make a claim under the bill of lading. In the context of the international sale of goods, the same is also true of a buyer who has to decide whether he/she should take up and pay for the bill of lading tendered by his/her seller. Even if the sale contract requires the tender of a copy of the charterparty referred to for payment together with the bill of lading,[6] the buyer will not be certain about the terms of carriage on tender of documents if such future amendments to the charterparty are also capable of being incorporated. Thus, the first question has a knock-on effect on the reliability and transferability of bills of lading in international sale of goods, given the buyer's rational reluctance to accept a contract of carriage whose terms are exposed to future changes.

The question as to whether a charterparty that has been rectified, rescinded or become null and void can be incorporated is important in three respects: first, if the answer to this question is 'no', pursuant to the rules of incorporation, the holders will have a potential plea when seeking to defeat incorporation. Secondly, from the perspective of shipowners seeking to bind the holders with their respective charterparties, the answer to this question has an impact on their decision as to whether they should try to keep their charterparties in force for incorporation purposes. Finally, the answer to this question reveals the nature of the incorporation of charterparties into bills of lading: is it the incorporation of only the contractual provisions that remain in effect in the contract from which they are incorporated, or is it the incorporation of a set of provisions which may not even originate from a contract?

This chapter will address the first step in the rules of incorporation to be followed by the holders before tracing down the missing parts of their respective contracts of carriage. It also provides guidance to carriers regarding the formal

[6] Where the sale contract is silent on this matter, the seller is not obliged to tender a copy of the charterparty referred to in the bill of lading. See *Finska Cellulosaforeningen v Westfield Paper Co Ltd* [1940] 2 All ER 473. See also Chapter 1, n 32. If, under the sale contract, the buyer is to arrange and pay for the carriage of the goods, the buyer cannot insist on the tender of a certain type of transport document in particular form, since these matters are entirely within the control of the buyer. See *Glencore v Lorico* [1997] 2 Lloyd's Rep 386 (CA).

requirements of incorporation that need to be fulfilled in order to use the provisions of a charterparty against the holders. In this chapter, the following issues will be examined: first, the question of whether a charterparty needs to be specified in the incorporation clause for its incorporation into the bill of lading will be analysed. The outcome of this analysis will be that, save in exceptional circumstances, the charterparty has to be identified in US law, while there is no such requirement under English law. With reference to this requirement in US law, further discussions will be made on how the charterparty needs to be identified for incorporation. At this stage, reference will also be made to the canons of construction with a view to discussing how ambiguous and inaccurate statements in the incorporation clauses are dealt with under English law and US law. Secondly, given that the charterparty need not be identified under English law and exceptionally under US law, the issue of which charterparty is to be chosen for incorporation when the bill of lading is of no assistance will be examined. Thirdly, for the purposes of deciding whether there are any other formal requirements for a charterparty to be incorporated, the question will be: can a bill of lading incorporate a charterparty that (1) is not reduced to writing before the bill of lading is issued, (2) is contained in or evidenced by fax, telex or email exchanges, (3) is amended before or after the bill of lading is issued, or (4) is rescinded, terminated or becomes null and void?

The first part of this chapter will discuss the question of whether US and English rules of incorporation require charterparties to be specified under the bill of lading.

I. Does the Charterparty Need to be Identified in the Bill of Lading?

A. Overview

A bill of lading is not the only guidance for the holder to find the terms of carriage in their entirety, where it has an incorporation clause. The position of such a holder is made worse by the fact that the incorporation clauses typically do not even provide the details of the charterparty to be incorporated. This problem frequently arises where the vessel is subject to more than one charterparty. On the question of why the incorporation clauses are habitually left blank in such cases, HHJ Diamond QC in *The Heidberg* said:[7]

> Typically the owner has no knowledge of the sub-charter and the shipper has no knowledge of the head charter. One may suspect that in these circumstances the date has not been filled in since the parties, or more probably their agents at the port of shipment,

[7] *The Heidberg* [1994] 2 Lloyd's Rep 287, 308.

were unable to agree which charter-party was to be identified in the bill. If each had been asked, each would have given a different answer.

Against this backdrop, an astute bill of lading holder would pause to consider whether the bill of lading could incorporate before starting to be concerned about which charterparty could potentially be incorporated. At this initial stage, it is not so much a question of which charterparty is sought to be incorporated as much as whether *any* charterparty can be incorporated through an incorporation clause that does not identify any charterparty. If the lack of, or insufficiency of, charterparty details in the bill of lading prevents incorporation, the question of which charterparty will not arise. Hence, a holder whose bill of lading does not meet such formal requirements will not need to be concerned with any other rules of incorporation. Whether or not there are such formal requirements under the rules of incorporation, the holders may also need to consider whether the incorporation clause can be rendered void for uncertainty: this question will arise in cases where the details contained therein are inaccurate and/or where the words of incorporation are somewhat ambiguous.

As a starting point, the question will be whether US law and English law require the charterparty to be specified in the incorporation clause for incorporation. Thereafter, the extent to which inaccuracies or ambiguities in the incorporation clause can be fatal to incorporation will be analysed. Finally, considering the likelihood of encountering such omissions in practice, a further analysis will be conducted into the possibility of incorporating a charterparty in cases where the terms of the contract of carriage, including the incorporation clause, are mistakenly not printed on the reverse side of the bill of lading.

B. Is there a Condition to Identify the Charterparty?

From the standpoint of the holders, the rule that the charterparty has to be identified in the bill of lading for its incorporation is favourable in many respects. Even though this requirement does not guarantee obtaining a copy of the relevant charterparty,[8] it at least provides reliable guidance to the holders whilst they are seeking a copy of the charterparty. With this requirement, it also becomes likely that the holders will be subject to a firm contractual position vis-à-vis their respective carriers. The practical explanation for this is that the incorporation clause cannot in most cases properly identify a charterparty which is not yet in existence by the time the bill of lading is issued. This requirement thus urges the

[8] See *Thyssen Inc v M/V Markos N* 1999 AMC 2515 (SDNY 1999) *aff'd sub nom Thyssen Inc v Calypso Shipping Corp SA* 310 F 3d 102 (2d Cir 2002), *cert denied* 123 SCt 1573, 155 L Ed 2d 312 (US 2003), which involved a carrier who refused the request of the holder to have a copy of the charterparty referred to. A similar situation also arose in the English case of *The Wadi Sudr* [2009] 1 Lloyd's Rep 666, where the request of the shipowner who was also the carrier under the bill of lading to have a copy of the voyage charterparty was rejected. Nonetheless, the bill of lading was held to incorporate the voyage charterparty.

carrier to conclude the charterparty by the time the bill of lading is issued and also to overcome the practical barriers mentioned by HHJ Diamond QC in *The Heidberg*.[9]

As between the shipowner and charterer, the condition to identify the charterparty for incorporation also has a significant impact on their legal relations. This is especially the case where the charterer is required by the terms of the charterparty to issue bills of lading with an effective incorporation clause.[10] In these circumstances, the charterer's obligation to issue and present[11] such a bill of lading will be harder to satisfy where the rules of incorporation require that the charterparty be sufficiently identified in the bill of lading.[12] Depending on the terms of the charterparty, the charterer's failure to satisfy this obligation may give the shipowner the right to refuse to sign the bill of lading.[13] Furthermore, to the extent that the bill of lading imposes on the shipowner greater obligations than those assumed under the charterparty, the shipowner will in most cases be entitled to recover from the charterer the losses that he/she incurred vis-à-vis the holder.[14]

i. The Position in US Law

In US law, the general rule is that identification of the charterparty in the bill of lading is a condition for incorporation. Approaching the question of

[9] See n 7.

[10] See, for instance, clause 20(b) of the Asbatankvoy Charterparty.

[11] In some cases, it may be the charterer who issues and signs the bill of lading without having to present it to the master or to the shipowner's agent for signature; see, for instance, *The Heidberg* [1994] 2 Lloyd's Rep 287, 311.

[12] See for English law, *The Garbis* [1982] 2 Lloyd's Rep 283 and for US law, *Field Line (Cardiff) v South Atlantic SS Line* 201 F 301, 306 (5th Cir 1912).

[13] If a charterparty requires the master to sign bills of lading 'as presented', the master is entitled to refuse to sign those bills of lading which are 'manifestly' inconsistent with the charterparty and/or which contain extraordinary terms. See under English law *The Ikariada* [1999] 2 Lloyd's Rep 365, 372; *The Berkshire* [1974] 1 Lloyd's Rep 185, 188; *The Anwar Al Sabar* [1980] 2 Lloyd's Rep 261, 265. Where a charterparty contemplates that the bill of lading to be issued thereunder will have a particular content, such as the details of the charterparty for incorporation purposes, the master will have the right to refuse to sign a bill of lading that does not provide those details. For English law, see *The Garbis* [1982] 2 Lloyd's Rep 283, 288. In US law, the master's obligation to sign the bill of lading as presented survives even in cases where the bill of lading conflicts with the provisions of the charterparty. Where the charterparty requires that the charterparty be identified in the bill of lading, it is likely that the master's refusal to sign a bill of lading that does not contain such identification will not constitute a breach. See *Field Line (Cardiff) v South Atlantic SS Line* 201 F 301, 306–07 (5th Cir 1912). See also J Cooke et al, *Voyage Charters*, 3rd edn (London, Informa Law from Routledge, 2007) paras 21.118–21.125.

[14] In the context of voyage charters, these losses can be recovered on the basis of breach of contract. For English law, see *Moel Tryvan v Kruger* [1907] 1 KB 809 (CA). The reasoning adopted in *Moel Tryvan v Kruger* has generally been followed by US courts, see *Field Line (Cardiff) v South Atlantic SS Line* 201 F 301, 306–07 (5th Cir 1912). In the context of time charters, these losses can alternatively be claimed under an implied or express indemnity, see *The Caroline P* [1984] 2 Lloyd's Rep 466. For US law, see *D/S Ove Skou v Hebert* 365 F 2d 341 (5th Cir 1966).

incorporation under contract law principles[15] and fairness to the parties,[16] US courts require that the incorporation clauses make an adequate[17] and clear[18] reference to an identifiable[19] charterparty in 'unmistakable language'.[20] This requirement survives in cases where the vessel is subject to only one charterparty.[21] Moreover, such is the strictness of this rule that it finds application even in cases where it is the holder in favour of the incorporation of the charterparty terms into the bills of lading.[22] Where a bill of lading contains an incorporation clause but does not identify any charterparty, the courts raise the prima facie inference that there is no intention to incorporate any charterparty.[23]

It would appear that the underlying purpose of this rule is to alleviate, at least to some extent, the unfairness of binding the holders with charterparty terms that they have no means of knowing.[24] Since this relief is exclusively intended for such holders, US courts[25] depart from this rigid requirement (a) where the holder is certain about the charterparty that the bill of lading seeks to incorporate and (b) where the incorporation is invoked against a bill of lading holder who is not a 'stranger' to the relevant charterparty.[26] For present purposes, the operation of the first limb of the exception will first be explained briefly.

a. Is There Certainty as to Which Charterparty is Intended to be Incorporated?

On the question of the circumstances in which US courts can find that there is no confusion as to which charterparty is intended, the decision of US Court

[15] *Volgotanker Joint Stock Company v Vinmar International Limited* F Supp 2d, 2003 WL 23018790 (SDNY 2003); *Midland Tar Distillers, Inc v M/T Lotos* 362 F Supp 1311, 1313 (SDNY 1973).

[16] *The Michael Thanasis* 311 F Supp 170, 175 (DC Cal 1970).

[17] *Coastal States Trading Inc v Zenith, SA* 446 F Supp 330, 338 (SDNY 1977).

[18] *Dun Shipping Ltd v Amerada Hess Shipping Corp Hovensa LLC and ABC Corp* 234 F Supp 2d 291, 296 (SDNY 2002); W Poor, *American Law of Charter Parties and Ocean Bills of Lading*, 5th edn (New York, Matthew Bender, 1968) 72.

[19] *Volgotanker Joint Stock Company v Vinmar International Limited* F Supp 2d, 2003 WL 23018790 (SDNY 2003); *Southwestern Sugar & Molasses Co v Eliza Jane Nicholson* 1955 AMC 746 (SDNY 1954).

[20] See *Son Shipping Co Inc v De Fosse & Tanghe* 1952 AMC 1931, 1932 (2d Cir 1952); *Import-Export Steel Corp v Mississippi Valley Barge Line Co* 1966 AMC 237, 240 (2d Cir 1965). See also MF Sturley, *Benedict on Admiralty*, vol 2A (New York, Matthew Bender, 2007) s 184, paras 17-61, 17-62.

[21] *Hawkspere Shipping Company Limited v Intamex SA* 330 F 3d 225, 2003 AMC 1374 (4th Cir 2003); *Macsteel International USA Corp v M/V Jag Rani* 2004 AMC 220 (SDNY 2003).

[22] See eg *United States v Cia Naviera Continental SA* 1962 AMC 2403 (SDNY 1962).

[23] *Amoco Oil Company v MT Mary Ellen* 1982 AMC 1758, 1761 (SDNY 1981); *Amoco Overseas Co v ST Avenger* 1975 AMC 782, 387 F Supp 589 (SDNY 1975).

[24] *New York Marine Managers Inc v Ektrans Int'l Transp & Trade Inc* 1989 WL 4030 (SDNY 1989); M Davies (ed), *Jurisdiction and Forum Selection in International Maritime Law: Essays in Honour of Robert Force* (The Hague, Kluwer Law International, 2005) 28–29.

[25] Arbitrators sitting in New York under the rules of the Society of Maritime Arbitrators also generally adopt this view; see *In Re Arbitration between Amoco Transport Company and Amoco Iran Oil Company* SMA No 2315 (10 October 1986).

[26] *Associated Metals and Minerals Corp v M/V Venture* 554 F Supp 281, 282 (DC La 1983); *Amoco Overseas Company v ST Avenger* 1975 AMC 782, 789 (SDNY 1975); *Keytrade USA Inc v Ain Temouchent M/V* 404 F 3d 891 (5th Cir 2005); *Coastal States Trading Inc v Zenith SA* 446 F Supp 330 (SDNY 1977).

of Appeals for the Fifth Circuit in *Cargill Ferrous International v Sea Phoenix* is illustrative.[27] There, Serene, the owners of *The Sea Phoenix*, time chartered the vessel to Western Bulk, which in turn entered into a voyage charterparty with Cargill. As between Cargill and Serene, the contract of carriage was contained in a bill of lading. Serene sought to compel Cargill to arbitrate pursuant to the arbitration clause in the voyage sub-charterparty, relying on the incorporation clause in the bill of lading. Although the incorporation clause was left blank, the Court found that the holder, who was also the sub-charterer and the shipper, had no confusion that the bill of lading sought to incorporate the voyage sub-charterparty, including the arbitration clause therein. In support of this finding, they said:[28]

> Cargill received and continued to hold the bills of lading issued pursuant to the Cargill-Western Bulk voyage charter … Second, the agent who signed the bills of lading … received its agency authority solely from a term in the voyage charter. Third, the bills of lading indicate freight is to be paid pursuant to the charter party. This provision depends on the incorporation of the Cargill-Western Bulk voyage charter to retain any meaning. Fourth, the Cargill-Western Bulk voyage charter, the only charter that Cargill signed, requires all bills of lading issued under the voyage charter to incorporate, among other things, the voyage charterer's arbitration clause.

Similar facts arose in *Keytrade USA Inc v Ain Temouchent M/V.*[29] There, the owners of the *Ain Temouchent*, CNAN, time chartered the vessel to Progress Bulk. Thereafter, a voyage charterparty was entered into between Progress Bulk and Keytrade AG ('KAG'). The holder of the bill of lading was Keytrade USA ('KUSA'). Given that the sale contract between KAG and KUSA was not an 'arm's length transaction', the Court considered KUSA, the holder, as if it were KAG, who was both the shipper and the sub-charterer. For this reason, KUSA was thus held to be not a 'stranger' to the voyage sub-charterparty—a point that will be discussed below. For present purposes, suffice it to say that the holder was held to have no confusion that the bill of lading sought to incorporate the voyage charterparty. On this matter, the Court said:[30]

> It is the voyage charter that specifies a Congen bill of lading was to be used. See Clause 9. It is the voyage charterparty that describes how the bill of lading should be marked vis-a-vis freight. See Clause 18 (mandating markings of 'clean 'on board'/freight payable as per charterparty'). It is the voyage charter that grants the captain of the *Ain Temouchent* the authority to sign the bill of lading. See Clause 9. Indeed, there is nothing in the CNAN/Progress Bulk time charter that speaks of the bill of lading. With only one (of two) charter parties speaking to shipment and bill of lading, it is difficult to discern how there could be 'confusion' as to which charterparty the bill of lading's incorporation clause referred.

[27] See *Cargill Ferrous International v Sea Phoenix* 2003 AMC 1027, 325 F 3d 695 (5th Cir 2003). See also *Coastal States Trading Inc v Zenith SA* 446 F Supp 330 (SDNY 1977).

[28] See 2003 AMC 1027, 325 F 3d 695, 699 (5th Cir 2003).

[29] *Keytrade USA Inc v Ain Temouchent M/V* 404 F 3d 891 (5th Cir 2005).

[30] 404 F 3d 891, 896 (5th Cir 2005).

Although this inquiry would appear to rest entirely on the voyage charterparty, the Court in *Keytrade USA Inc v Ain Temouchent M/V* further stated that 'analyzing the bill of lading is a fundamental component of our analysis'.[31] The main reason for this is that a bill of lading that does not contain an incorporation clause cannot incorporate, irrespective of the holder's actual notice of the intended charterparty. Nonetheless, the decisions in *Keytrade USA Inc v Ain Temouchent M/V* and *Cargill Ferrous International v Sea Phoenix* suggest that, by and large, this particular inquiry entails looking at the terms of all the charterparties relevant to the voyage. A further point to note is that in both cases it was the shipowner who sought to compel the voyage sub-charterparty provisions against the holder who had actual notice of the charterparty. The shipowners were obviously not party to these voyage sub-charterparties. These facts raise the question of whether the courts would have taken the same view had the holders sought to invoke the provisions of their respective voyage charterparties against the shipowners.

Similar considerations arise where the vessel is subject to one charterparty and a contract of affreightment. *Amoco Overseas Co v ST Avenger*[32] involved a charterparty that was entered into between the shipowner ('Ocean Couriers') and Amoco Trading International Limited ('ATI'). Prior to this charterparty, ATI had entered into a contract of affreightment with Amoco Overseas Oil Co ('Overseas'). A dispute arose between Ocean Couriers, as carrier under the bill of lading, and Overseas, as the holder. Although the incorporation clause in the bill of lading left blank the date of the charterparty to which it referred, the Court held that Overseas had 'no confusion concerning who in fact was the charterer on this voyage and which charterparty governed the rights of the charterer vis-a-vis the shipowner'.[33] Negotiations between ATI and Ocean Couriers clearly showed that the parties intended the bill of lading to incorporate the charterparty. Given that ATI and Overseas were inextricably intertwined for the reasons explained below,[34] Overseas was held to have no confusion that the voyage charterparty was to be incorporated into the bill of lading.

b. Is the Holder a Stranger to the Intended Charterparty?

On the question of circumstances in which a holder is not treated as a stranger to the charterparty, the decision of US Court of Appeals for the Fifth Circuit in *Cargill Ferrous International v Sea Phoenix* is again of assistance.[35] There, the Court took the view that the holder, who was also the shipper, was not a 'stranger' to the voyage sub-charterparty that the bill of lading sought to incorporate. The

[31] 404 F 3d 891, 895 (5th Cir 2005).

[32] *Amoco Overseas Co v ST Avenger* 1975 AMC 782, 387 F Supp 589 (SDNY 1975).

[33] 1975 AMC 782, 387 F Supp 589, 591 (SDNY 1975).

[34] See Section I.B.i.b below.

[35] See 2003 AMC 1027 (5th Cir 2003). See also *Coastal States Trading Inc v Zenith SA* 446 F Supp 330 (SDNY 1977).

reason for this was that the holder was also the charterer of the intended voyage sub-charterparty.[36]

US case law also suggests that a holder that is only 'affiliated'[37] with the charterer can in some cases equally be treated as not a stranger to the intended charterparty. The same is also true of the agent[38] or the alter ego[39] of the charterer. In *Amoco Oil Co v MT Mary Ellen*,[40] Amoco Oil Co, which consigned a cargo of oil for transportation under a shipowner's bill of lading, brought a cargo claim against the shipowner, as carrier. The shipowner sought to compel Amoco Oil Co to arbitrate pursuant to the arbitration clause in the charterparty that they concluded with Amoco Transport Co. The bill of lading did not provide any details of this charterparty, although the charterparty contemplated that it would be incorporated into the bill of lading. The shipowners submitted that there was no need to identify the charterparty in the incorporation clause, for the holder was not a stranger to the charterparty. In support of this, they further submitted that the holder was the alter ego of the charterer and thus had notice of the charterparty. The Court did not accept these submissions and held that the requirement to identify the charterparty had to be satisfied in this case. Drawing guidance from the decision in *Coastal States Trading Inc v Zenith SA*,[41] the Court found no such alter ego relationship between the charterer and the holder. In arriving at this conclusion, the Court relied on the fact that the business operations of the charterers and the holders were quite separate, and that the transactions between the parties were made on an arm's-length basis.

When deciding against incorporation, the Court in *Amoco Oil* also relied on the fact that there was no attempt to identify the charterparty in the bill of lading: this was taken to mean that there was no intention to incorporate the charterparty into the bill of lading.[42] Given that the holder was not a party to the charterparty and that the bill of lading did not contain any details of the charterparty, the holder's mere awareness of the charterparty did not amount to an acceptance of the terms of the charterparty.[43]

[36] *Cargill Ferrous International v Sea Phoenix* 2003 AMC 1027 (5th Cir 2003).

[37] See *Amoco Overseas Co v ST Avenger* 387 F Supp 589 (SDNY 1975). See also Davies (ed) (n 24) 28.

[38] *Keytrade USA Inc v Ain Temouchent M/V* 404 F 3d 891 (5th Cir 2005).

[39] See *Amoco Overseas Co v ST Avenger* and *Coastal States Trading Inc v Zenith SA* 446 F Supp 330 (SDNY 1977). Even though in both cases the courts did not find that there was an alter-ego relationship between the holder and the relevant charterer, the views therein support this proposition.

[40] *Amoco Oil Co v MT Mary Ellen* 1982 AMC 1758, 529 F Supp 227 (SDNY 1981).

[41] See 446 F Supp 330 (SDNY 1977). See also *Fisher v International Bank* 282 F 2d 231 (2d Cir 1960), where the application of the alter ego theory was extensively discussed.

[42] 1982 AMC 1758, 529 F Supp 227, 229 (SDNY 1981).

[43] ibid.

However, in *Amoco Overseas Co v ST Avenger*,[44] the Court found a 'close connection'[45] between the bill of lading holder, Overseas, and the charterer, ATI. In support of this finding, the Court said:[46]

> ATI and Overseas are two of a complex network of corporate affiliates ... doing business under the name 'Amoco' and ultimately owned by Standard Oil Company (Indiana) ('Standard'). Included in the network are Amoco Oil Company, a subsidiary of Standard which purchases and distributes petroleum products within the United States, and Amoco International Oil Company ('AIO'), a wholly owned subsidiary of Standard charged with overseeing and controlling all Amoco's transactions with respect to purchase, sale and transportation of crude oil outside North America ... Overseas functions primarily to purchase crude oil for sale to Amoco Oil Company ... ATI functions to purchase and sell crude oil for distribution outside the United States, but also ... arranges transportation of some of the oil which Overseas purchases and sells ... The method in which this network operates is relevant to the question before the court. Neither ATI nor Overseas has any employees, and the two corporations operate from the same office space. The work of the corporations is performed by employees of AIO, on loan to one another of the affiliates pursuant to a formal employee loan agreement ... And an employee of AIO handles the transportation arrangements, whether these be for ATI in its own purchases and sales of oil, or for ATI in its capacity as charterer for Overseas' shipment of oil.

This close connection illustrated by the Court led to the incorporation of the charterparty arbitration clause into the bill of lading, although the charterparty was not correctly identified in the bill of lading.[47] Although not 'unmistakable', this failed attempt at sufficiently identifying the charterparty was treated as an expressed intention in the bill of lading to incorporate a charterparty. To these findings, the Court also added that the holder had no confusion as to which charterparty the bill of lading sought to incorporate—due to the reasons explained above.[48] Thus, coupled with the incorporation clause, which indicated an intention to incorporate, the holder's knowledge of the intended charterparty led the Court to find in favour of incorporation.

It is also worth considering again the decision in *Keytrade USA Inc v Ain Temouchent M/V*.[49] There, the US Court of Appeals for the Fifth Circuit held that the holder was not a stranger to the intended sub-charterparty because there was

[44] 1975 AMC 782, 387 F Supp 589 (SDNY 1975).

[45] See also *Astra Oil Co Inc v Rover Navigation Ltd* 2003 AMC 2415 (2d Cir 2003), where the Court's finding of 'close connection' between the charterer and the holder led to the incorporation of the charterparty into the bill of lading.

[46] 1975 AMC 782, 387 F Supp 589, 591 (SDNY 1975).

[47] 387 F Supp 589 (SDNY 1975).

[48] ibid, at 591. See also Section I.B.i.a above.

[49] 404 F 3d 891 (5th Cir 2005).

an agency relationship between the holder, KUSA, and the sub-charterer, KAG. On the finding of this agency relationship, the district court said:[50]

> KAG owns ninety percent of KUSA's stock. Except for Michael Moosman (KUSA's president and ten-percent shareholder), KUSA's entire board consists of KAG officers and directors. Since KUSA's inception in October 2000, KUSA has bought all of its imports and nearly all of its supply through its parent. KUSA's president works closely with KAG on all its imports ... KUSA decides which contracts to enter based on what is most profitable for the Keytrade 'group.' KUSA does not charter its own vessels, but instead relies on KAG to handle this aspect of the import process. The *Ain Temouchent* charter was handled in the same manner as other Keytrade imports to the United States. In response to a request by KUSA, KAG finds a supplier. Once it was determined that the supplier's price met with KUSA's approval, KAG contracted with the supplier and started looking for a vessel to ship the cargo. The shipment was insured under a blanket insurance policy that covers the Keytrade group as a whole. At the time cargo was loaded onto the vessel, title passed from the supplier to KAG and simultaneously from KAG to KUSA. Although KAG prepares purchase contracts and invoices in connection with its shipments to KUSA, it does not demand full payment from KUSA in cases such as this one, where KUSA must sell for less than the contract price. KUSA, communicating through KAG, was active in the *Ain Temouchent* voyage from the start ... a 'recap' of the charter was sent to both KAG and KUSA; the charter party itself was not sent to either KAG or KUSA. The 'recap' itself states, that disputes are subject to arbitration. When the vessel stopped in Dubai, Moosman of KUSA immediately began working through Andrea Vaterlaus of KAG, in an effort to get the vessel moving. They discussed re-routing the shipment. But there was no discussion of which company (KAG or KUSA) would bear the additional costs, if any. Although a loss might be KUSA's in the first instance, it ultimately would fall to KAG. Thus, KUSA is far from the bona fide holder-in-due-course who is innocent of the voyage charter terms.

On the whole, when deciding whether the holder is a stranger to the charterparty that the bill of lading seeks to incorporate, a number of issues need to be considered. As is clear from the quoted part of the judgment, this includes: the corporate structures and operations of the relevant holder and charterer, which are in almost all cases corporate entities, the way in which the relevant charterparty is entered into and performed, and if relevant, the way in which the sale contract between the charterer and the holder is concluded and performed and the terms of that sale contract.

c. Where Do These Rules Take Us?

To summarise, the decision in *Amoco Overseas Co v ST Avenger* illustrates what factors come into play when deciding whether the holder is a stranger to the charterparty that the bill of lading seeks to incorporate.[51] The decision further

[50] See F Supp 2d, 2003 WL 122312, *2 (ED La 2003). This finding was not contested on appeal. Hence, the US Court of Appeals for the Fifth Circuit was left with the question of whether there was any confusion as to which charterparty was intended to be incorporated, see 404 F 3d 891, 893–94 (5th Cir 2005). For this issue, see Section I.B.i.a above.

[51] *State Trading Corp of India Ltd v Grunstad Shipping Corp (Belgium) N/V* 582 F Supp 1523, 1524 (SDNY 1984); *Keytrade USA Inc v Ain Temouchent M/V* 404 F 3d 891, 894 (5th Cir 2005); *Cargill Ferrous International v Sea Phoenix* 325 F 3d 695, 698 (5th Cir 2003); *Cementos Andinos Dominicanos*

illustrates that this inquiry entails a fact-driven analysis.[52] The approach taken in this decision is also consistent with the long line of cases where the courts consistently asked:[53] 'Is the charterparty clearly identified in the bill of lading and does the holder of the cargo have actual or constructive notice of incorporation?'[54]

The second limb of this question somewhat supports the proposition that 'notice' is at the heart of the US rules of incorporation.[55] Although this proposition reflects the US position to some extent, it should not be taken to mean that 'notice' is the sole decisive factor for incorporation.[56] For the most part, the decision on the incorporation issue depends on the incorporation clause. The reason for this is twofold: first, 'unmistakable reference' to a charterparty in the incorporation clause yields constructive notice.[57] To put it differently, the element of notice does not come as an additional condition to satisfy where there is an unmistakable reference to a charterparty. In such circumstances, the holder is deemed to have known of the referred charterparty, although he/she may not have actual notice of the terms of the charterparty.[58] Thus, in *Thyssen Inc v M/V Markos*,[59] the unmistakable reference to a charterparty in the bill of lading led to the incorporation of the charterparty, although the holder's request to have sight of the charterparty had been refused by the carrier. Secondly, a bill of lading that does not contain an incorporation clause is fatal to incorporation, irrespective of the holder's actual notice of the intended charterparty.[60]

In light of these observations, carriers seeking to achieve incorporation have two options: one is to establish that the incorporation clause contains an 'unmistakable reference' to a charterparty; the other is to prove that, despite the lack of an 'unmistakable reference', there is *no confusion* as to the charterparty that the bill of lading seeks to incorporate, and that the holder is not a 'stranger' to the

SA v East Bulk Shipping SA 2006 AMC 1121 (SDNY 2006); *Volgotanker Joint Stock Company v Vinmar International Ltd* F Supp 2d, 2003 WL 23018798, *6 (SDNY 2003); *Thyssen Inc v M/V Markos N* 1999 AMC 2515 (SDNY 1999) *aff'd sub nom Thyssen Inc v Calypso Shipping Corp SA* 310 F 3d 102 (2d Cir 2002) *cert denied* __ US __, 123 SCt 1573, 155 L Ed 2d 312 (US 2003); *Kaystone Chemical Inc v Bow-Sun* F Supp 1989 WL 39498, *2 (SDNY 1989); *Continental UK Ltd v Anagel Confidence Compania Naviera, SA* 658 F Supp 809, 812–13 (SDNY 1987); *The Rice Company (Suisse), SA v M/V Nalinee Naree* 2008 AMC 1152, 1162 (5th Cir 2008).

[52] *Energy Transport Ltd v MV San Sebastian* 348 F Supp 2d 186, 204 (SDNY 2004); *Fairmont Shipping Ltd v Primary Industries* F Supp, 1987 WL 10389 (SDNY 1987).

[53] *Midland Tar Distillers Inc v M/T Lotos* 362 F Supp 1311, 1313 (SDNY 1972).

[54] ibid. See also *Continental Insurance Company v M/V Nikos N* 2002 AMC 1287, 1290 (SDNY 2002); *Continental Florida Materials Inc v M/V Lamazon* 334 F Supp 2d 1294, 1297 (SDFla 2004); *Salim Oleochemicals Inc v M/V Shropshire* 169 F Supp 2d 194, 198 (SDNY 2001); *Energy Transport Ltd v MV San Sebastian* 348 F Supp 2d 186, 204 (SDNY 2004).

[55] See also Davies (ed) (n 24) 27.

[56] See *A/B Olson & Wright v Foresta Trading Corporation, Arbitration at New York* 1928 WL 58500 (arbit), 1929 AMC 19 and *Amoco Oil Company v MT Mary Ellen* 529 F Supp 227, 1982 AMC 1758, 1761 (SDNY 1981).

[57] *Steel Warehouse Co v Abalone Shipping Ltd of Nicosai* 1998 AMC 2054, 2057 (5th Cir 1998).

[58] ibid.

[59] 1999 AMC 2515 (SDNY 1999) *aff'd sub nom Thyssen Inc v Calypso Shipping Corp SA*, 310 F 3d 102 (2d Cir 2002), *cert denied* __ US __, 123 SCt 1573, 155 L Ed 2d 312 (US 2003).

[60] ibid. The same is also true in English law, see *Serraino v Campbell* [1891] 1 QB 283, 297, where the Court gave no weight to the fact that the bill of lading holders had actual notice of the charterparty terms due to their being the charterer.

intended charterparty.[61] In assessing these issues, US courts consider both the incorporation clause and the issue of notice.

ii. The Position Under English Law and Some Comparative Remarks

Under English law, the incorporation issue is addressed within the realms of contract construction.[62] It is well settled that a charterparty need not be identified in the bill of lading for its incorporation.[63] Thus, a pre-printed incorporation clause itself is sufficient for the inference that the bill of lading seeks to incorporate an 'identifiable' charterparty.[64]

When compared with their counterparts under English law, the US rules of incorporation on this particular issue would appear more favourable to the holder than the carrier. Although the US rules do not guarantee that the holder will obtain a copy of the relevant charterparty, it at least urges the carrier to clearly identify in the bill of lading which charterparty is to be incorporated. This identification in the bill of lading rules out the possibility of disputes between the holder and the carrier as to which charterparty is incorporated. Furthermore, from the time of taking up the bill of lading, the holder also is kept alert as to the carrier's intention to incorporate a charterparty. It is probably because of these salutary results that the condition to identify the charterparty is also recognised under the Rotterdam Rules: Under Article 76 of the Rules, where a charterparty or a similar contract contains an arbitration clause, a transport document that is issued under such a contract can incorporate the arbitration clause provided that: (a) the document identifies the parties to and the date of the contract and (b) it incorporates by specific reference the arbitration clause in the contract.[65]

Although the requirement as to the identification of the charterparty has these attractions, to ensure that the charterparty is sufficiently identified in the bill of lading could be a difficult task. This is especially the case where the charterparty under which the bill of lading is to be issued requires the master to sign the bill of lading 'as presented'.[66] Unless the charterparty expressly requires that the bill of lading to be presented for signature contain some particular details of the charterparty, it is unlikely that the charterparty will be identified in the bill of lading.[67] Similar problems arise where the charterparty authorises the charterer either expressly or by implication to issue and sign a shipowner's bill of lading for the

[61] *Keytrade USA Inc v Ain Temouchent M/V* 404 F 3d 891, 894 (5th Cir 2005); *Cargill Ferrous International v Sea Phoenix* 325 F 3d 695, 698 (5th Cir 2003).

[62] *The Annefield* [1971] P 168, 179.

[63] *The Garbis* [1982] 2 Lloyd's Rep 283, 287; *The Ikariada* [1999] 2 Lloyd's Rep 365, 372; *The San Nicholas* [1976] 1 Lloyd's Rep 8, 12 (CA); *The SLS Everest* [1981] 2 Lloyd's Rep 389, 391–92 (CA).

[64] *The Annefield* [1971] P 168, 179.

[65] It is important to note that Art 76 applies to arbitration agreements in non-liner transportation. Much stricter rules apply in the case of liner transportation; see Art 75 of the Rules.

[66] See n 13.

[67] ibid.

master:[68] the shipowner in such cases would be anxious to have the details of his/her charterparty to be provided in the bill of lading, whilst the charterer may not be that vigilant about this matter. Another practical constraint is that the master or other persons who may be in charge of issuing bills of lading may not even be aware of the necessary charterparty details to make an 'unmistakable reference' to the charterparty that is sought to be incorporated. Furthermore, where the vessel is subject to more than one charterparty, there might even be disputes as to which charterparty should be identified in the bill of lading.

This requirement also loses its justification when one considers the possibility that it could even be applied to a holder who favours incorporation. Given that the main purpose of this requirement is to afford protection to the holders, why is it not waived in cases where doing so would be for the benefit of the holder? As will be recalled, exception to this requirement is recognised only (a) where there is no confusion as to which charterparty the bill of lading seeks to incorporate, and (b) where the holder is not a stranger to the charterparty. When determining whether the exception applies on these grounds, the courts conduct a fact-driven analysis. On the whole, what flows from the operation of this exception is that it creates a variable contractual position under bills of lading: a contractual position that depends on the circumstances of every subsequent holder. With bills of lading generally passing through the hands of numerous traders, to determine the carriage terms under bills of lading by reference to the actual position of every holder brings with it contractual uncertainty in these transferable instruments.

Given the need to identify the charterparty in the bill of lading where the question of incorporation is governed by US law, the question arises as to what constitutes sufficient identification. The discussions below will show how carriers need to identify their respective charterparties in bills of lading for incorporation under US law.

C. How is the Charterparty to be Identified in the Bill of Lading?

Charterers are frequently required by their charterparty to issue and present for signature[69] a bill of lading that incorporates the charterparty.[70] To fulfil this obligation, they undoubtedly need to know whether the bill of lading that they present can actually incorporate. In assessing this, charterers' considerations should vary depending on the rules of incorporation of the legal system governing the incorporation issue. Where English law governs the question of incorporation,

[68] In time charters, charterers generally have either express or implied authority to sign bills of lading for the master. For US law, see *Ariate Compania Naviera SA v Commonwealth Tankship Owners* 310 F Supp 416, 422 (SDNY 1970). For English law, see Cooke et al (n 13) para 18.176.

[69] See n 13.

[70] See, for instance, clause 20(b) of the Asbatankvoy Charterparty.

the charterer will not be in breach of this contractual obligation where the bill of lading that he/she presents for signature does not contain any charterparty details: provided that it contains an incorporation clause, a bill of lading can incorporate.

Different considerations arise where US law governs the question of incorporation. As will be recalled, the general rule under US law is that an incorporation clause is not of itself sufficient to trigger incorporation. The bill of lading must also properly identify the charterparty, failing which the charterparty cannot, in most cases, be incorporated. For the fulfilment of the identification requirement under US law, there should be an 'unmistakable reference'[71] to the charterparty that is sought to be incorporated. To this end, the stated particulars of the charterparty in the bill of lading should (1) unambiguously differentiate the charterparty,[72] (2) give a clear notice as to the carrier's intention to incorporate[73] and, finally, (3) attest the existence of the charterparty at the time of issuing the bill of lading.[74] Consequently, US case law suggests that the courts find unmistakable reference to a charterparty when the names of the parties to the charterparty, and the place and date of its making, are stipulated under the bill of lading.[75] Notably, it is also accepted that for an unmistakable reference, all these charterparty details need not necessarily be provided in the bill of lading: in a number of judicial decisions and arbitration awards, the date of charterparty itself is treated as sufficient to render the charterparty reference unmistakable.[76] Nevertheless, it is preferable to have all those particulars of the charterparty in the bill of lading.[77]

One should consider the possibility that the vessel can be subject to more than one charterparty and that all charterparties can be concluded on the same date. In such circumstances, the date of the charterparty is not usually sufficient

[71] *Son Shipping Co Inc v De Fosse & Tanghe* 1952 AMC 1931, 1932 (2d Cir 1952).

[72] In this respect, the charterparty details in the bill of lading are expected to make the charterparty both identifiable and specific, see *Volgotanker Joint Stock Company v Vinmar International Limited* F Supp 2d, 2003 WL 23018798.

[73] *United States v Cia Naviera Continental, SA* 1962 AMC 2403, 2407 (SDNY 1962).

[74] *Thyssen Inc v M/V Markos N* 1999 AMC 2515 (SDNY 1999) *aff'd sub nom Thyssen Inc v Calypso Shipping Corp SA* 310 F 3d 102 (2d Cir 2002), *cert denied* 123 SCt 1573, 155 L Ed 2d 312 (US 2003).

[75] ibid. See also *Associated Metals and Minerals Corp v M/V Venture* 554 F Supp 281, 282 (EDLa 1983).

[76] *Continental Insurance Company v M/V Nikos N* F Supp 2d, WL 530987 (SDNY 2002); *Thyssen Inc v M/V Markos N* 1999 AMC 2515 (SDNY 1999) *aff'd sub nom Thyssen Inc v Calypso Shipping Corp SA* 310 F 3d 102 (2d Cir 2002) *cert denied* 123 SCt 1573, 155 L Ed 2d 312 (US 2003); *Ibeto Petrochemical Industries Limited v M/T Beffen* 2007 AMC 213 (2d Cir 2007); *Steel Warehouse Co v Abalone Shipping Ltd of Nicosai* 1998 AMC 2054, 2058 (5th Cir 1998); *Hawkspere Shipping Company Limited v Intamex SA* 2003 AMC 1374 (4th Cir 2003); *United States Barite Corp v M/V Haris* 1982 AMC 925 (SDNY 1982); *United States v Cia Naviera Continental SA* 1962 AMC 2403, 2407 (SDNY 1962). R Force and M Davies, 'United States Maritime Law 2003' (2004) *Lloyd's Maritime and Commercial Law Quarterly* 196, 197. For arbitration awards that are in line with this approach see *In re Arbitration Between The Office of Supply, Government of the Republic of Korea and New York Navigation Company Inc* SMA No 654 (August, 1971); *In re Arbitration Between Alimentos Precocidos Guayana CA and Her An Shipping SA* SMA No 3468 (14 August 1998) and *In re Arbitration Between Cementos Andinos Dominicanos SA and East Bulk Shipping SA* SMA No 3993 (11 February 2008).

[77] See *Continental Insurance Company v Polish Steamship Company* 346 F 3d 281, 281–82 (2d Cir 2003).

to make an unmistakable reference.[78] When the date is not of itself sufficient to unambiguously differentiate the charterparty that the bill of lading seeks to incorporate, it becomes essential to provide other particulars of the charterparty in the bill of lading. No such necessity will arise, and therefore the charterparty date could amount to an 'unmistakable reference', if the holder happens to know which one of the charterparties is actually referred to in the bill of lading.[79]

Although the date of the charterparty is a strong tool to satisfy the identification requirement, it does not follow, however, that the place of making the charterparty and the name of the parties to it are insufficient. Any of these particulars can create an 'unmistakable' reference, as long as they meet the criteria in the surrounding circumstances.[80] When assessing whether there is an unmistakable reference to a charterparty, the courts will thus consider the factual circumstances of each case.[81] However, statements such as 'to be used with charterparties', 'as per relevant/applicable charterparty', 'freight prepaid', or an explicit reference to a charterparty form will not have any role to play.[82]

It is clear from these observations that US courts do not require a meticulous degree of precision in identifying the charterparty. There is no requirement that all charterparty details be stated exhaustively in the bill of lading. A charterparty can effectively be identified by providing the names of parties to the charterparty and the date and place of its making. As will be recalled, the requirement will in most cases be satisfied when the bill of lading contains only the date of the charterparty. Therefore, there is some flexibility afforded in identifying the charterparty for incorporation purposes.

Having stated the standards for identifying the charterparty, a further question is whether the bill of lading can incorporate when the charterparty details provided therein are inaccurate or ambiguous.

D. Inaccurate and/or Ambiguous References

Ambiguities and inaccuracies are commonplace in commercial contracts, including contracts of carriage contained in or evidenced by bills of lading. The wide use of standard-form bills of lading minimises the risks of having ambiguous provisions in bills of lading, although this does not completely rule out that risk,

[78] *Volgotanker Joint Stock Company v Vinmar International Limited* F Supp 2d, 2003 WL 23018798 (SDNY 2003); *Joo Seng Hong Kong Co v S/S Unibulkfir* 493 F Supp 35, 40 (SDNY 1980).

[79] *National Material Trading v M/V Kaptan Cebi* 1998 AMC 201 (DSC 1997).

[80] *Steel Warehouse Co v Abalone Shipping Ltd of Nicosai* 1998 AMC 2054, 2058 (5th Cir 1998).

[81] *Energy Transport Ltd v MV San Sebastian* 348 F Supp 2d 186, 204 (SDNY 2004).

[82] See *MISR Ins Co v M/V Har Sinai* 1978 AMC 1223 (SDNY 1977). In this context, the argument that a particular bill of lading form is a sufficient reference to a charterparty was rejected despite the fact that such a bill of lading form was designed to be issued under a specific charterparty form. *Steel Warehouse Co v Abalone Shipping Ltd of Nicosai* 1998 AMC 2054, 2058 (5th Cir 1998); *Macsteel International USA Corp v M/V Jag Rani* F Supp 2d, 2003 WL 22241785 (SDNY 2004); *Continental Insurance Company v Polish Steamship Company* 2003 AMC 2718, 2721 (2d Cir 2003).

with typewritten provisions frequently inserted into bills of lading. Even more common are inaccurate representations and statements in bills of lading. Where the stated charterparty details contain some ambiguities or inaccuracies or where the language of the incorporation clause is unclear, the question will arise as to whether such flaws can debar incorporation. A closer look will be taken at the US and English rules of incorporation to address this issue.

i. Ambiguities and Inaccuracies in the Stated Particulars of the Charterparty

Given that US law requires an unmistakable reference to a charterparty, the holders usually succeed in their attempts at frustrating incorporation in the absence of an accurate and unambiguous identification of a charterparty in the bill of lading.[83] Such flaws in the bill of lading may be ignored if the bill of lading also contains some unambiguous and accurate charterparty details that can unmistakably identify the charterparty. In such cases, the bill of lading will be able to incorporate the identified charterparty.[84] In this context, the courts will be more inclined to favour incorporation if the charterparty date, the strongest tool to identify and differentiate a charterparty,[85] is correctly stipulated therein.[86]

Given that US courts dispense with the identification requirement where the holder is not a 'stranger' to the charterparty, the inaccuracies and ambiguities in the stated details of the charterparty do not necessarily rule out incorporation.[87] Provided that the holder does not have any confusion as to the identity of the charterparty to be incorporated, the courts decide in favour of incorporation despite the flaws in the stated particulars of the charterparty in the bill of lading.[88]

Somewhat surprisingly, even in the case of a holder who is a stranger to the charterparty, the courts may refuse to treat the flaws in the identification as a barrier to incorporation. They may do so if the holder happens to know which charterparty is referred to in the incorporation clause. In *The Kaptan Cebi*,[89] the owners chartered the vessel to 'Concept Carriers', which in turn sub-chartered the vessel to 'OSKMET' for the carriage of goods from Russia to the United States. OSKMET entered into the latter charterparty for the fulfilment of a sale contract that it entered into with 'NMT'. Concluded on the same day, both charterparties contained a London arbitration clause. NMT brought a cargo claim against the owners under the bill of lading. The bill of lading was on the Congenbill 2007 form, and there was thus an incorporation clause on the reverse side of the bill of lading. NMT sought to resist the incorporation of the arbitration clause of the

[83] *Coastal States Trading Inc v Zenith Navigation SA* 446 F Supp 330 (SDNY 1977).
[84] *Continental UK Ltd v Anagel Confidence Compania Naviera, SA* 1987 AMC 2012 (SDNY 1987).
[85] See n 78.
[86] See *Continental UK* 1987 AMC 2017 (SDNY 1987).
[87] *Amoco Overseas Co v ST Avenger* 1975 AMC 782, 789 (SDNY 1975).
[88] ibid.
[89] 1998 AMC 201, F Supp 1997 WL 91500 (DSC 1997).

sub-charterparty into the bill of lading on the grounds that only the date of the charterparty was provided in the bill of lading. Although the Court accepted that the identification of the charterparty was ambiguous, with both charterparties concluded on the same day, the holder was bound by the arbitration clause of the sub-charterparty. The Court expected the holder to know which charterparty was meant in the incorporation clause for the following reasons:[90]

> NMT acknowledges that it purchased the cargo from OSKMET, who was obligated to deliver it from Kerch, Russia to a U.S. port to be designated by NMT. NMT was also aware that OSKMET would be chartering a vessel for delivery of the cargo and was not a vessel operator. There was a charter-party agreement between Concept Carriers and OSKMET dated October 5, 1995, whereby OSKMET chartered the KAPTAN CEBI to transport the cargo from Kerch to Georgetown. It is, therefore, apparent that this was the charter-party to which the ocean bill of lading was referring as the 'Charter-Party dated October 5, 1995.' Furthermore, the charter-party also listed the discharging port or place as 'Georgetown.' Since the sales confirmation by which NMT contracted to sell to Georgetown Steel was dated November 3, 1995, it may be reasonably inferred that the listing of final destination as Georgetown is further evidence of NMT's knowledge of which charter contract was being incorporated into the bill of lading.

Different considerations arise under English law, where there are some ambiguities and/or inaccuracies in the stated particulars of a charterparty in the bill of lading. Unlike the position in US law, English courts do not require any precise description of the charterparty in their bills of lading. Thus, ambiguous statements regarding the particulars of the charterparty do not prevent incorporation, nor do inaccurate charterparty details. As was suggested in the case of *The Merak*, such inaccuracies in the bill of lading will not be rectified,[91] but instead will be treated merely as surplus, unless they point to another charterparty in the chain of charterparty contracts.[92]

To view the overall picture, it is important to raise one question: what is the practical impact of these rules on the position of carriers and bill of lading holders? For those holders who wish to avoid incorporation, it is well worth raising the ambiguities and inaccuracies in the stated charterparty details where US law governs the incorporation issue. From the standpoint of carriers, the US rules of incorporation pose more challenges in achieving incorporation in the case of erroneous or ambiguous charterparty details in the bill of lading. This is simply because the chances of proving that the holder is in a position to know the actual identity of the charterparty are rather slim.

No such difficulties arise for carriers when the governing law is English law. Ambiguities and mistakes in the charterparty details do not normally prevent

[90] 1998 AMC 201, F Supp 1997 WL 915000, *4 (DSC 1997).

[91] On the question of why the doctrine of rectification does not generally find room for application in bills of lading, see n 92.

[92] See *The Merak* [1965] P 223 (CA), where the bill of lading mistakenly referred to 'clause 32' of the relevant charterparty instead of 'clause 30', which was the arbitration clause. The Court refused to correct the mistake and treated the reference merely as surplus.

incorporation. It follows that the English rules of incorporation, with respect to this issue, do not stand out as favourable to the holder, as they do under US law. This surely has the probable effect of making well-advised holders less inclined to bring forward these matters to thwart incorporation.

Having discussed US law and English law governing this issue, the focus will now be on the question of whether a bill of lading is apt to incorporate if the incorporation language therein is unclear.

ii. Ambiguous Incorporation Language

Unlike false descriptions or ambiguities in the stated particulars of a charterparty, the flaws in the incorporation language may not, at first, appear to debar incorporation. However, when the meaning of the incorporation clause is dubious, it may well be worth raising this matter to frustrate incorporation. This raises the question of the circumstances in which such an argument can succeed.

In both jurisdictions, unclear incorporation language does not, in most cases, stand as a barrier to incorporation. For a bill of lading to incorporate, the incorporation language only needs to manifest the intention to make the charterparty part of the bill of lading.[93] Consequently, carriers are forgiven for their unclear language in the incorporation clause to the extent that their intention to incorporate is objectively ascertainable from the clause.[94] When the 'plain language'[95] in the incorporation clause makes such an intention evident, both US and English courts thus give effect to this intention, despite some ambiguities in the clause.[96] Where the intention is less evident, the courts prefer to give a 'commercially

[93] For US law, *Klos v Lotnicze* 133 F 3d 164, 168 (2d Cir 1997) quoting *Swamiathan v Swiss Air Transport Co Ltd* 962 F 2d 387 (5th Cir 1992); *Cabot Corporation v SS Mormacscan* 441 F 2d 476, 478–79 (SDNY 1971), *cert denied*, 404 US 855, 1987 AMC 565, where the Court emphasised the importance of the 'clarity of language' when ascertaining the intention of the parties. See also Restatement (Second) On Contracts, §200. For English law, see *The Starsin* [2004] AC 715, 722, 737 (HL); *The Eurymedon* [1975] AC 154, 169 (PC); *The Nema (No 2)* [1982] AC 724, 736 (HL).

[94] For English law, see *The Starsin* [2004] AC 715, 722, 737 (HL); *The Eurymedon* [1975] AC 154, 169 (PC); *The Nema (No 2)* [1982] AC 724, 736 (HL). See also *Reardon Smith Line Ltd v Hansen-Tangen* [1976] 2 Lloyd's Rep 621, 625 (CA); *Vitol BV v Compagnie Europeene des Petroles* [1988] 1 Lloyd's Rep 574, 576; *BBC 1 v Ali* [2002] 1 AC 251, 259 (HL). For US law, *Klos v Lotnicze* 133 F 3d 164, 168 (2d Cir 1997) quoting *Swamiathan v Swiss Air Transport Co Ltd* 962 F 2d 387 (5th Cir 1992); *Cabot Corporation v SS Mormacscan* 441 F 2d 476, 478–79 (SDNY 1971), *cert denied*, 404 US 855, 1987 AMC 565. See also *Energy Transport Ltd v MV San Sebastian* 348 F Supp 2d 186, 203 (SDNY 2004).

[95] *United States v Donovan* 348 F 3d 509, 512 (6th Cir 2003).

[96] For English law, see *The SLS Everest* [1981] 2 Lloyd's Rep 389, 391 (CA); *Modern Building Wales Ltd v Limmer & Trinidad Co Ltd* [1975] 1 WLR 1281, 1289 (CA). For US law, see Restatement (Second) On Contracts, §202(1). See also *Royal Insurance Company of America v Orient Overseas Container Line Ltd* 525 F 3d 409, 421 (6th Cir 2008).

sensible'[97] and 'reasonable'[98] meaning to the incorporation clause. In so doing, they take into account inter alia the overall context of the contract[99] and the understanding of a 'sophisticated' businessman engaged in the shipping business.[100] In doing so, however, the courts do not rewrite or dispense with the words used by the parties 'in the clearest and most exceptional cases'.[101]

These US and English approaches need to be viewed in light of the fact that it is not uncommon for commercial men in the shipping market to use shorthand writings and unclear expressions. When extracting the meaning of these expressions, drawing guidance from 'custom or past practices of parties' is a long-established approach particularly adopted by arbitrators.[102] US courts also consider 'course of dealings', 'usage of trade' and 'course performance' to attribute a meaning to the words,[103] where there is more than one meaning that could reasonably be given to the provision.[104] Similarly, English courts admit evidence of trade custom and usage only when the meaning of words is unclear.[105]

In *The SLS Everest*, the bill of lading holder unsuccessfully argued that the incorporation clause was not apt to incorporate when the clause read 'freight and

[97] For English law, *Pagnan SPA v Tradax Ocean Transportation* [1987] 2 Lloyd's Rep 342, 351 (CA); *Mannai Investment Co Ltd v Eagle Star Life Assurance Co Ltd* [1997] AC 749, 771 (HL); *Miramar Maritime Corp v Holborn Oil Trading Ltd* [1984] AC 676, 682 (HL); *The Antaios* [1985] AC 191, 201. For US law, see *Fishman v LaSalle National Bank* 247 F 3d 300, 302; *Fleet National Bank v H&D Entertainment Inc* 96 F 3d 532, 538 (1st Cir 1996) *cert denied*, 117 SCt 1335 (US 1997); *National Tax Institute Inc v Topnotch at Stowe Resort and Spa* 388 F 3d 15, 19 (1st Cir 2004).

[98] Under English law, the reasonableness is to be assessed by considering the practical effect of the provision or the contract, *President of India v Jebsens (UK) Ltd* [1991] 1 Lloyd's Rep 1, 9 (HL), per Lord Goff of Chieveley. In this context, in choosing meaning to be ascribed to the term, English courts may prefer the one which leads to reasonable consequences, if the parties' intention is not clear enough to proceed upon the unreasonable meaning, *L Schuler AG v Wickman Machine Tool Sales Ltd* [1974] AC 235, 251 (HL). See also *Rainy Sky SA v Kookmin Bank* [2012] 1 Lloyd's Rep 34, para 14. However, the courts cannot refuse to enforce a provision merely because they believe it unreasonable, *The Irbenskiy Proliv* [2005] 1 Lloyd's Rep 383, 387. In US law, there is a strong preference for the reasonable meaning, see Restatement (Second) On Contracts, §203(a), Restatement (First) On Contracts §236. See also *North American Construction Corp v The United States* 56 Fed Cl 73, 82; *Ludwig Honold Mfg Co v Fletcher* 405 F 2d 1123, 1131 (3rd Cir 1969); *Bruce v Lumbermens Mutual Casualty Company* 222 F 2d 642, 645 (4th Cir 1955).

[99] For English law, *Adamastos Shipping Co Ltd v Anglo-Saxon Petroleum Co* [1959] AC 133, 158 (HL); *Sirius International Insurance Co v FAI General Insurance Ltd* [2004] 1 WLR 325 (HL). For US law, *McAdams v Massachusetts Mutual Life Insurance Co* 391 F 3d 287, 299 (1st Cir 2004); *Gomez v Rivera Rodriguez* 344 F 3d 103, 121 (1st Cir 2003); Restatement (Second) On Contracts §202, comments (b) and (d).

[100] For US law, *Steel Warehouse Co v Abalone Shipping Ltd of Nicosai* 1998 AMC 2054, 2056 (5th Cir 1998); *Energy Transport Ltd v MV San Sebastian* 348 F Supp 2d 186, 203 (SDNY 2004). For English law, *The Annefield* [1971] P 168, 177 (CA); *The Starsin* [2004] AC 715, 737 (HL); *Modern Building Wales Ltd v Limmer & Trinidad Co Ltd* [1975] 1 WLR 1281 (CA).

[101] For English law, see *The Pacific Champ* [2013] 2 Lloyd's Rep 320, 333, per Eder J. A similar view is taken in US law, see Restatement (First) On Contracts, §235.

[102] See *In re Arbitration Between The Office of Supply, Government of The Republic of Korea and New York Navigation Company, Inc* SMA No 654 (August 1971).

[103] Restatement (Second) On Contracts §203(b).

[104] See *Metric Constructors Inc v National Aeronautics and Space Administration* 169 F 3d 747, 752 (Fed Cir 1999); *Teg-Paradigm Environmental Inc v United States* 465 F 3d 1329, 1338 (Fed Cir 2006).

[105] *Thor Navigation Inc v Ingosstrakh Insurance Co Ltd & Anor* [2005] 1 CLC 12, 26.

other condition [there was a blank] including the exoneration clause'.[106] Despite the ambiguous language, the intention to incorporate was obvious, and the Court did not hesitate to give effect to the clause as if it contained the full incorporation wording.[107] In a similar vein, the US Court in *Lowry & Co v SS Le Moyne D'Iberville* did not treat the incorporation clause as superfluous and gave effect to it completely, although it did not contain the words 'incorporated by reference' or any similar wording.[108]

As is clear from these observations, the *contra proferentem* rule has little or no weight in interpreting the incorporation clauses, although the application of the rule to bills of lading is generally accepted.[109] Since the courts in both jurisdictions do not require any meticulous clarity in meaning of these provisions, it is only in the rarest cases that bills of lading are treated as inapt for incorporation due to the flawed incorporation language therein. It therefore follows that where a charterparty is appropriately identified in the bill of lading, the courts will be more inclined to find bills of lading as competent for incorporation with a view to giving effect to the 'main purpose' of the incorporation clause.[110] When errors and/or ambiguities are only in the language of the incorporation clause, the chances of defeating incorporation by attacking the incorporation wording would thus appear rather slim.

A further question is whether the courts can find in favour of incorporation where the omission goes so far as to leave the reverse side of the bill of lading, where the incorporation clause is typically found, unprinted. Given that such bills of lading would lack the printed carriage provisions, including the incorporation clause, it poses a challenge for carriers to argue that incorporation should be allowed. Can such a bill of lading incorporate, even in the absence of a printed incorporation clause on its reverse side?

[106] *The SLS Everest* [1981] 2 Lloyd's Rep 389, 391 (CA).

[107] ibid. See also *Adamastos Shipping Co Ltd v Anglo-Saxon Petroleum Co* [1959] AC 133, 161 (HL) and *The Irbenskiy Proliv* [2005] 1 Lloyd's Rep 383, 388.

[108] *Lowry & Co v SS Le Moyne D'Iberville* 253 F Supp 396, 398 (SDNY 1966). See also *Son Shipping Co v De Fosse* 199 F 2d 687, 688–89 (2d Cir 1952); *Gronstadt v Withoff* 21 F 253 (SDNY 1884). This view is also generally adopted by maritime arbitrators sitting in New York, see *In Re Arbitration between Alpine Shipping of Monrovia and Palm Shipping Co* SMA No 1485 (22 October 1980) where the arbitrators took the view that the incorporation clause was sufficient to incorporate a charterparty, although the language of the clause did not contain the word 'incorporate' or any word to that effect. But see *Production Steel of Illinois v SS Francios LD* 294 F Supp 200 (SDNY 1968).

[109] For US law, see *Royal Insurance Company of America v Orient Overseas Container Line Ltd* 525 F 3d 409, 424–25 (6th Cir 2008) *cert denied* 129 SCt 299 (US 2008). However, it must be borne in mind that when there is already a meaning given to a particular provision under bills of lading pursuant to case law or legislation, this rule may not have any application, Restatement (Second) On Contracts §206, comment (b). Similarly, English courts are also vigilant in applying this rule in the context of bills of lading: *The Irbenskiy Proliv* [2005] 1 Lloyd's Rep 383.

[110] For English law, see *Glynn v Margetson* [1893] AC 351, 357 per Lord Halsbury. This perspective is also taken in US law, *Williams v Metzler* 132 F 3d 937, 947 (3rd Cir 1997). See also *Capitol Bus Co v Blue Bird Coach Lines Inc* 478 F 2d 556, 560 (3rd Cir 1973).

iii. Is the Omission to Print the Incorporation Clause on the Bill of Lading Fatal to Incorporation?

The crucial point here is this: imagine a bill of lading that makes it clear on its front that it is on a well-known standard form. If the reverse side of this bill of lading—on which the incorporation clause is typically found—is by some mischance left blank, can such a bill of lading incorporate? Would this question be answered differently if the bill of lading were not on a well-known standard form and/or if a charterparty were clearly identified on the front side of the bill of lading?

Since the omission to print the reverse side of the bill of lading leaves the bill of lading with almost no written conditions of carriage, the initial question is how US and English courts fill this contractual lacuna. The case law in both jurisdictions suggests that the courts will prefer to imply a contract.[111] The provisions of this contract will be determined pursuant to the answer to one question: which carriage provisions would have been stipulated on the reverse side of the bill of lading had the carrier not left it unprinted?[112] Of those provisions, the courts will only imply the provisions that are usual and reasonable.[113]

What flows from these observations is that commercial men should expect to be bound by the carrier's terms to the extent that they are reasonable and usual, although the terms of carriage are not contained in the bill of lading. Falling back on our scenario—where the reverse side of a bill of lading on a well-known form, such as the Congenbill 2007 form, is left blank—what terms will be implied into the bill of lading? Given that reasonable commercial men would be expected to regard the blank reverse side of the bill of lading as mere oversight, it is likely that the courts will imply standard terms of carriage in the Congenbill 2007 form. In so doing, they will treat the standard incorporation clause in the Congenbill 2007 form as if it were printed on the reverse side.[114]

[111] In English law the courts can imply a term in order to give 'commercial efficacy' to the contract, see *The Arctic Trader* [1996] 2 Lloyd's Rep 449, 452. Under US law it is accepted that a contract or term may be implied when there is 'course of dealing', 'usage of trade' and 'course of performance' manifesting such an intention, see Restatement (Second) On Contracts §4, comment (a), Uniform Commercial Code §1-201(b)3, §1-303. See also *Ventura Maritime Co Ltd v ADM Export Co* 44 F Supp 2d 804, 806 (EDLa 1999) quoting *Luckenbach SS Co v American Mills Co* 24 F 2d 704, 705 (5th Cir 1928).

[112] For US law, see ibid. See also *Interline v Zim Israel Navigation Ltd* F Supp 2d, 2000 WL 1060445 (NDCal 2000); *New Hampshire Insurance Co v Seaboard Marine Ltd* F Supp 1992 WL 33861 (SDFla 1992); *Royal Insurance Co v Sea-Land Services Inc* 50 F 3d 723, 728 (9th Cir 1995). For English law, see *Pyrene Company Ltd v Scindia Steam Navigation Company Ltd* [1954] 1 Lloyd's Rep 321, 333.

[113] See ibid. For US law, see also *Encyclopaedia Britannica Inc v Hong Kong Producer* 422 F 2d 7 (2d Cir 1969). Under English law, the constructive notice generally has no application in commercial contracts, *Manchester Trust v Furness* [1895] 2 QB 539, 545. However, this proposition is held not applicable where the terms referred to are usual, *The Njegos* [1935] 53 Ll L Rep 286, 296. See also, M Özdel, 'Incorporation of Charterparty Clauses into Bills of Lading: Peculiar to Maritime Law?' in M Clarke (ed), *Maritime Law Evolving* (Oxford, Hart Publishing, 2013) 181–95.

[114] For a similar view under English law, see N Gaskell, *Bills of Lading: Law and Contracts* (London, Informa Law from Routledge, 2000) para 21.27, quoting *The Hai Hing* [2000] 1 Lloyd's Rep 300; and

There are three main grounds for this solution: first, the holders of such a bill of lading have sufficient notice of the incorporation clause in the Congenbill 2007 form given the heading on the face of the bill of lading form, that is to say 'Congenbill 2007' and the words 'to be used with charterparties' under the heading. Both these statements on the front of the bill of lading amount to sufficient notice, for they direct the holders to the usual and readily accessible standard terms of carriage in the Congenbill 2007 form. Secondly, the carrier's omission to print the carriage terms on the reverse side cannot be seen as deliberate by the holders, who are treated as prudent businessmen in both jurisdictions.[115] Thirdly, the provisions of the Congenbill 2007 form can readily be considered as 'the carrier's usual terms' in both jurisdictions.

As regards the third ground, the question arises as to what constitutes 'the carrier's usual terms'. To address this issue, a closer look must be taken at the English Court of Appeal decision in *Interfoto Picture Library v Stiletto Visual Programmes Ltd*[116] and the decision of the US Court of Appeals for the Fifth Circuit in *Luckenbach SS Co v American Mills Co.*[117] In these decisions, the Courts took the view that the contract terms could only be treated as 'usual' if they are in line with 'common business practice', the 'course of dealings between the parties' or with the nature of the contract.[118] In this respect, the holders engaged in shipping and trade are reasonably to be expected to know the bill of lading terms when any of these circumstances arise.[119] When considered in light of these explanations, the provisions in the Congenbill 2007 form clearly comes under 'the carrier's usual terms' given its wide use in practice.

R Merkin, *Arbitration Law*, 3rd edn (London, Informa Law, 2004) para 5.20 quoting *Stensted Shipping v Shenzen Nantian Oil Mills* [2000] All ER (D) 1175.

[115] For US law, see *Steel Warehouse Co v Abalone Shipping Ltd of Nicosai* 1998 AMC 2054, 2056 (5th Cir 1998). For English law, *The Starsin* [2004] AC 715, 737 (HL).

[116] *Interfoto Picture Library v Stiletto Visual Programmes Ltd* [1989] QB 433, 445. See also E Macdonald, 'The Duty to Give Notice of Unusual Contract Terms' (1988) *Journal of Business Law* 375, 380–81.

[117] *Luckenbach SS Co v American Mills Co* 24 F 2d 704, 705 (5th Cir 1928).

[118] For English law, see Macdonald (n 116). For US law, see *Luckenbach SS Co v American Mills Co* 24 F 2d 704, 705 (5th Cir 1928). See also *American Home Assurance Co v TGL Container Lines Ltd* 347 F Supp 2d 749, 761 (NDCal 2004), where the fact that there was no 'previous course of dealings between the parties' was not taken into account, *Interline v Zim Israel Navigation Ltd* F Supp 2d, 2000 WL 1060445 (NDCal 2000). On the contrary, see *Royal Insurance Co v Sea-Land Services Inc* 50 F 3d 723, 728 (9th Cir 1995) and *Russul Corp v Zim American Integrated Shipping Services Co* 2009 WL 3247141 (SDNY 2009), where the Courts relied heavily on the previous dealings of the parties.

[119] In this context, it should be noted that the concept of usualness is narrower than reasonableness, as the test for the latter also includes examination of the effect of the provision, and purpose of the contract: F Lorenzon, 'When Is a CIF Seller's Carriage Contract Unreasonable?—Section 32(2) of the Sale of Goods Act, 1979' (2007) 13 *Journal of International Maritime Law* 241, 244, quoting *Tsakiroglou & Co Ltd v Noblee Thorl Gmbh* [1962] AC 93, 121–22. The US law position is also similar, *Stamm v Barclays Bank of New York* 960 F Supp 724, 729 (SDNY 1997) where it is stated that 'evaluating the reasonableness of ... clauses, a court must analyze the contract in which they are found, including the benefits to both offeree and offeror flowing from those clauses'. Nonetheless, it can scarcely be argued that this difference has any effect on the current analysis, since the courts do not generally imply unreasonable terms. For US law, see Uniform Commercial Code §1-303(e), for English law, *The Reborn* [2009] 1 CLC 909, 916.

Could it then be concluded that such a bill of lading can incorporate a charterparty? It is clear in US law that, whether printed or implied, the incorporation clause is, of itself, insufficient to incorporate a charterparty. The general rule is that, for incorporation, the incorporation clause should be coupled with an 'unmistakable reference' to a charterparty in the bill of lading.[120] Leaving aside the cases where the holder is not a stranger to the charterparty, such a bill of lading is thus apt to incorporate only if the charterparty is adequately identified on its face. A contrary approach is taken in US law where the holder is not a 'stranger' to the charterparty. Hence, as with the position under English law, the implied incorporation clause will be sufficient for incorporation.

Since these conclusions are based on the assumption that the bill of lading is on the Congenbill 2007 form, different considerations will arise where the bill of lading is not on a form that has such a wide acceptance and use throughout the world. Where the standard terms used for the bill of lading are neither common nor readily accessible by the holder, it will be far more difficult for carriers to persuade the court that their standard terms, which include an incorporation clause, should be implied into the bill of lading.

On the whole, these observations suggest that the failure of carriers to print the carriage conditions, including the incorporation clause, on the reverse side of the bill of lading, does not necessarily preclude incorporation. By and large, the consequences of such a failure depend on the factual circumstances of the case.

Whether implied or express, an incorporation clause itself cannot provide any guidance to the holder as to which charterparty is to be incorporated. Where a bill of lading does not identify the charterparty to be incorporated and where the vessel is subject to more than one charterparty, is it for carriers to decide which charterparty is to be incorporated? Or alternatively, do the rules of incorporation tell which charterparty should be incorporated?

II. Which Charterparty is Deemed to be Referred to in the Bill of Lading?

A. Overview

The question of which charterparty is purported to be incorporated is one of the simplest questions if a charterparty is clearly identified in the bill of lading. The same is also true in cases where the vessel is only subject to one charterparty. Where there is more than one charterparty, it is likely that disputes will arise as to which charterparty should be chosen for incorporation. As will be recalled, US

[120] *Son Shipping Co Inc v De Fosse & Tanghe* 1952 AMC 1931, 199 F 2d 687 (2d Cir 1952).

law dispenses with the requirement as to the identification of the charterparty in the bill of lading only in exceptional circumstances. The result of this is that the holders do not have to predict which charterparty is to be incorporated when the bill of lading does not identify any charterparty.

Under US law, the question of which charterparty is to be incorporated becomes relevant only where the holder is not a 'stranger' to the charterparty that the bill of lading seeks to incorporate. With these considerations in mind, there are two key questions: first, is the holder certain about the charterparty that the bill of lading seeks to incorporate? After determining the intended charterparty under this question, the next question is: is the holder a 'stranger' to this charterparty? Having already discussed the circumstances in which a holder is not treated as a 'stranger' to the charterparty, our focus will now be on choosing the charterparty to be incorporated.

Under English law, the practical significance of the question of which charterparty is to be chosen for incorporation is different. Since charterparties need not be identified in bills of lading for their incorporation, bills of lading frequently do not contain any charterparty details. When this is the case, the answer to this question has a significant impact on the legal position of holders vis-à-vis their respective carriers. This question is also of significance to all carriers who wish to know whether the rules point to the charterparty that they would wish to incorporate. Carriers would be more inclined to have their own charterparties incorporated into bills of lading since they may not know whether the terms of other charterparties in the chain secure their rights, as their own charterparties would. Whether they wish to achieve the incorporation of another charterparty or of their own charterparties, the rules of incorporation will, in any case, be of assistance in persuading the court or the tribunal for the incorporation of the charterparty that they favour.

The preferences of the holders for the charterparty to be incorporated also vary depending on the factual circumstances of each case and on the provisions of the charterparties that could potentially be incorporated. To achieve the incorporation of the charterparty that they favour, the holders also need to rely on the particular rules of incorporation, which will be analysed below.

B. The Position under US Law

In US law, where no charterparty is identified in the bill of lading, the general rule is that the courts do not treat the incorporation clause as an expressed intention to incorporate a charterparty. Instead, they conduct a fact-driven analysis to decide whether such an intention actually exists. Thus, where the holder happens to know which charterparty the bill of lading seeks to incorporate, the incorporation clause is taken to have referred to this particular charterparty.[121] This approach

[121] For more discussions on this issue, see Sections I.B and I.C above.

raises two key questions in order to find the relevant charterparty: first, in what circumstances is it possible for the holder to be certain about which charterparty is meant in the incorporation clause? Secondly, how could this be proved?

With respect to the former question, it is clear in US law that such circumstances may arise in cases where the holder is not a 'stranger' to the charterparty. It follows that a holder could be certain about the charterparty to be incorporated if he/she is the charterer of that particular charterparty,[122] or if he or she has a 'close relationship' with such charterer.[123] For the purposes of this analysis, US courts take the view that a holder who is the transferee of the bill of lading is presumed to be a stranger to the charterparty that the bill of lading seeks to incorporate. There is good reason for the courts to raise such a presumption in favour of the holders, who are generally not in a position to know which charterparty is sought to be incorporated.[124]

As for the latter question, a holder is usually deemed to be certain about the incorporation of a particular charterparty if the charterparty to which he/she is not a 'stranger' contains provisions as to its incorporation into the bill of lading.[125] In establishing certainty, US courts have refused, however, to take the view that there should necessarily be an express statement to that effect in the charterparty.[126] Thus, the courts have found that a holder is certain about this matter where an intention to incorporate the charterparty can be inferred from the charterparty provisions.[127] The charterparty provisions that can raise such an inference include the provisions on the form and content of the bill of lading to be issued thereunder, as well as those delegating the authority to issue the bill of lading.[128] For such an inference, the courts do not require that the form and content of the bill of lading issued be in strict compliance with the provisions of the charterparty.[129]

Consequently, in *Cargill Ferrous International v Sea Phoenix M/V*, a number of facts supported the Court's finding that the holder, who was also the shipper, had no confusion about the incorporation of the voyage sub-charterparty.[130] This finding was based on three grounds: first, the holder was the charterer of the sub-charterparty; secondly, the agent who signed the bill of lading obtained his/her agency authority from this particular contract; thirdly, unlike the head time

[122] *Cargill Ferrous International v Sea Phoenix M/V* 2003 AMC 1029 (5th Cir 2003).

[123] See Sections I.B and I.C above.

[124] *General Authority for Supply Commodities v SS Capetan Costis I* 631 F Supp 1488 (SDNY 1986); *Macsteel International USA Corporation v M/V Jag Rani* F Supp 2d, 2002 WL 22241785 (SDNY 2003); *Continental Florida Materials Inc v M/V Lamazon* 334 F Supp 2d 1294 (SDFla 2004), aff'd (11th Cir 2005).

[125] *Cargill Ferrous International v Sea Phoenix M/V* 2003 AMC 1027, 1030 (5th Cir 2003).

[126] *Keytrade USA Inc v Ain Temouchent M/V* 404 F 3d 891, 894 (5th Cir 2005) and *State Trading Corp of India Ltd v Grunstad Shipping Corp (Belgium) N/V* 582 F Supp 1523 (SDNY 1984). In both cases, the courts partly relied on a charterparty provision which stated that 'any Bill of Lading signed by the master of agent shall be without prejudice to the charterparty'.

[127] ibid.

[128] ibid. See also *Cargill Ferrous International* 2003 AMC 1027, 1030 (5th Cir 2003).

[129] *Keytrade USA, Inc. v Ain Temouchent M/V* 404 F 3d 891, 894 (5th Cir 2005).

[130] See *Cargill Ferrous International* 2003 AMC 1027, 1030 (5th Cir 2003).

charterparty, the voyage sub-charterparty contained a provision that it would be incorporated into any bill of lading issued thereunder.

A closer look at the US case law further suggests that extrinsic evidence can be admissible to establish certainty. In *Coastal States Trading Inc v Zenith Navigation* the shipowner's bill of lading was held to refer to the sub-charterparty. The shipowner successfully compelled the holder—who was also the shipper—'Trading', to arbitrate pursuant to the arbitration clause in the sub-charterparty. The sub-charterparty was entered into between Trading and Coscol. The intention of Trading to accomplish the incorporation of the sub-charterparty was established by the testimonies of their employees.[131] On this matter, the Court said:[132]

> Since this evidence concerning the charter party to which the bill of lading makes reference comes, in considerable measure, from Trading's own employees, Trading is hardly in a position to claim surprise or unfair advantage in a holding that the bill of lading incorporates the terms of the EXXONVOY 69 voyage charter party.

A similar approach was also adopted in *Amoco Overseas Co v ST Avenger*.[133] The case involved a charterparty that was entered into between the owner of *ST Avenger* and Amoco Trading International ('ATI'), and a contract of affreightment made between ATI and Amoco Overseas Co. When choosing between these contracts for incorporation purposes, the Court relied heavily on the pre-contractual negotiations of the charterer and the shipowner. This led to the decision that the incorporation clause should be taken to refer to the charterparty.

Obviously, the rule provides a perplexing solution to the question of which charterparty is deemed to be incorporated.[134] Although the rule can be justified on the basis that it makes the holders subject to the charterparty provisions of which they have notice, it blurs the line between charterparties and bills of lading, which are separate contracts. Those provisions negotiated between the parties to the charterparty are separate from those in the bill of lading. This is why an incorporation clause is needed to make the charterparty part of the bill of lading. When this is accepted, it becomes difficult to justify why being the charterer of the relevant charterparty should necessarily make this party bound by the charterparty provisions also in the bill of lading context. This approach also loses sight of the fact that, even though parties to the charterparty may have intended to incorporate their contracts into the bill of lading, the bill of lading may simply not achieve incorporation.[135] In other words, this approach undermines the logical difference between seeking to incorporate a contract and failing or being able to do so.

[131] See *Coastal States Trading Inc v Zenith Navigation* 446 F Supp 330 (SDNY 1977). On the contrary, evidence on the pre-contractual negotiations between the parties is not admissible under English law in resolving which charterparty is presumed to be incorporated, see *The Heidberg* [1994] 2 Lloyd's Rep 287, 309.

[132] 446 F Supp 330, 339 (SDNY 1977).

[133] 1975 AMC 782, 785 (SDNY 1975).

[134] For a similar view, see Justice Garza EM, in his dissenting judgment in *Cargill Ferrous International v Sea Phoenix M/V* 2003 AMC 1027, 1042 (5th Cir 2003).

[135] ibid.

A further point of criticism arises with respect to the decision in *The Sea Phoenix*. The decision is not congruent with the US rule of incorporation that for the bill of lading to incorporate a particular charterparty, the holder should be certain as to the incorporation of that charterparty.[136] While holding in favour of the charterparty to which the holder was not a 'stranger', the Court in *The Sea Phoenix* case gave weight to the fact that this was the only charterparty which contained provisions regarding the content of the bill of lading to be issued. With respect, this fact does not sufficiently establish that the holder was certain as to the incorporation of his/her charterparty into the bill of lading. Since the holder is not a stranger to just one charterparty, how could he/she know which other charterparties, if any, contain provisions on incorporation?

In *The Sea Phoenix* case, had there been more than one charterparty stipulating that it be incorporated into the bill of lading, the Court would have perhaps decided against incorporation. This result is rather unattractive from the perspective of a holder who is not a 'stranger' to only one of those relevant charterparties. A holder in such circumstances would be unable to foresee whether the bill of lading incorporated his/her charterparty or whether it was inapt for incorporation due to the provisions in other charterparties.

C. The Position under English Law

Perhaps with a view to promoting certainty in contracts contained in bills of lading, the solutions offered under English law are more straightforward than those offered in US law. Under English law, a bill of lading without any charterparty details can incorporate a charterparty.[137] Where the incorporation clause does not identify the charterparty to be incorporated, English courts do not engage in an inquiry to find which charterparty the shipper and the carrier intended to incorporate:[138] their decisions mainly rest on the presumed intention of the original parties to the bill of lading. Even more importantly, the courts never turn their attention to the actual position of the holder to see whether the holder has notice of the charterparty to be incorporated.[139]

With the leading judgment in *The San Nicholas*, a general presumption in favour of the head charterparty is recognised where there is more than one

[136] *The Rice Company SA v M/V Nalinee Naree* 2008 AMC 1152, 1161 (5th Cir 2008).

[137] *The Sevonia Team* [1983] 2 Lloyd's Rep 640, 644; *The Garbis* [1982] 2 Lloyd's Rep 283, 288.

[138] *The Heidberg* [1994] 2 Lloyd's Rep 287, 309–11. But see *Quark Ltd v Chiquita Unifrutti Japan Ltd and Ors* QBD (Com Ct) (Andrew Smith J), 25 April 2005 *(The Vinson)* 677 *Lloyd's Maritime Law Newsletter* 1.

[139] *The San Nicholas* [1976] 1 Lloyd's Rep 8 (CA). But see *Smidt v Tiden* (1973–74) LR 9 QB 446 where the conflict with regard to the intention of the shipper and the carrier as to the charterparty sought to be incorporated was held to prevent incorporation. This approach was later abandoned with the decision in *The San Nicholas*, see B Eder et al, *Scrutton on Charterparties and Bills of Lading*, 22nd edn (London, Sweet & Maxwell, 2011) para 6-018.

charterparty in the picture.[140] The justification for this rule ('rule of thumb') is made on the grounds that it is generally shipowners who act as contractual carriers in bills of lading.[141] This justification is in harmony with the main purpose of the incorporation clauses, which purpose is to enable shipowners to turn to and face bill of lading holders on the same terms as their respective charterparties. Following this main purpose, it is submitted that the presumption should shift to the sub-charterparty, if any, where it is the charterer who acts as contractual carrier in the bill of lading.[142] Whether or not the bill of lading is a shipowner's bill of lading, English law shifts the presumption to the voyage sub-charterparty, where the head charterparty is a time charterparty.[143] This rule was established by the decision in *The SLS Everest.*[144] The rationale behind this shift is that voyage charterparties are, by their nature, more akin to bill of lading contracts, as opposed to time charterparties,[145] which contain more inapposite provisions such as hire.[146]

i. The Application of the Presumptions

These explanations raise one further question: are these rules, which are based on the presumed intention of the parties, always applied regardless of the factual circumstances of the case? The answer to this question is not as straightforward as it might at first seem in the wake of the decision in *The Heidberg.* There, HHJ Diamond QC took the view that neither *The San Nicholas* nor *The SLS Everest* would be followed, when it made commercially more sense not to do so.[147]

[140] See *The San Nicholas* [1976] 1 Lloyd's Rep 8 (CA). The presumption readily supports the proposition that the incorporation clause is of itself sufficient to reflect the intention to incorporate a charterparty, *The Sevonia Team* [1983] 2 Lloyd's Rep 640, 644. Even in cases where the factual circumstances of the case leave English courts in doubt as to which charterparty is actually sought to be incorporated, they will, in any case, assume that one of the charterparties concerned is intended to be incorporated. This position was previously to the contrary, see *The Nai Matteini* [1988] 1 Lloyd's Rep 452; *Smidt v Tiden* (1973–74) LR 9 QB 446.

[141] See *The San Nicholas* at 11. In general terms, an unqualified signature of a master or his agent makes the bill of lading an owner's bill of lading, see *The Rewia* [1991] 2 Lloyd's Rep 325 (CA). But see *Elder Dempster v Paterson Zochonis* [1924] AC 522 (HL), where the bill of lading was held to be a charterer's bill, despite the master's unqualified signature on the bill of lading. Demise and identity of carrier clauses on the reverse side of the bill of lading may be decisive of this matter, see *The Berkshire* [1974] 1 Lloyd's Rep 185; *The Venezuela* [1980] 1 Lloyd's Rep 393. However, where the carrier is clearly identified on the face of the bill of lading, this identification will be decisive irrespective of an identity of carrier or demise clause, if any, on the reverse side, see *The Starsin* [2004] AC 715, 779 (HL).

[142] For a similar view see G Treitel and FMB Reynolds, *Carver on Bills of Lading*, 3rd edn (London, Sweet & Maxwell, 2011) para 30-027.

[143] But see *The Heidberg* [1994] 2 Lloyd's Rep 287, 312.

[144] [1981] 2 Lloyd's Rep 389, 392 (CA).

[145] ibid.

[146] ibid. See also *The Nanfri* [1978] 1 Lloyd's Rep 581, 591.

[147] See *The Heidberg* [1994] 2 Lloyd's Rep 287, 312. This is also supported by the fact that while interpreting commercial contracts, the courts presume that the parties could not have intended to create a result which is extremely unfair, commercially unsound or of no effect, see *The Miramar* [1984] AC 676 (HL).

a. *The Vinson*

The circumstances in which the courts could depart from these presumptions were later illustrated in *The Vinson*. There, a shipowner ('Quark'), who was also the carrier in the bill of lading, unsuccessfully objected to the incorporation of the sub-time charterparty providing for London arbitration.[148] Apart from this charterparty, which was entered into between the time charterers ('Eco') and Sunline Shipping Ltd ('Sunline'), there were two others: the head time charterparty made between Quark and Eco and the contract of affreightment ('the COA'), which was concluded between Sunline as operator and Laysun as shipper. The bill of lading was issued on the Congenbill form. In order to compel the holder to arbitrate in New York, the carrier sought to justify the incorporation of any of these two latter contracts, with both the COA and the head time charterparty containing a New York arbitration clause.

The carrier did not meet with success in this case, with the decision of Andrew Smith J that the sub-time charterparty was incorporated, despite the rule established in *The San Nicholas*. Andrew Smith J did not choose the head time charterparty mainly because it was designed for Quark's participation in the pool agreement. Thus, he found the provisions therein not apt for incorporation into the bill of lading. Furthermore, he took the view that, although none of the three charterparties was particularly appropriate for incorporation, the sub-time charterparty had the 'most appropriate terms' for incorporation.

In arriving at this conclusion, Andrew Smith J relied on four main grounds. First, the bill of lading was on the Congenbill form, instead of the Reefer Bill of Lading form that the COA called for. Secondly, the incorporation clause in the bill of lading expressly referred to the law and arbitration in the incorporation clause. Only in the sub time charterparty were there provisions both on choice of law and arbitration. Thirdly, although pre-printed, an express reference to a charterparty was made in the bill of lading, and this was taken to indicate an intention not to incorporate the COA. Finally, despite the fact that the COA contained a provision in respect of freight, the provision was held to be obscure and inapplicable in the bill of lading context.

Andrew Smith J in *The Vinson* sought to ascertain the actual intention of the original parties to the bill of lading. With respect, this approach deviated from the traditional approach of English courts based on the presumed intention of the parties. His consideration of all the three charterparties with a view to finding the 'most appropriate' one for incorporation was also far from traditional.[149] The inquiry into finding the 'most appropriate charterparty' went beyond the boundaries established by the decision in *The SLS Everest*. In the latter case, the presumption was shifted to the sub-voyage charterparty on the grounds

[148] *Quark Ltd v Chiquita Unifrutti Japan Ltd and Ors* QBD (Com Ct) (Andrew Smith J), 25 April 2005, (2005) *(The Vinson)* 677 *Lloyd's Maritime Law Newsletter* 1.

[149] For a similar view, see *The Heidberg* [1994] 2 Lloyd's Rep 287, 312.

that the head charterparty was a time charterparty, and that it was by its nature inapposite for incorporation, whereas the Court in *The Vinson* sought to find the most appropriate one, although none of the three charterparties was particularly appropriate for incorporation.

Probably due to these departures from the well-accepted rules of incorporation, Andrew Smith J in *The Vinson* sought to justify the decision by treating the surrounding facts as 'unusual'.[150] This makes it evident that his decision on incorporation can neither be taken as a rule, nor be treated as a restriction to the application of the presumptions established under *The SLS Everest* and *The San Nicholas*. It therefore follows that a departure from the presumptions should only become possible in the presence of unusual and distinct facts, making it commercially 'sensible' not to resort to those presumptions.[151] As the decision in *The Vinson* suggests, this may be the case where the presumptions under *The SLS Everest* and *The San Nicholas* point to a charterparty whose incorporation cannot have any meaningful effect within the context of the bill of lading. A departure from the presumptions in those cases would be justifiable for two reasons. First, the parties cannot reasonably be presumed to have intended to incorporate a charterparty that does not have a meaningful effect in the bill of lading context. Secondly, such a departure would be necessary in order to give the incorporation clause a 'commercially sensible' meaning.[152]

b. *The Wadi Sudr*

Another confusing twist in determining which charterparty is to be incorporated was seen in the case of *The Wadi Sudr*.[153] There, the vessel *Wadi Sudr* was successively time chartered, sub-time chartered and voyage chartered. A dispute arose between the holder and the carrier under a shipowner's bill of lading that contained an incorporation clause. One of the issues before Gloster J was which charterparty was to be incorporated into the bill of lading. Neither the holder nor the carrier suggested the sub-time charterparty be incorporated. This left Gloster J with two candidates for incorporation.

Her decision on the incorporation of the voyage sub-sub-charterparty was based on three grounds.[154] Of these grounds, only one was a true reflection of the traditional approach of English courts towards the incorporation issue. This ground was that many of the terms of the head time charterparty would be inapposite in the bill of lading context. The second ground was similar to that adopted by Andrew Smith J in *The Vinson*: the voyage charterparty was a contract of affreightment on voyage terms for the carriage of the goods in question. Looking

[150] This was mainly because the head time charterparty was part of the pool agreement between the shipowner and head charterer.
[151] For a similar view, see *The Heidberg* [1994] 2 Lloyd's Rep 287, 312.
[152] See n 97.
[153] [2009] 1 Lloyd's Rep 666.
[154] ibid, at para 111.

at the particular terms of the voyage charterparty, Gloster J thus found this charterparty 'more appropriate' for incorporation. As regards the third ground, Gloster J pushed the boundaries even further, relying on the fact that the holder was also the charterer of the voyage charterparty, to which his supply agreement with a buyer also referred. This line of reasoning came very close to that applied by US courts. With respect, it was at odds with the well-established rule under English law that the holder's actual position, including his/her other contractual arrangements, should not have any role to play when addressing the incorporation issue. Thus, the mere fact that the holder was the voyage charterer did not justify reading the incorporation clause in the bill of lading as if it had referred to the voyage charterparty. The reference to the voyage charterparty in the holder's contract of sale with a buyer also did not support such reading, given that all these contracts were distinct and separate from each other.

ii. The Application of the Presumptions in the Case of a Chain of Charterparties

Leaving aside the exceptional circumstances, in which not following the presumptions can commercially make more sense, the presumptions established in *The San Nicholas* and *The SLS Everest* should be applied, to the extent possible. Thus, where the picture involves one voyage sub-charterparty and one voyage sub-sub-charterparty, the bill of lading should be deemed to refer to the sub-charterparty, as opposed to the voyage sub-sub-charterparty. To choose the voyage sub-charterparty would be in accordance with the presumptions in *The San Nicholas*, which points to the charterparty that is the highest charterparty in the hierarchy, and in *The SLS Everest*, which favours voyage charterparties as opposed to time charterparties. In the absence of unusual facts, there is no reason to depart from the presumptions, particularly since the consistent application of these presumptions should be upheld to promote certainty in bills of lading.

Where the vessel is subsequently time chartered, sub-time chartered and voyage sub-sub-chartered, as was the case in *The Wadi Sudr*, which charterparty should be chosen for incorporation? Pursuant to the decision in *The Wadi Sudr*, the voyage sub-sub-charterparty must be chosen. Doing so would not be a departure from the presumptions: applying the decision in *The SLS Everest*, the presumption should shift to the voyage sub-sub charterparty, for it has, by its nature, more apposite terms for incorporation. This solution is also in line with the decision in *The San Nicholas:* given that there is only one apposite charterparty in such a chain of charterparties, the 'rule of thumb' does not apply.

The presumptions will not be helpful, however, in finding the charterparty where there is no hierarchy between charterparties, and where all of them are equally apposite. These circumstances may arise in cases where there are slot charterparty agreements, under which the shipowner lets not the entire vessel but spaces thereof to a number of parties. As a solution to this, guidance can be drawn from *National Navigation Co v Endesa Generacion SA*, where it is suggested that the bill of lading be matched with the charterparty 'which governed the contractual relations between the original parties to the bill of lading and in pursuance of which the bill was issued'.[155] The first limb of this suggestion is problematic, for there may not always be a charterparty between the shipper and the carrier. Nonetheless, the suggestion can be taken to mean this: the bill of lading should be matched with the charterparty which contains provisions as to its issuance and/or which covers the same goods carried under the bill of lading.[156]

iii. The Commercial Impact of The San Nicholas *and* The SLS Everest

The major consequence flowing from the general presumption, which favours the head charterparty, is that the holder bears the risk of the head charterer's failure to pay the freight or hire[157] and/or other sums due under the head charterparty. This result has adverse effects on particularly the holder who is the sub-charterer of the vessel.[158] With the incorporation of the head charterparty into the bill of lading, the holder's payment to the charterer does not discharge the holder from liability for payment vis-à-vis the shipowner under a shipowner's bill of lading:[159] a holder who has paid freight to the charterer is at risk of paying freight also to the shipowner under a shipowner's bill of lading that incorporates the head charterparty.[160] When seeking to avoid this risk, it would be rather difficult for the holder to establish that the head charterer collected the freight from the holder as agents of the shipowner.[161] In this respect, a freight-prepaid stamp appearing on the bill of lading can effectively estop the shipowner from claiming freight against the holder under the bill of lading.[162] However, if the holder knows that freight remains due under the incorporated charterparty, the freight-prepaid stamp will not estop the carrier from claiming freight against such a holder.[163]

From the perspective of a holder who is also the sub-charterer of the vessel, the presumption in favour of the incorporation of the sub-charterparty is clearly more favourable. Payment of freight to the charterer pursuant to the sub-charterparty provisions discharges the holder's liability vis-à-vis the ship-

[155] ibid, at para 110. As will be recalled the decision of the Commercial Court on incorporation was overturned by the Court of Appeal on other grounds, see Chapter 1, n 48.

[156] On this matter, see also *The Ikariada* [1999] 2 Lloyd's Rep 365, 372. There, the Court took the view that bills of lading should incorporate the charterparty under which the goods are carried.

[157] This is relevant in cases where the vessel is only time chartered or where she is first time chartered and then sub-time chartered.

[158] The same is also true of the holder who entered into a contract of affreightment with the sub-charterers, and made payment to such parties.

[159] It must be noted, however, that consignees or endorsees cannot automatically be subject to the obligations under the bill of lading, unless they qualify as a 'lawful holder of the bill of lading' within the meaning of s 5(2) of COGSA 1992 and they assume liabilities by virtue of s 3(1) thereof.

[160] As was the case in *The Constanza M* [1980] 1 Lloyd's Rep 505, affirmed in [1981] 2 Lloyd's Rep 147.

[161] *The Constanza M* [1980] 1 Lloyd's Rep 505, 514.

[162] *The Indian Reliance* [1997] 1 Lloyd's Rep 52; *Cho Yang Shipping Co Ltd v Coral (UK) Ltd* [1997] 2 Lloyd's Rep 461, 463; *The Nanfri* [1979] 1 Lloyd's Rep 201.

[163] *The Indian Reliance* [1997] 1 Lloyd's Rep 52.

owner when the bill of lading incorporates the sub-charterparty.[164] With the incorporation of the sub-charterparty provisions, including the provisions as to freight, into the bill of lading, the charterer is deemed to have received freight on behalf of the shipowner under the bill of lading.[165] On this matter, Rix J (as he then was) in *The Indian Reliance* said:[166]

> In my judgment the expression 'Freight payable as per charterparty' did incorporate cl 9 of the sub-charter, so as to make freight payable to the nominated account. Whether that is to be treated as a payment due to Cosemar [the charterer] or due to the owners but payable to Cosemar does not, I think, for present purposes matter, but I would be inclined to say the latter.

From the standpoint of the holder who is also the sub-charterer, the presumption in favour of the head charterparty may appear one-sided: in the case of a shipowner's bill of lading, it should be the shipowner's duty to clearly identify his/her charterparty in the bill of lading in order to be able to invoke his/her charterparty provisions also against the holder.[167] From this perspective, the presumption in favour of the head charterparty would appear to prejudice the shipowner by favouring the shipowner's choice over that of the shipper.[168] Favouring the head charterparty may raise objections also because one may expect the *contra proferentem* rule to prevent the resolution of the ambiguity, which arises from the failure of the shipowner to identify the charterparty, for the benefit of the holder.

Nonetheless, it is submitted that the application of the presumption should be upheld. The justification is the operation of the *contra proferentem* rule in bills of lading: although English courts recognise the application of the rule in the context of bills of lading,[169] they usually do not bring this rule into play if this could run the risk of undermining the commercial purpose of a particular provision therein.[170] Given the commercial purpose of the incorporation clauses—to

[164] *The Indian Reliance* [1997] 1 Lloyd's Rep 52, 57–58.

[165] ibid. However, the shipowner can intercept to claim its right directly from the shipper who is also the sub-charterer at any time before payment has been made to the charterer. *The Bulk Chile* [2013] 2 Lloyd's Rep 38 (CA) at para 24 per LJ Tomlinson, applying the dicta of Rix LJ in *The Spiros C* [2000] 2 Lloyd's Rep 319, 322. Freight-prepaid stamp on the bill of lading does not prevent the owner from intercepting payment, see *The Nanfri* [1979] 1 Lloyd's Rep 201, 210. However, clause 8 of the New York Produce Exchange (NYPE) form or a similar employment clause could arguably prevent the shipowner from exercising such a right where the time charterer is not in default of his/her payment obligations, see *The Bulk Chile*, above, at paras 28 and 29.

[166] [1997] 1 Lloyd's Rep 52, 57–58.

[167] See *The Heidberg* [1994] 2 Lloyd's Rep 287, 312. See also the dissenting judgment of Justice Garza EM in *Cargill Ferrous International v Sea Phoenix M/V* 2003 AMC 1027, 1046 (5th Cir 2003).

[168] For a similar view see Treitel and Reynolds (n 142) para 3-028. It must be noted that the intention of the shipper will be to incorporate the sub-sub-charterparty, if the shipper is the sub-sub-charterer. However, for ease of reference the analysis will be made upon the assumption that the picture involves a head charterparty and a sub-charterparty.

[169] For English law, see *The Irbenskiy Proliv* [2005] 1 Lloyd's Rep 383, 386 and *The Starsin* [2004] AC 715, 779 (HL). For US law, see *Royal Insurance Co of America v Orient Overseas Container Line Ltd* (6th Cir 2008) *cert denied*, 129 SCt 299 (US 2008); *Encyclopaedia Britannica, Inc v Hong Kong Producer* 1969 AMC 1741, 1752 (2d Cir 1969).

[170] *The Irbenskiy Proliv* [2005] 1 Lloyd's Rep 383, 388.

enable the shipowner to turn and face the holder on the same terms as his/her charterparty—a presumption that favours the head charterparty is clearly justifiable. Thus, the *contra proferentem* rule should not be applied in these cases to rule out the presumption.

Furthermore, it is also difficult to argue that this rule is one-sided, for two reasons. First, shippers usually have no interest in the incorporation issue, let alone the incorporation of any charterparty. This is best understood by looking at the position of a shipper who is also a CIF seller under a contract sale. Unless otherwise agreed in the sale contract, or in the letter of credit that incorporates UCP600, such sellers can tender for payment a bill of lading that does not identify the charterparty to be incorporated.[171] On receiving payment, they will typically lose their interest in the goods. Thus, it is unlikely that the question of which charterparty will be a matter of concern to them even in cases where their contract of carriage is under a bill of lading.[172] Secondly, given that shippers are the parties to draft and present the bill of lading for signature, they may, in some cases, have the opportunity to identify the charterparty they wish to incorporate.[173]

By and large, these observations justify the rule in *The San Nicholas* and also prompt one question: is English law actually in need of the exception established in *The SLS Everest*, which shifts the presumption from the head time charterparty to the voyage sub-charterparty? The views against this presumption can to some extent be supported on two grounds. First, having two different presumptions can complicate the issue, leading to uncertainty in bills of lading as contracts of carriage. Secondly, in view of the fact that the objective of *The SLS Everest* is to protect the holders from inapposite provisions, one can argue that they can equally be safeguarded from such terms under the consistency test[174] and the rule of manipulation.[175]

Despite the force of these arguments, there are weightier reasons to justify the view that English law is in need of the ruling in *The SLS Everest*. Time

[171] Under UCP600, such a bill of lading is acceptable insofar as it can be defined as a 'Charter Party Bill of Lading', see Art 22.

[172] Where a shipowner's bill of lading remains in the hands of a shipper who is also the sub-charterer of the vessel, such a shipper can sue the shipowner under the bill of lading.

[173] See also Cooke et al (n 13) para 18.61. It will be recalled that shippers have no right to present a bill of lading which contains the date of their respective charterparties, where the relevant head charterparty provides that the bill of lading to be presented for signature contain the details of the head charterparty. However, when the relevant charterparty requires the master to sign the bill of lading 'as presented', the shipper will be in a relatively better position, given that, in such cases, they are merely obliged to present a bill of lading that does not contain 'extraordinarily and manifestly' inconsistent provisions, see n 13. Whether shippers are actually entitled to insert their respective charterparties into the bill of lading depends on the 'proper construction' of the charterparty, see *The Garbis* [1982] 2 Lloyd's Rep 283. See also Eder et al (n 139) para 6-041. Nonetheless, when the vessel is time chartered under a charterparty that requires the master to sign the bill of lading 'as presented', the vessel owner cannot in most cases insist on inserting their charterparty details into the bill of lading, see *The Nanfri* [1979] 1 Lloyd's Rep 201, 206.

[174] C Debattista, *Bills of Lading in Export Trade*, 3rd edn (Haywards Heath, Tottel Publishing, 2008) para 8.17.

[175] ibid.

charterparties have more inapposite terms than voyage charterparties, and many of their provisions make little sense in the context of bills of lading. Above all, *The SLS Everest* is more helpful in maintaining the commercial efficacy of incorporation clauses when compared to the consistency test and the rules of manipulation: neither of these rules may prove as satisfactory as the rule established in *The SLS Everest.* When all inapposite terms are first incorporated and then jettisoned from the bill of lading, it is likely that there will be no charterparty provision applicable in the bill of lading, despite the incorporation clause. The presumption established in *The SLS Everest* prevents the incorporation of an inapposite charterparty in the first place and thus facilitates the incorporation of an apposite one. Hence, a charterparty that is more workable in the bill of lading context is incorporated with the effect that there will be more chances for the incorporated provisions to survive in the bill of lading.

There are also other practical reasons why the presumption under *The SLS Everest* decision should be upheld. Shifting the presumption to a voyage sub-charterparty produces results that are in harmony with the recognised contractual position of time charterers vis-à-vis their respective shipowners. In particular, the exception is in accordance with the 'delegation theory' established under *The Spiros C.*[176] On this theory, Rix LJ in *The Spiros C* said:[177]

> In my judgment, when a shipowner contracts that his freight should be payable as per a charterparty, he intends, and it is common ground with his shipper that he does so, that at any rate until he steps in to claim his freight upon the failure of his time charterer, the whole manner or mode of the collection of the freight should be delegated to the time charterer.

The delegation theory is founded on the premise that shipowners should in principle look only to their time charterers to recover hire, with the time charterers being delegated to collect the freight on behalf of the shipowners. On even a quick glance at the theory, one can easily see that it is in line with the presumption in two main respects. First, both have the effect of placing the risk of the time charterer's failure to pay the sums due under the time charterparty on the shipowner. Secondly, neither of these rules prevents the shipowner from exercising its right to claim the bill of lading freight from the shipper who is also the sub-charterer at any time before the freight has been paid pursuant to the sub-charterparty.[178]

A further point to make is the commercial impact of favouring the incorporation of the sub-voyage charterparty where there is a head time charterparty and a voyage sub-sub-charterparty. It is true to say that neither the shipowner nor

[176] See *The Spiros C* [2000] 2 Lloyd's Rep 319. This line of thought was also followed in *The Bulk Chile* [2013] 2 Lloyd's Rep 38 (CA). See paras 24 and 25 of the judgment.

[177] [2000] 2 Lloyd's Rep 319 at para 39.

[178] However, depending on its wording, an employment clause in a time charterparty could arguably restrain a shipowner from demanding payment of bill of lading freight to be made directly to itself until the time the charterer is in default of its payment obligations under the charterparty. See n 176.

the shipper may have any interest in incorporating the voyage sub-charterparty, particularly since neither of them is a party to it. Nevertheless, to accept that the incorporation clause is taken to refer to the sub-voyage charterparty makes commercial sense, especially when it is viewed against the background of the 'delegation theory':[179] with time charterers being treated as responsible towards their respective shipowners for the collection of freight, it is commercially sensible to read the incorporation clause as if it incorporates the sub-charterparty, as opposed to the sub-sub-charterparty. This view also promotes certainty, for it is in harmony with both presumptions under *The San Nicholas* and *The SLS Everest*.

It is true to say that, when this suggestion is followed, the holder who is also the sub-sub-charterer will be at the risk of paying freight also to the shipowner under a shipowner's bill of lading. This, however, does not justify choosing a voyage sub-sub-charterparty for incorporation purposes, given that a similar adverse effect has already been created and is prevalent with the general presumption under *The San Nicholas*. Furthermore, it is hard to suggest that to favour the sub-charterparty strips the holder of any protection. In such circumstances, the holders can seek redress against their respective sellers under contracts of sale: for payment, they can specifically require tender of a freight-prepaid bill of lading. This will, to a great extent, prevent the risks of making double payment for the carriage of goods.[180]

Having discussed which charterparty is to be chosen for incorporation where the bill of lading is silent as to the identity of the charterparty, further inquiry is necessary: is the charterparty so chosen actually capable of being incorporated into the bill of lading? This will be discussed below.

III. Is the Charterparty Capable of Being Incorporated?

A. Overview

Through the eyes of a bill of lading holder who is not familiar with the customary ways of concluding charterparties in shipping practice, it may well be expected that the charterparty to which the bill of lading refers is a formal written agreement. Furthermore, such a holder may fairly presume that the relevant charterparty has already been concluded by the time the bill of lading is made out. However, a great number of charterparties in practice are concluded over the telephone or by telex, fax or email exchanges, with the terms later being recapitulated in a 'fixture recap' telex, fax or email. It is very common for charterparties that were concluded by

[179] See Cooke et al (n 13) para 18.61, where similar arguments were raised.
[180] See n 164.

such means to be set out in a formal charterparty long after the bill of lading has been issued. It is even possible to see charterparties that have not been reduced to any form of writing by the time the bill of lading is issued.[181]

Evidently, the incorporation of charterparties that have been concluded in any of these ways poses difficulties for bill of lading holders. One of the problems is that when the charterparty is contained in or evidenced by a series of fax, telex or email exchanges, it becomes highly unlikely that the holder will be able to see the terms of a charterparty in such form. Where the concluded charterparty is not in any written form, this becomes simply impossible. From the perspective of the holder, the form of the charterparty is of importance because it may also help the holder frustrate the incorporation of the charterparty.

Just as with many other contracts in commerce, it is also possible that the charterparties to which the incorporation clause refers may not be in effect as a result of their being repudiated, rescinded or invalidated. Given that such a charterparty is not in force even between its original parties, should this contract be allowed to become part of the bill of lading and be effective between the parties to the bill of lading? This question may be answered in the affirmative given that to determine the incorporation issue on the basis of the contractual status of the incorporated contract would make this inquiry overly technical and somewhat complicated. No matter which view is taken, this issue reveals what carriers and holders should understand from incorporation: is it merely incorporation of some provisions, or is it incorporation of an effective contract into another contract?

This section will discuss four critical issues. At the outset, the issue of whether charterparties need to be in formal written form for incorporation will be analysed. Thereafter, the question will be whether the charterparty needs to be concluded by the time the bill of lading is issued. Given that charterparties are frequently altered or rectified, the issue of the extent to which such charterparties can be incorporated will then be discussed. Finally, the focus will be on the possibility of incorporating charterparties that are rescinded, terminated or which have become null and void.

B. What Forms of Charterparty can be Incorporated?

It will be recalled that the rules of incorporation in relation to this issue are of significance to holders. The chances of being shown the charterparty terms referred to increase when the rules of incorporation require a formal written charterparty, and stricter rules of incorporation make the incorporated charterparty terms more ascertainable. However, from the perspective of carriers, strict rules of incorporation would bring more difficulties in achieving incorporation, given that in many cases charterparties are concluded over the telephone, or by fax,

[181] *The Heidberg* [1994] 2 Lloyd's Rep 287.

telex or email exchanges, with the terms later being set out in a 'fixture recap'.[182] As part of this practice, the provisions under fixture recaps are carried to a formal charterparty long after the contract is actually concluded.[183] Above all, the eventual stage of having a formal charterparty is usually reached after the relevant bill of lading has been issued[184] and endorsed to a third party. The other possibility is that these contracts may not even be concluded by the time the bill of lading is issued, and they may even remain in the form of electronic communications.

This common practice of concluding charterparties brings challenges to holders, who reasonably expect to have a firm contractual position under their respective contracts of carriage as from the time when bills of lading have been endorsed to them. In order to see the extent to which their expectations are met under US law and English law, the first question is whether an oral charterparty can be incorporated. The next step will be to discuss whether other forms of charterparty can be incorporated into bills of lading.

i. Oral Charterparties

It is well established in both English law and US law that oral charterparties cannot be incorporated into bills of lading.[185] Thus, for a charterparty to be incorporated, it must be reduced to writing by the time the bill of lading is issued. From the standpoint of the holders, this requirement has salutary effects, for it allows the incorporation of only those provisions that can be ascertained from the time when the bill of lading was issued.[186]

There is a solid legal underpinning against the incorporation of oral charterparties: parol evidence is not admissible to alter bill of lading terms. This is best understood and supported by the English Court of Appeal decision in *Leduc v Ward*[187] and by the US Supreme Court decision in *The Delaware*.[188] In the former case, the Court refused to hold that verbal agreements made between the carrier and the shipper were binding upon the endorsees of the bill of lading.[189] In so doing, they sought to afford protection to the endorsees who take up the bill

[182] *The Petr Schmidt* [1995] 1 Lloyd's Rep 202.

[183] See, for instance, *The Heidberg* [1994] 2 Lloyd's Rep 287.

[184] See *The Spiros C* [2000] 2 Lloyd's Rep 319 (CA); *The Heidberg* at 310.

[185] For US law, see R Lord, *Williston on Contracts*, vol 11, 4th edn (Rochester, NY, Lawyers Cooperative Publishing, 2012) §30:25; For English law see *The Heidberg* [1994] 2 Lloyd's Rep 287 at 310. See also Treitel and Reynolds (n 142) para 30-030 quoting *Excess Insurance Co Ltd v Mander* [1997] 2 Lloyd's Rep 119, 127.

[186] For US law, see *Macsteel International USA Corp v M/V Jag Rani* 2004 AMC 220, 222 (SDNY 2003). For English law, *The Garbis* [1982] 2 Lloyd's Rep 283, 287.

[187] *Leduc v Ward* (1888) LR 20 QBD 475. As between the shipper and carrier, the bill of lading is only evidence of contract of carriage. For this reason, oral agreements can form part of the contract of carriage between these parties, *The Ardennes* [1951] 1 KB 55. For a similar view under US law, see *The Delaware* 81 US 579 (US 1871).

[188] US 579 (US 1871). For a similar view, see *Western Lumber Manufacturing v US* 1926 AMC 91, 93 (NDCal 1925).

[189] *Leduc v Ward* (1888) LR 20 QBD 475.

of lading by merely considering its face value.[190] Under US law, inadmissibility of oral agreements in the context of bills of lading was also recognised in *The Delaware.*[191] There, the Court did not admit parol evidence showing an agreement to carry cargo on deck on the grounds that the contract of carriage was contained in the bill of lading. It naturally flows from these decisions that bills of lading cannot incorporate an oral charterparty, given that provisions in bills of lading cannot be varied by verbal agreements.

The incorporation issue is usually tied up with disputes on incorporation and enforcement of charterparty forum selection clauses. This makes it necessary to ask one question: are there any formal requirements under English law and US law for the enforcement of forum selection clauses? If this question is answered in the affirmative, the next question is: are the formal requirements in harmony with the rules of incorporation? As regards the formal requirements, arbitration agreements under English law, section 5 of the 1996 Act dictates that only those arbitration agreements that are in writing come within the scope of the Act. For the purposes of the application of the US Federal Arbitration Act 1925 ('the 1925 Act'), arbitration agreements also need to be in writing.[192] Despite this tendency on formalities in both legal systems, pure oral arbitration agreements are nevertheless treated as valid at English common law and under US law, although such agreements are outside the 1996 Act and the 1925 Act. The result of this is that, although valid, oral arbitration agreements cannot benefit from these statutes, which would have facilitated their enforcement.[193]

On exclusive jurisdiction agreements, those that are purely oral are enforceable under US law.[194] A quick glance at the English common law suggests that the position is the same.[195] On closer examination of the position under English law, it will be seen that reference should also be made to Article 23 of Council Regulation (EC) No 44/2001 on Jurisdiction and the Recognition and Enforcement of Judgments in Civil and Commercial Matters ('the Regulation'). Article 23(1) provides that where parties to a dispute in relation to a civil or commercial matter designate the courts of a Member State, the court chosen shall have jurisdiction provided that two conditions are satisfied: first, at least one of the parties to the jurisdiction agreement must be domiciled in an EU Member State. Secondly, the

[190] For a similar view see *The Heidberg* [1994] 2 Lloyd's Rep 287.

[191] 81 US 579 (US 1871). But see *Hellenic Lines Ltd v US* 1975 AMC 697, 712 (2d Cir 1975), where the Court took the view that, as between the carrier and the shipper, the bill of lading could hardly be treated as a complete contract of carriage.

[192] See 9 USC §2.

[193] For English common law, see the Departmental Advisory Committee on Arbitration (DAC) Report on Arbitration Bill 1996 ('the DAC Report') para 32. See also s 81(2)(a) of the 1996 Act. For US law, see *Tuca v Ocean Freighters Ltd* 2006 AMC 1455 (EDLa 2006).

[194] See *Chateu des Charmes Wines Ltd v Sabate USA Inc* 328 F3d 528, 531 (9th Cir 2003) quoted in F Sparka, *Jurisdiction and Arbitration Clauses in Maritime Transport Documents* (Heidelberg, Springer, 2009) 100.

[195] See *Baghlaf Al Zafer Factory Co BR for Industry Ltd v Pakistan National Shipping Co (No 1)* [1998] CLC 716 quoted in D Joseph, *Jurisdiction and Arbitration Agreements and their Enforcement*, 2nd edn (London, Sweet & Maxwell, 2010) para 3.44.

jurisdiction agreement must comply with the requirements as to the form of jurisdiction agreements under subsections (1) and (2) of Article 23. The designated court's assumption of jurisdiction by virtue of Article 23 is nonetheless subject to Article 27, which is part of the *lis pendens* rule.[196] Under the latter Article, the court that has been seised of proceedings first is given priority to rule on its own jurisdiction.[197] In essence, the combined effect of these Articles is this: the court designated shall not have jurisdiction by virtue of Article 23 where the court of another Member State has been seised of proceedings first and established its jurisdiction pursuant to the Regulation.

With the revised Regulation ('the Recast Regulation')[198] due to take effect as of 10 January 2015, attention must also be drawn to Article 25 of the Recast Regulation, which is the counterpart of Article 23 of the Regulation. The Recast Regulation brings with it significant changes on jurisdiction and the recognition and enforcement of judgments in civil and commercial matters. On the enforcement of jurisdiction agreements, the domicile requirement is abolished. Thus, where the courts of a Member State are designated in a jurisdiction agreement, the courts chosen shall have jurisdiction irrespective of the domicile of the parties to the agreement. The requirement as to the form of jurisdiction agreements for enforcement purposes remains the same in the Recast Regulation, although the question of who decides the validity of a choice of court agreement will be answered differently. 'In order to enhance the effectiveness of exclusive choice of court agreements',[199] the Recast Regulation creates an exception to the *lis pendens* rule.[200] With this newly created exception, the court chosen in the exclusive jurisdiction agreement has, in principle,[201] priority to determine the validity of the agreement, as well as its applicability to the dispute before it.[202] To put it another way, where a court of a Member State chosen in an exclusive jurisdiction agreement is seised, the courts of other Member States shall stay proceedings for the chosen court to rule on its jurisdiction. Leaving the question of who decides, both the Regulation and the Recast Regulation ('the Regulations') require the jurisdiction clause to be evidenced in some form of writing.[203] The formal requirements for jurisdiction agreements under the Regulations are discussed elsewhere in

[196] For the *lis pendens* rule under the Regulation, see Arts 27–30 of the Regulation. For the *lis pendens* rule under the Recast Regulation, see Arts 29–34 of the Recast Regulation.

[197] See Case C-116/02 *Erich Gasser GmbH v MISAT SRL* [2003] ECR I-14693, [2005] QB 1.

[198] Regulation (EU) No 1215/2012 of the European Parliament and of the Council of 12 December 2012 on jurisdiction and the recognition and enforcement of judgments in civil and commercial matters (recast).

[199] See para 22 of the Preamble to the Recast Regulation. A jurisdiction agreement that falls within the scope of Art 25 shall be treated as exclusive unless the parties have agreed otherwise, see Art 25(1) of the Recast Regulation. This provision is also found in Art 23(1) of the Regulation.

[200] See n 196.

[201] See Art 31(4) of the Recast Regulation.

[202] See, in particular, subsections (2) and (3) of Art 31 of the Recast Regulation. For the position under the Regulation, see Arts 23 and 27 of the Regulation.

[203] See subsections (1) and (2) of Art 23 of the Regulation, and subsections (1) and (2) of Art 25 of the Recast Regulation.

this book. For present purposes, suffice it to say that a purely oral jurisdiction agreement is not enforceable under the Regulations.[204]

As is clear from these observations, it is vital for jurisdiction and arbitration agreements to be reduced to some form of writing for enforcement. This situation is in harmony with the rule of incorporation that an oral charterparty cannot be incorporated into the bill of lading. The hostility of the courts towards the incorporation of oral charterparties is readily explicable. It would make little sense to allow the incorporation of oral forum selection agreements: as has been discussed, the enforcement of these agreements is either problematic or impossible.

The explanations made so far show that much turns on the form of the charterparty referred to and that charterparties must be in some form of writing for incorporation. However, to say that charterparties must be in some form of writing is not of much assistance. It naturally raises the question of what the constituent elements of a 'written' charterparty are. It is now timely to discuss the legal position under US law and English law.

ii. *Charterparties Contained in or Evidenced by Fax, Telex or Email Exchanges*

Charterparties are commonly concluded by fax, telex or email exchanges. Although this practice adds layers of complexity in defining what constitutes a written charterparty for incorporation purposes, it is well established in shipping and trade. Where a charterparty referred to in the bill of lading is a formal, executed contract, the holder may have more chances of being shown a copy of the charterparty. Where a charterparty is only evidenced by telex, fax or email exchanges and is not even set out in a fixture recap, the holder's chances of seeing the terms reduce significantly.

Both English and US courts have sensibly preferred to keep pace with the customary ways of concluding charterparties in shipping and trade practices. Thus, the courts have firmly taken the view that charterparties the terms of which have been recapitulated in a 'fixture recap' telex or fax message are 'in writing' for incorporation purposes.[205] Thus, in the English case of *The Epsilon Rosa*, a charterparty that was only recapitulated in a 'fixture recap' telex by the time the bill of lading was issued was treated as in writing. In *The Epsilon Rosa* a formal, executed charterparty was drawn up after the bill of lading was issued, while in *The Channel Ranger* the charterparty remained in a 'fixture recap' email message.[206] Males J in *The Channel Ranger* was equally receptive to the incorporation of the

[204] ibid.

[205] For English Law, see *The Epsilon Rosa* [2002] 2 Lloyd's Rep 701, affirmed in [2003] 2 Lloyd's Rep 509. For US law, see *Thyssen Inc v M/V/Markos N* 1999 AMC 2515 (SDNY 1999) *aff'd sub nom Thyssen Inc v Calypso Shipping Corp SA* 310 F 3d 102 (2d Cir 2002) *cert denied* 123 SCt 1573, 155 L Ed 2d 312 (US 2003), quoting *Great Circle Lines Ltd v Matheson & Company Ltd* 1982 AMC 2321, 2328 (2d Cir 1982).

[206] *The Channel Ranger* [2014] 1 Lloyd's Rep 337.

charterparty in the form of an email, although no formal charterparty was ever drawn up.[207] Across the Atlantic, the courts have taken a similar line. In *Thyssen Inc v M/V Markos N*, the Court held that a 'fixture recap' that refers to a standard form charterparty is sufficient for present purposes, even in the absence of a final written contract.[208]

However, both US and English cases suggest that a charterparty in the form of a fixture recap telex, fax or email can only be treated as written where the fixture recap (a) clearly sets out the terms of the charterparty, or (b) makes a clear reference to a written charterparty.[209] In this respect, the requisite element of 'clarity' is satisfied in cases where the reference or the provisions contained in the recap message can sufficiently form a charterparty whose terms are reasonably ascertainable.[210] On the question of what references could make the charterparty terms ascertainable, the position under US and English law is: where the reference directs the holder to a standard charterparty form or to a written contract, such a reference is sufficient to form a written charterparty for incorporation purposes.[211] Consequently, even though a fixture recap telex, fax or email may not stipulate the terms of a charterparty in their entirety, a mere reference to a charterparty in such messages satisfies the writing requirement, as long as the reference therein points to a set of written terms.[212]

As naturally flows from the observations above, US and English courts do not call for a signed charterparty agreement for incorporation. A mere fixture recap contained in an email, fax or telex can be treated as a 'written' charterparty, if it has the required content.[213] The same approach should also be followed in cases

[207] ibid, at 339. It should be noted that the decision has been referred to the Court of Appeal.

[208] *Thyssen Inc v M/V/Markos N* 1999 AMC 2515 (SDNY 1999) *aff'd sub nom Thyssen Inc v Calypso Shipping Corp SA* 310 F 3d 102 (2d Cir 2002) *cert denied* 123 SCt 1573, 155 L Ed 2d 312 (US 2003).

[209] See n 208.

[210] For English law, see *The Epsilon Rosa* [2002] 2 Lloyd's Rep 701 and *The Channel Ranger* [2014] 1 Lloyd's Rep 337. For US law, see *JS & H Construction Company v Richmond County Hospital Authority* 473 F 2d 212, 215 (5th Cir 1973) quoted in Lord (n 185) §30:25.

[211] For English law, see *The Petr Schmidt* [1995] 1 Lloyd's Rep 202 and *The Channel Ranger* [2014] 1 Lloyd's Rep 337. For US law, see *Thyssen Inc M/V/Markos N* 1999 AMC 2515 (SDNY 1999) *aff'd sub nom Thyssen Inc v Calypso Shipping Corp SA* 310 F 3d 102 (2d Cir 2002) *cert denied* 123 SCt 1573, 155 L Ed 2d 312 (US 2003).

[212] For English law, see *The Petr Schmidt* [1995] 1 Lloyd's Rep 202 and *The Channel Ranger* [2014] 1 Lloyd's Rep 337. For US law see *Thyssen Inc M/V/Markos N aff'd sub nom Thyssen Inc v Calypso Shipping Corp SA* 310 F 3d 102 (2d Cir 2002) *cert denied* 123 SCt 1573, 155 L Ed 2d 312 (US 2003) and also *Continental Insurance Company v M/V Nikos N* 2002 AMC 1287 (SDNY 2002).

[213] For US law, see *Carnival Cruise Lines Inc v Shute* 499 US 585 (US 1991). For the position at English common law, see *The Petr Schmidt* [1995] 1 Lloyd's Rep 202. On the question of the concluding of a binding contract by telex, fax or email exchanges, English and US courts are divided. Where the exchanges demonstrate a 'meeting of minds' on the 'essential part' of the charter, US courts find that there is a binding charterparty, regardless of a fixture recap made 'subject to details': *Great Circle Lines Ltd v Matheson & Company Ltd* 1982 AMC 2321, 2328 (2d Cir 1982); *US Titan Inc v Guangzhou Zhen Hua Shipping Co* 2001 AMC 2080 (2d Cir 2001). The position under English law is diametrically opposite to that of US law. While a recap telex, fax or email can itself form a contract, a recap fixture which is 'subject to details' does not amount to a binding contract, see *The Junior K* [1988] 2 Lloyd's Rep 583; *The CPC Galia* [1994] 1 Lloyd's Rep 68. For a recent example, see *The Pacific Champ* [2013] 2 Lloyd's Rep 320.

where a charterparty has been concluded by fax, telex or email exchanges, without the terms being recapitulated in a fixture recap. As long as its terms are reasonably ascertainable, there is no reason why a charterparty in the latter form should not be incorporated. These observations lead to the conclusion that there are no rigid rules of incorporation as to the form of the charterparty to be incorporated. This accepted, a closer look must now be taken at the rules of formality designed for forum selection agreements. This will show the extent to which the forum selection clauses incorporated into the bill of lading can be binding upon the bill of lading holders.

iii. Formal Requirements of Forum Selection Clauses: English Law

Under English law, the formal requirements for forum selection agreements are no tighter than those envisaged under the rules of incorporation. A quick glance at the required form of arbitration agreements under the 1996 Act suggests that the requirement of writing is even more relaxed than that found under English rules of incorporation. Under section 5 of the 1996 Act, the writing requirement is satisfied where the arbitration agreement (a) is concluded in writing, whether or not it is signed by the parties,[214] (b) is made by exchange of communications in writing, such as exchange of faxes, telexes or emails,[215] or (c) is evidenced in writing.[216]

In brief terms, the writing requirement under the English rules of incorporation is much stricter than that under the 1996 Act in two main respects: under the Act, first, an arbitration agreement recorded by any means is treated as in writing;[217] secondly, an arbitration agreement is also treated as in writing if it is concluded in a way other than in writing but refers to terms that are in writing.[218] Conversely, under the English rules of incorporation the charterparty must be reduced to writing. As will be recalled, an oral charterparty is not capable of being incorporated, whether recorded or not, and thus it cannot be binding upon the holder.

As regards the writing requirement for jurisdiction agreements under the Regulation, attention must be drawn to Article 23(2) of the Regulation. The provision states that electronic communications providing 'a durable record of the agreement' are qualified as in writing. Pursuant to this provision, the Court in *The Posejdon* viewed an English jurisdiction clause in the Towhire form as 'written' under Article 23. There was a general reference to the Towhire form in the recap telex, and this was held sufficient for the purposes of the requirement.[219] Also, the Court went on to hold that the recap telex reflected the deal between the parties,

[214] See s 5(2)(a) and 5(3) of the 1996 Act.
[215] See s 5(2)(b) and 5(5) of the 1996 Act.
[216] See s 5(2)(c) and 5(4) of the 1996 Act.
[217] See s 5(6) of the 1996 Act.
[218] See s 5(3) of the 1996 Act. See also the DAC Report, paras 31–40.
[219] *The Posejdon* [2010] 1 Lloyd's Rep 384.

with no objection being made to its terms within a reasonable time.[220] The counterpart of Article 23(2) of the Regulation is found in Article 25(2) of the Recast Regulation on the same terms.

With these considerations in mind, can it be said that a charterparty forum selection clause, which is incorporated into the bill of lading, is deemed to have satisfied the writing requirement? As is clear from section 5 of the 1996 Act, Article 23(2) of the Regulation and Article 25(2) of the Recast Regulation, forum selection agreements in various forms are treated as in writing. This has the effect that a forum selection agreement that is qualified as in writing becomes binding upon the immediate parties to the agreement. Where such an agreement is incorporated into the bill of lading, could it also be treated as in writing vis-à-vis the holders?

On this question, some useful guidance can be drawn from the European Court of Justice (ECJ) decision in *The Tilly Russ*.[221] There, the ECJ held that the jurisdiction clause printed on the reverse side of the bill of lading was to be considered as 'in writing' between the shipper and the carrier, provided that both parties had consented to be bound by the clause.[222] In this sense, they suggested that the required consent would be present in cases where (1) the bill of lading was signed by both parties, (2) the printed jurisdiction clause in the bill of lading was the result of a prior oral jurisdiction agreement, or (3) the clause was the result of an established course of dealings between the parties.[223] The opinion of the Court in *The Tilly Russ* needs to be viewed in light of the fact that shippers hardly ever sign the bills of lading.[224] Thus, carriers in most cases are not able to establish consent based on the second limb of the test propounded by the decision in *The Tilly Russ*. *The Tilly Russ* was decided long before the entry into force of the Regulation. The decision was based on Article 17 of the Convention of 27 September 1968 on Jurisdiction and Enforcement of Judgments in Civil and Commercial Matters, which contained no reference to 'usages of international trade and commerce' at the time this dispute was litigated. With the adoption of the Accession Convention of 1978, the phrase referred to was added to the Article, and it was later clarified in the Convention of San Sebastian of 26 May 1989.

To assess whether the incorporated and express jurisdiction agreements are enforceable in bills of lading, attention must now be drawn to Article 23(1)(c) of the Regulation.[225] The provision contains a more relaxed rule of formality for jurisdiction agreements where the parties are engaged in trade and commerce.

[220] ibid, at paras 60–61.

[221] Case C-71/83 *The Tilly Russ* [1984] ECR 2417; [1985] QB 931.

[222] ibid. See also Case C-24/76 *Estasis Salotti Colzani Aimo E Gianmario Colzani v RUWA Polstereimaschinen Gmbh* [1976] ECR 1831; [1997] CLC 168.

[223] See Case C-71/83 *The Tilly Russ* [1984] ECR 2417; [1985] QB 931 at 953.

[224] Y Baatz, 'The Conflict of Laws' in Y Baatz (ed), *Maritime Law* (London, Sweet & Maxwell, 2011) 14.

[225] The Regulation has been the successor to Art 17 of the Convention on Jurisdiction and Enforcement of Judgments 1968. There is no complete succession precisely because the Convention is applicable to legal proceedings that ensued before 1 March 2002 and to the cases falling within the

For present purposes, what the provision suggests is this: a jurisdiction clause in a bill of lading that accorded to the usage of trade and commerce—such as a bill of lading on an international standard form—should be binding upon the shipper, whether or not he/she signed the bill of lading. Jurisdiction agreements, whether express or incorporated, are commonplace in international standard form bills of lading. With this widely known and regularly observed usage of jurisdiction agreements in such bills of lading, there is no reason why these agreements should not be treated as in writing vis-à-vis the shipper, who is the original party to the bill of lading. The same conclusion will also flow from Article 25(1)(c) of the Recast Regulation, which contains the same provision as that in Article 23(1)(c).

To support this conclusion, a more persuasive authority is the decision of the ECJ in *Transporti Castelletti Spedizioni Internazionali SpA v Hugo Trumpy SpA*.[226] There, the ECJ held that original parties to the bill of lading, namely the shipper and the carrier, would be presumed to have consented to the jurisdiction clause in the bill of lading that was in a form that accorded to the usage of trade and commerce.[227] They further suggested that it was for the national courts to determine the usages for the purposes of this assessment.[228]

Leaving aside shippers, when the position of consignees and endorsees of bills of lading is considered, the question will be: could an express or an incorporated jurisdiction clause in a bill of lading be equally treated as in writing vis-à-vis such parties? To answer this question, the main guidance is again the ECJ decision in *The Tilly Russ*.[229] The decision further suggests that where the jurisdiction agreement is deemed to have satisfied the formalities as between the original parties to the bill of lading, the same agreement will be equally qualified as in writing as between carriers and consignees/endorsees.[230] This is, however, subject to the satisfaction of one condition: the consignees/endorsees must have succeeded to the rights and obligations of the respective shippers pursuant to the relevant national law.[231] Hence, in *The Tilly Russ*, the ECJ said:

> [A]cquisition of the bill of lading could not confer upon the third party more rights than those attaching to the shipper under it. The third party holding the bill of lading thus becomes vested with all the rights, and at the same time becomes subject to all the obligations, mentioned in the bill, including those relating to the agreement on jurisdiction.[232]

jurisdiction of Denmark, which has not acceded to the Regulation; see A Briggs and P Rees, *Civil Jurisdiction and Judgments*, 5th edn (London, Informa Law from Routledge, 2009) para 1-04.

[226] Case C-159/97 *Transporti Castelletti Spedizioni Internazionali SpA v Hugo Trumpy SpA* [1999] ECR I-1597; [1999] ILPr 492.

[227] ibid, at 510–11.

[228] ibid, at 518.

[229] Case C-71/83 [1984] ECR 2417; [1985] QB 931.

[230] ibid, at 954.

[231] ibid. See also *Siboti K/S v BP France SA* [2003] 3 Lloyd's Rep 364, para 41.

[232] ibid. See also Case C-159/97 *Transporti Castelletti Spedizioni* [1999] ECR I-1597 at 510; *Siboti K/S v BP France* [2003] 2 Lloyd's Rep 364, para 41.

So far as English law is concerned, rights and obligations under bills of lading can be transferred to consignees and endorsees of bills of lading. By virtue of the English COGSA 1992, 'the lawful[233] holder of a bill of lading' to whom the bill of lading has been transferred, is deemed to have succeeded to 'all rights of suit' under the bill of lading as if he/she had been a party to that contract.[234] For consignees/endorsees to be treated as a lawful holder, they must have the bill of lading in their possession.[235] By the Act, the word 'holder' is used to refer to endorsees to whom the bill of lading has been transferred either in full or blank, as well as consignees.[236] While the lawful holders succeed to 'all rights of suit' on transfer of bills of lading, liabilities therein are transferred to these parties when they take a step, as defined under section 3(1) of COGSA 1992, to enforce the contract of carriage.[237] Bills of lading referred to in COGSA 1992 do not include 'straight bills of lading'.[238] Nonetheless, this type of bill of lading is treated as a seawaybill for the purposes of application of COGSA 1992.[239] The upshot of this is that consignees of such bills of lading can equally succeed to the rights and obligation of the shipper under the bill of lading.[240]

Under English law, it is therefore possible for the consignees/endorsees to succeed to the rights and obligations of shippers under the bill of lading. When this happens, it will be become possible for the carrier to compel the holder to litigate pursuant to the jurisdiction clause in the bill of lading. Where a consignee/endorsee ('a holder') does not succeed to the rights of the shipper pursuant to the relevant national law, the decision in *The Tilly Russ* suggests that Article 23(1)(c) will not operate. Thus, a jurisdiction clause in a bill of lading, whether express or incorporated, will not be treated as 'written' vis-à-vis such holders, unless their consent to the jurisdiction clause is established by virtue of Article 23(1)(a) or 23(1)(b) of the Regulation.[241] These conclusions will also be followed after the entry into force of the Recast Regulation, with Article 25(1) containing the same provisions as those in Article 23(1) of the Regulation.

None of the complexities above arises in the case of arbitration clauses in bills of lading. Excluded from the scope of the Regulation and of the Recast

[233] See s 5(2).

[234] See in particular ss 1(2), 2(1) and 5(2) of COGSA 1992.

[235] See s 5(2).

[236] ibid.

[237] See *The Berge Sisar* [1998] 2 Lloyd's Rep 475 (CA).

[238] See s 1(2)(a).

[239] See *AP Moller-Maersk v Sonaec Villas* [2011] 1 Lloyd's Rep 1.

[240] However, on transfer of a straight bill of lading, the shipper's rights under the bill of lading do not extinguish, see s 2(5). This situation is diametrically opposed to that of the shipper who has transferred an order bill of lading to the consignee, see s 2(5)(a). See also *AP Moller-Maersk v Sonaec Villas*, quoting C Debattista, *Southampton on Shipping Law* (London, Informa Law from Routledge, 2008) 101.

[241] See Case C-159/97 *Transporti Castelletti Spedizioni* [1999] ECR I-1597 at paras 81–82, and Case C-71/83 *The Tilly Russ* [1984] ECR 2417 at 953. See also Case C-387/98 *Coreck Maritime GmBH v Handelsveem* [2000] ECR I-9337; [2001] CLC 550.

Regulation,[242] enforcement of arbitration agreements under English law has been and will remain straightforward. A consistent line of English judicial decisions suggests that an arbitration agreement incorporated into the bill of lading is binding upon the holder, even though he/she is not the original party to the agreement.[243] Furthermore, when an arbitration agreement is duly incorporated, the holders are deemed to have intended to arbitrate their disputes just as if they were the actual parties to the agreement.[244] Thus, in *The Nerano*, the holder unsuccessfully argued that the incorporated arbitration agreement referring to the disputes between the owner and charterer was not an agreement 'in writing' as between the carrier and the holder.[245] The holder's main contention was that when the wording of the agreement was adapted to that of the bill of lading,[246] the agreement could no longer be treated as 'in writing'. In other words, when the agreement was read as if it referred to the disputes between the holder and the carrier, this change of words rendered the agreement not in writing. The Court dismissed these submissions, holding that the incorporated arbitration agreements with such adapted wording would still be treated as in writing and will be binding upon the holders.

iv. Formal Requirements of Forum Selection Clauses: The US View

In sharp contrast to the observations above, US courts to date have adopted a more conservative approach: the incorporated arbitration clauses which refer to the disputes between the parties to the charterparty are not in principle treated as enforceable against the parties to the bill of lading.[247] In *The Rice Company SA v M/V Nalinee Naree*, the Court thus refused to hold that the shipowner was bound by the arbitration clause in the sub-voyage charterparty which was incorporated into the shipowner's bill of lading.[248] The Court's decision hinged on the wording of the arbitration clause that merely referred to the disputes arising between the actual parties to the sub-voyage charterparty.

Where an incorporated arbitration clause does not contain such restrictive language, US courts have been more receptive to its application to the parties to bills of lading. In *Thyssen v M/V Markos*,[249] the Court held that the holder was bound by the incorporated arbitration clause where the clause referred to any disputes arising under the charterparty or the bill of lading issued thereunder. The

[242] See Art 1(1)(d) of the Regulation and Art (1)(2)(d) of the Recast Regulation.

[243] *The Nerano* [1996] 1 Lloyd's Rep 1, 3; *The Rena K* [1979] QB 377, 391.

[244] See *The Delos* [2001] 1 Lloyd's Rep 703.

[245] There, the holder relied on the Arbitration Act 1975, which was in effect during the litigation. This statute was later succeeded by the Arbitration Act 1996. For present purposes, the decision in *The Nerano* is still relevant, for there is no substantial difference between these statutes on this matter.

[246] For the rule of manipulation, see Chapter 3.II.

[247] The exception to this has been recognised only for those cases where the holder is also the charterer of the charterparty referred to, which contained an arbitration clause. Chapter 3.II.B.

[248] *The Rice Company SA v M/V Nalinee Naree* 523 F3d 528, 2008 AMC 1152 (5th Cir 2008).

[249] 1999 AMC 2515 (SDNY 1999).

decision in *Thyssen* must be viewed in light of the fact that US courts do not in principle compel parties to arbitrate disputes that they have not agreed to refer to arbitration.[250] The general view of the courts has been that arbitration agreements could only bind non-parties in rare circumstances.[251] As the decision in *Thyssen v M/V Markos* suggests, the incorporation of arbitration clauses into bills of lading is an example of such rare circumstances.

At this juncture, a further question arises: should a charterparty arbitration clause incorporated into a bill of lading be treated as in writing vis-à-vis a holder that is not a party to the charterparty? In such cases, is an incorporated charterparty arbitration clause 'in writing' within the meaning of Chapter I of Title 9 United States Code ('USC'), which contained the Federal Arbitration Act, 1925 ('the 1925 Act'), Chapter II of 9 USC, which incorporated the New York Convention, 1958 and Chapter III of 9 USC, which implemented the Panama Convention, 1976? To address this issue, it is necessary to discuss first the scope of application of the 1925 Act and of the Conventions.

Arbitration agreements between the citizens of the United States fall outside the scope of the New York Convention by virtue of 9 USC §203. Accordingly, the 1925 Act, which is enshrined in Chapter I of 9 USC, is applicable to these parties. However, where the majority of the parties to the arbitration agreement are the citizens of the Panama Convention States, this Convention comes into play and governs the issues of formality.[252]

On a quick glance at the 1925 Act and the Conventions, it would appear that the writing requirement envisaged in the 1925 Act could be given the widest possible meaning. The 1925 Act does no more than state the requirement of writing, leaving to the courts the issue of what actually makes an arbitration agreement in writing.[253] On the writing requirement, a much tighter provision is Article 2(2) of the New York Convention, which states that 'The term "agreement in writing" shall include an arbitral clause in a contract or an arbitration agreement, signed by the parties or contained in an exchange of letters or telegrams'. On the interpretation of the writing requirement under the New York Convention, US courts are divided. Pursuant to the decision in *Kahn Lucas Lancaster Inc v Lark International Ltd*,[254] an arbitration clause in a contract is binding if the clause is the result of an arbitration agreement either signed by both parties or contained in an exchange of letters or telegrams. However, the decision in *Sphere Drake Ins PLC v Marine Towing Inc* was that in the case of an arbitration clause in a contract,

[250] *Painewebber Incorporated v Bybyk*, 81 F 3d 1193, 1198 (2d Cir 1996); *United Steelworkers of America v Warrior & Gulf Navigation Co* 363 US 574, 582 (US 1960).

[251] *Bridas SAPIC v Government of Turkmenistan* 345 F 3d 347, 355–56 (5th Cir 2003).

[252] See part B-35 of the Panama Convention, and 9 USC §305.

[253] See, for instance, *Valero Refining Inc v M/T Lauberhorn* 1987 AMC 2100, 2105 (5th Cir 1987). There, the arbitration clause in an unsigned charterparty was held to be in writing within the meaning of the Federal Arbitration Act 1925 ('the FAA') and was enforceable between the parties.

[254] *Kahn Lucas Lancaster Inc v Lark International Ltd* 186 F 3d 210 (2d Cir 1999).

the requirement of signature by the parties or an exchange of letters or telegrams does not apply.[255]

A similar rule of formality is also found in Article 1 of the Panama Convention. Unlike the wording of Article 2(2) of the New York Convention, Article 1 of the Panama Convention does not leave open the possibility of two different interpretations.[256] The result of this is that, under the latter Convention, the writing requirement is met where a contract that contains an arbitration clause or an arbitration agreement is signed by both parties or is contained in an exchange of letters, telegrams or telexes.

Just as with Article 2(2) of the New York Convention, Article 1 of the Panama Convention also raises the question of the extent to which arbitration agreements could be treated as in writing vis-à-vis third parties. In the context of the incorporation of arbitration clauses into bills of lading, this issue is of great significance: only in exceptional cases does the holder of a bill of lading happen to be also the party to the incorporated charterparty, including the agreement to arbitrate contained therein. Should the writing requirements in the Conventions be interpreted in such a way that these holders can be bound by the incorporated arbitration clauses?

Given that US courts do not in principle compel parties to arbitrate the disputes that they have not agreed to refer to arbitration, it would appear that the answer to this question must be 'no'. If this is harsh from the standpoint of carriers, the application of the restrictive interpretation of the writing requirement under the New York Convention or that of Article 1 of the Panama Convention is in fact even harsher: the carrier would be expected to establish that the arbitration clause is the result of an arbitration agreement either (1) signed by the carrier and the holder, or (2) contained in an exchange of communications between the holder and carrier.[257] Recently, Judge Tauro of the federal district court of Massachusetts in *Maroc Fruit Board SA v M/V Vinson*[258] followed this line of thought, when holding that the shipper was not bound by the charterparty arbitration clause incorporated into the bill of lading. Given the absence of the shipper's signature on the bill of lading, the judge took the view that the arbitration agreement did not satisfy the writing requirement under the New York Convention. His reliance on Chapter II of 9 USC, which implemented the New York Convention, was based on the fact that both the shipper and the carrier were foreign parties.

In *Instituto Cubano De Establizacion Del Azucar v T/V Golden West*[259] and *Federal Insurance Company and Turbana Corp v MV Audacia*, the Courts also

[255] *Sphere Drake Ins PLC v Marine Towing Inc* 16 F 3d 666, 1994 AMC 1581 (5th Cir 1994). For more discussions on this topic, see M Davies, 'Litigation Fights Back: Avoiding the Effect of Arbitration Clauses in Charterparty Bills of Lading' (2004) 35 *Journal of Maritime Law and Commerce* 618.

[256] See Davies (n 255).

[257] ibid.

[258] *Maroc Fruit Board SA v M/V Vinson* 2012 WL 2989195 (D Mass 2012).

[259] *Instituto Cubano De Establizacion Del Azucar v T/V Golden West* 1957 AMC 1481 (SDNY 1957).

adopted a similarly conservative approach.[260] The Courts in these decisions took the view that neither the holders nor the carriers could be compelled to arbitrate their disputes by reason of an incorporated arbitration agreement to which they were not parties. The Court in the latter decision took this stance, although the scope of the incorporated arbitration agreement was not confined to the disputes between its actual signatories.

These conservative approaches raise the question of why parties to the bill of lading cannot simply be deemed to have consented to arbitrate where the bill of lading contains an express or incorporated arbitration clause. To establish the actual consent of every subsequent holder to the arbitration clause is not only impractical but also inconsistent with the workings of shipping and trade practice. Perhaps due to these weaknesses, the more compelling US authorities, such as *Thyssen*, take a more liberal view.[261] They treat the incorporated arbitration clauses as binding upon the holders provided that the clause refers to disputes arising between the parties to the bill of lading.[262] With this view, they recognise, albeit silently, that the concept of deemed consent could come into play in the case of arbitration clauses incorporated into bills of lading. Most notably, this tendency towards the enforcement of arbitration clauses in bills of lading is best illustrated by the US Supreme Court decision in *Vimar Seguros y Reaseguros SA v M/V Sky Reefer* (‘*The Sky Reefer*’).[263] There, the arbitration agreement printed on the reverse side of the bill of lading was held to be binding upon the endorsee, who neither signed the bill of lading, nor individually negotiated the terms therein. Although the parties in *The Sky Reefer* were not both American citizens, the arbitration agreement was governed by Chapter I of 9 USC. This was also the case in *Thyssen*.

On the enforcement of jurisdiction agreements incorporated into the bill of lading, the decision of the US Supreme Court in *Carnival Cruise Lines v Shute*[264] is also of assistance. There, the Court took the view that the jurisdiction clause in a cruise ticket was binding upon the passenger, although the passenger did not negotiate the terms of the ticket, including the jurisdiction clause. What naturally flows from this decision is that an express or incorporated jurisdiction clause in bills of lading should be binding upon a bill of lading holder, although the holder has not actually consented to be bound by it. Given that a bill of lading holder is generally far more sophisticated than a cruise passenger, there is no reason why a

[260] *Federal Insurance Company and Turbana Corp v MV Audacia* 1987 AMC 566 (SDNY 1986).

[261] See *Thyssen Inc M/V/Markos N aff'd sub nom Thyssen Inc v Calypso Shipping Corp SA* 310 F 3d 102 (2d Cir 2002) *cert denied* 123 SCt 1573, 155 L Ed 2d 312 (US 2003). See also, *Citrus Marketing Board of Israel v M/V Ecuadorian Reefer* 754 F Supp 229 (DMass 1990); *Union Carbide Corporation v M/T Monte Carmelo* F Supp 2d, 2002 WL 31812676 (SDNY 2002); *Cementos Andinos Dominicanos SA v East Bulk Shipping SA* 2006 WL 846551 (SDNY 2006); *Vimar Seguros y Reaseguros SA v M/V Sky Reefer, et al* 1994 AMC 2513 (1st Cir 1994) *aff'd* 515 US 528 (US 1995).

[262] For further discussions on this matter, see Chapter 3.III.

[263] *Vimar Seguros y Reaseguros SA v M/V Sky Reefer, et al* 1994 AMC 2513 (1st Cir 1994), *aff'd* 515 US 528 (US 1995).

[264] *Carnival Cruise Lines v Shute* 499 US 585 (US 1991).

jurisdiction clause incorporated into a bill of lading should not be treated as 'in writing' vis-à-vis the holder.

v. Rules of Formality: Where Do They Take Us?

The observations reveal that there are different writing requirements in the context of the rules of incorporation and of the enforcement of forum selection clauses. From the standpoint of a carrier seeking to incorporate and enforce arbitration clause vis-à-vis a bill of lading holder, the legal position in both jurisdictions is actually less complex than it seems. Where a charterparty meets the writing requirement under the applicable rules of incorporation and is also incorporated into the bill of lading with its forum selection clause, the clause will in most cases be treated as in writing vis-à-vis the holder.

On forum selection clauses, it would appear that there is a tendency in both jurisdictions to relax the formalities for their enforcement. A similar relaxation of formalities can also be seen in the recent incorporation cases in both jurisdictions: the courts have been receptive to the incorporation of charterparties contained in a fixture recap even in the absence of a final written contract signed by the parties. From the carriers' perspective, this situation removes the necessity of drafting a formal charterparty, although they still need to pay particular attention to the time of concluding the charterparty for incorporation purposes. This will be discussed below.

C. Do We Need an Already Concluded Charterparty by the Time the Bill of Lading is Issued?

Having identified the formalities, a further question is: when should charterparties in the required form need to come into existence for the purposes of incorporation? The practical importance of this issue is that to allow carriers to incorporate charterparties that have not yet sprung into existence when the bill of lading is issued would be similar to giving these parties a blank cheque. They would be given an unfettered right to bind the holders to the terms of charterparties, regardless of when they come into existence. Evidently, this would greatly undermine the sanctity of incorporation clauses, for the bill of lading is expected to provide ascertainable and specific provisions from the time it is issued. The same is also true of bills of lading, which are expected to provide a firm contractual position to the holders vis-à-vis the carriers.[265] For these reasons, it is tempting to say that incorporation clauses should not be interpreted in such a way that future charterparties can be incorporated.

Before taking any stance on this issue, it should be recalled that the bill of lading does not always start life as a contract of carriage in cases where it is issued to

[265] For a similar view, see *The Northern Progress (No 2)* [1996] 2 Lloyd's Rep 319, 326.

a shipper who is a charterer of the vessel. Thus, one can argue that commercial certainty is not necessarily prejudiced by incorporating a charterparty that is concluded after the bill of lading is issued. If this is accepted, then the question will be: when should the charterparty be concluded for incorporation? Should it be by the time the bill of lading is endorsed to a third party,[266] or prior to the holder's first demand to see a copy?[267] Could it then be said that specific account should be given of the time when the bill of lading starts to function as a contract of carriage?

i. English Law

From a general contract law perspective, the incorporation of a contract that has yet to be concluded is not an unlikely eventuality. However, this can only be achieved under English law with an incorporation clause that manifests the intention of the parties to incorporate as such.[268] Accordingly, unless there is an express provision to the contrary, general words of incorporation are not apt to import a contract that has yet to be concluded.[269] However, English case law suggests that such incorporation is allowed in exceptional circumstances, where two conditions are met. First, the logical sequence of the transactions must make it impossible to conclude the contract to be incorporated before the incorporating contract is executed.[270] Secondly, the terms of the contract to be incorporated must be usual and reasonable.[271]

In the context of bills of lading, English courts have taken a similar line. Their approach to date has been to allow the incorporation of only those charterparties that are concluded and reduced to a written form by the time the respective bills of lading are made out.[272] This rule mainly has its roots in *The Heidberg*, where HHJ Diamond QC stood against incorporation of an oral charterparty that was not accurately reduced to a written form before the bill of lading was issued.[273] On the question of what qualifies as a 'written' charterparty, it must be recalled that a more persuasive and well-recognised authority is *The Epsilon Rosa*.[274] There, the Court of Appeal held that the charterparty was incorporated, even though it was

[266] For a similar view, see Treitel and Reynolds (n 142) para 3-028.

[267] ibid.

[268] See *Excess Insurance Co Ltd v Mander* [1997] 2 Lloyd's Rep 119, 127, where the Court refused to hold that the treaty was incorporated into the main agreement on the grounds that the agreement was executed four months before the treaty.

[269] ibid.

[270] See *The Northern Progress*, 326; *OK Petroleum AB v Vitol Energy SA* [1995] 2 Lloyd's Rep 160.

[271] See *OK Petroleum* [1995] 2 Lloyd's Rep 160 at 163. In this respect, the reasonableness is assessed on the basis of the nature of the main agreement, see *The Northern Progress* [1996] 2 Lloyd's Rep 319.

[272] See *The Heidberg* [1994] 2 Lloyd's Rep 287, 310; *Fidelitas Shipping Co v V/O Exportchleb* [1963] 2 Lloyd's Rep 113, 117 (CA); *The Spiros C* [2000] 2 Lloyd's Rep 319, 327 (CA); *The Epsilon Rosa* [2003] 2 Lloyd's Rep 509, 516 (CA). See also Treitel and Reynolds (n 142) para 3-028.

[273] See *The Heidberg* [1994] 2 Lloyd's Rep 287.

[274] HHJ Diamond QC in *The Heidberg* took the view that charterparties evidenced under fixture recap would not qualify for incorporation purposes, see ibid, at 311.

merely evidenced under a recap fixture telex made before the bill of lading was issued.[275]

The explanations made so far do not, however, throw light on the question of whether a charterparty that has yet to be concluded can be incorporated when an incorporation clause contains an express provision to that effect.[276] Should the incorporation clause be allowed to incorporate a charterparty that does not exist by the time the bill of lading is issued? If the intention to incorporate a future charterparty is made clear in the incorporation clause, the courts can do nothing but give effect to that intention. The key rule of construction is to give effect to the intention of the parties that can objectively be ascertained from the contract wording.[277] However, it is likely that English courts will be reluctant to read the incorporation clause as apt to incorporate a charterparty that did not exist at the time the bill of lading was issued. To read the incorporation clause as such would bring with it an unascertainable contract of carriage in the bill of lading. The courts will try to avoid this result given that to have such bills of lading in international trade would greatly undermine the reliability of the bills of lading as contracts of carriage. Consequently, incorporation clauses in bills of lading can rarely be said to be adequate for incorporating a contract that will come into existence in the future.

However, for those bills of lading that first start life as a mere receipt, should they be allowed to incorporate a charterparty that has been concluded before the bill of lading started to operate as a contract of carriage?[278] From a contract law perspective, there would appear to be no problems with allowing the incorporation of the charterparty in such cases—the incorporation would not create the risk of having unascertainable contract terms in the bill of lading. This would be problematic, however, given the way the bill of lading operates: unlike many other commercial contracts, it is difficult to determine exactly when the bill of lading turns into a contract of carriage. For this reason, the issue date of the bill of lading needs to be taken as a basis, not the time when the bill of lading started to operate as a contract of carriage. The issue date of the bill of lading, which is readily provided on its face, is a more reliable basis when determining by which time the charterparty to be incorporated must be concluded. Consequently, it is a sounder rule to require an already concluded charterparty at the time the bill of lading is issued, even though the bill of lading may have been surrendered to a shipper who would merely hold the same as a receipt.

Although well recognised, the need to have an already concluded charterparty by the time the bill of lading is issued is not set in stone. The rule may, in the future, be subject to an exception. On this issue, some useful guidance can be

[275] See *The Epsilon Rosa* [2003] 2 Lloyd's Rep 509, 516 (CA).

[276] Treitel and Reynolds (n 142) para 3-028.

[277] See *The Northern Progress* [1996] 2 Lloyd's Rep 319 at 329. See also *Credit Lyonnais Bank Nederland NV v Export Credits Guarantee Department* [1998] 1 Lloyd's Rep 19, 38 (CA).

[278] ibid.

drawn from the *obiter dictum* of Rix J (as he then was) in *The Northern Progress*,[279] which raises one possibility: the bill of lading can be taken to refer to a charterparty that has yet to be concluded, although the incorporation clause is silent on this matter. The bill of lading can thus be taken to such an extent that the logical sequence of the transactions justifies entering into a charterparty contract after the bill of lading is issued, and that the terms of the charterparty are usual and reasonable.[280]

Rix J's *obiter dictum* in *The Northern Progress* raises the question of the circumstances in which it could be deemed logical and justifiable to conclude a charterparty after the bill of lading is issued. A good example of this is the position of an FOB seller, whose buyer rejects the bill of lading[281] or fails to make a payment.[282] It is natural for the seller in such cases to enter into a charterparty with the shipowner after the bill of lading is issued, if his/her sale contract with a new buyer requires the seller to enter into a contract of carriage.[283] In light of these observations, should the unique position of such sellers justify the incorporation of a charterparty which was not concluded at the time the bill of lading was issued? *The Northern Progress* is a compelling authority to conclude that it should, so long as the referred charterparty contains usual and reasonable provisions.

Since this suggested exception has not yet been applied to any case, the general rule that the charterparty must be concluded by the time the bill of lading is issued still remains intact. Accordingly, the holders are well protected as a result of this firm stance, creating non-variable carriage terms in bills of lading as from the time they are made out. Having seen where English law stands on this issue, the next section will focus on the position under US law.

ii. US Law

From a general contract law perspective, there are two main hurdles preventing incorporation of a contract that will be concluded in the future. The main barrier is one of the US rules of incorporation, which requires that the incorporation clause specifies the contract to be incorporated without leaving any doubt as to its identity.[284] It can, therefore, seem unlikely that a contract that is yet to be concluded can be incorporated. Nonetheless, in *Lamb v Emhart Corp*, such a contract was held to be incorporated, inter alia, because the incorporation clause expressly provided that contractual rights of the parties were to be contingent

[279] [1996] 2 Lloyd's Rep 319, 328.

[280] ibid.

[281] See *Ventura Maritime Co Ltd v ADM Export Co* 1998 AMC 1676 (EDLa 1999) where a similar situation arose.

[282] As in *AP Moller-Maersk A/S v Sonaec Villas Cen Sad Fadoul and Others* [2011] 1 Lloyd's Rep 1.

[283] ibid.

[284] See *Chiacchia v National Westminster Bank USA* 124 AD 2d 626, 628 (2d Dep't 1986). See also *Painewebber Incorporated v Bybyk* 81 F 3d 1193 (2d Cir 1996), quoted in Lord (n 185) §30:25.

upon the contracts to be concluded in the future.[285] Another compelling reason for finding in favour of incorporation was that both parties had the opportunity to examine the formation of these future agreements and assented to provisions in these agreements after their formation.[286] Hence, the Court in *Lamb v Emhart Corp* distinguished the case from those where one party to an agreement seeks to incorporate into the agreement a number of contracts that he/she will conclude in the future with third parties.[287]

On the applicability of *Lamb v Emhart Corp* to the bill of lading cases, it is clear that the decision can seldom find room for application. In general terms, the case of *Lamb v Emhart* is not applicable, particularly because of the requirement that the bill of lading make an 'unmistakable' reference to an already concluded charterparty.[288] Nonetheless, this conclusion cannot be followed where the holder is not a 'stranger'[289] within the meaning of the US rules of incorporation. The requirement of unmistakably specifying the charterparty disappears in the case of such a holder, as do the time constraints to execute the same.[290] When these circumstances arise, it is therefore likely that US courts will be more inclined to incorporate a future charterparty. This result also draws support from the decision in *Lamb v Emhart* simply because such bill of lading holders have the chance to examine the formation of the charterparty referred to and to see its terms.[291] It here proves valuable to recall that, for a future charterparty to be incorporated, *Lamb v Emhart* also calls for the assent of the parties to the subsequent agreement. Nonetheless, this requirement must not be given any weight in the context of bills of lading: on becoming a holder, the holders should be deemed to have consented to the bill of lading terms.[292]

From a general perspective, the rule as to the time for the conclusion of the charterparty to be incorporated favours holders. It saves the holder from being a party to a contract of carriage that does not provide a firm contractual position, as well as increasing the reliability of bills of lading in international trade. From the perspective of carriers, though, this time constraint is yet another hurdle to overcome to achieve incorporation. In considering time limits, carriers also need to know whether any similar time restrictions could apply when they seek to incorporate a charterparty that has been amended or rectified.

[285] *Lamb v Emhart Corp* 47 F 3d 551 (2d Cir 1995).

[286] ibid, at 558. In addition to their knowledge on these provisions, the Court also found the existence of their assent to the provisions on the basis of their subsequent conduct, mainly evidenced in the correspondence between the parties.

[287] ibid.

[288] See *Thyssen Inc v M/V Markos* 1999 AMC 2515, 2518 (SDNY 1999) *aff'd sub nom Thyssen Inc v Calypso Shipping Corp SA* 310 F 3d 102 (2d Cir 2002) *cert denied* 123 SCt 1573, 155 L Ed 2d 312 (US 2003).

[289] *Cargill Ferrous International v Sea Phoenix M/V* 2003 AMC 1027 (5th Cir 2003); *Keytrade USA, Inc v Ain Temouchent M/V* 2005 AMC 948 (5th Cir 2005).

[290] See *Ventura Maritime Co Ltd v ADM Export Co* 1998 AMC 1676 (EDLa 1999).

[291] 47 F 3d 551 (2d Cir 1995).

[292] For a similar view see *Ventura Maritime Co Ltd v ADM Export Co* 1998 AMC 1676 (EDLa 1999).

D. The Incorporation of Charterparty Terms that have been Amended or Rectified

It is timely to examine the formalities and time restrictions envisaged in respect of the incorporation of amended or rectified charterparties. For present purposes, the key questions will be: for an altered or rectified charterparty provision to be incorporated, under which form should the provision be evidenced and until when should it be rectified or amended? As regards the incorporation of amended charterparties, the required form of amendments will initially be discussed. The next step will then be to look at the conditions with respect to the time of making the amendments. Finally, the extent to which a rectified charterparty can be incorporated will be analysed.

i. The Required Form Amendments

Both English and US cases suggest that only those amendments that are 'in writing' within the meaning of the rules of incorporation are suitable for incorporation. Under English law, the major underpinning for this is the decision in *The Heidberg*—the decision which establishes the key rule that oral charterparties cannot be incorporated.[293] When ruling against the incorporation of an oral charterparty, HHJ Diamond QC in *The Heidberg* relied heavily on the decision in *Leduc v Ward*, where it was held that verbal arrangements between the shippers and carriers could not vary the bill of lading terms.[294] Taking this case as a basis, HHJ Diamond QC acknowledged that oral agreements, including oral charterparties, could not be binding upon the transferees of the bill of lading. In so doing, he sought to give a certain level of protection to the transferees who take up and pay for bills of lading on their face value. Viewed in that light, the reasoning in *The Heidberg* is sufficient to act as a barrier also to the incorporation of oral amendments to charterparties.

Similar considerations arise also under US law. In *The Pelotas*,[295] the Court adopted a similar reasoning to that in *Leduc v Ward*, when holding that the carrier was liable vis-à-vis the holder of the bill of lading for deviation. The Court refused to admit evidence showing that some of the shippers had actual knowledge of the carrier's proposed deviation. The Court further took the view that neither the knowledge of shippers nor their verbal arrangements with the carrier could vary the bill of lading provision requiring the carrier to sail directly to the destination. The decision in *The Pelotas* also signalled the strenuous efforts of US courts to protect the holders' reliance on bills of lading. Consequently, the ruling is persuasive authority for the suggestion that verbal charterparty amendments cannot be treated as part of bills of lading by way of incorporation.

293 [1994] 2 Lloyd's Rep 287.
294 (1888) LR 20 QBD 475.
295 *The Pelotas* 1933 AMC 1188 (5th Cir 1933).

While seeking to afford protection to the holders, both US and English courts have refrained, however, from taking excessively rigid approaches. Thus, the courts have refused to confine the meaning of written amendments to formal addenda that contain the signature of the relevant parties.[296] Consequently, just as with those charterparties contained in fixture recap telexes, emails and faxes,[297] amendments in such forms are also taken as 'in writing' for incorporation purposes.[298] Nonetheless, as with charterparties in these forms, such amendments can only overcome the writing requirement to the extent that the amended terms are ascertainable.[299]

There may be another stumbling block for carriers when seeking to achieve the incorporation of an amendment to a charterparty. The decision in *Fidelitas Shipping Co v V/O Exportchleb* suggests that, if the holder is provided with a copy of the charterparty, this should also include the amendment. This requirement may come as a surprise given that the English rules of incorporation are not based on notice.[300] Such a requirement is likely to be imposed onto a carrier on the other side of the Atlantic, where the rules of incorporation are to some extent based on notice.[301]

By and large, the rule that oral amendments to the charterparty cannot be incorporated is justified by reference to the fragile position of the holders, ie consignees/endorsees. This raises two questions: first, can an oral amendment be incorporated into the bill of lading where the bill of lading remains in the hands of shippers? Secondly, can an oral amendment be incorporated in cases where doing so would be to the benefit of the holder? As regards the first question, guidance must be drawn from the decision in *The Spiros C.*[302] There, the shipper effected the payment of freight pursuant to the verbal amendment to the sub-charterparty, which was made between himself/herself as the sub-charterer and the time charterer. The shipowner claimed freight from the shipper under the bill of lading, arguing that the bill of lading merely incorporated the sub-charterparty without the verbal alteration to it. There was no question that the bill of lading incorporated the sub-charterparty,[303] the dispute was whether the verbal amendment as to the method of payment of freight was also incorporated. The Court of Appeal refused the shipowner's claim, holding that the verbal amendment was

[296] For English law, see *Fidelitas Shipping Co v V/O Exportchleb* [1963] 2 Lloyd's Rep 113 (CA). For US law, see *Japan Sun Oil Co Ltd v The M/V Maasdijk* 1995 AMC 726 (EDLa 1994). As regards US law, it must also be added that incorporation is defined as making reference to a document that could be an unsigned paper, see *In re Prudential Insurance Co of America*, 148 SW 3d 124, 135 (Tex 2004).

[297] For English law see, *The Epsilon Rosa* [2003] 2 Lloyd's Rep 509. For US law, see *Thyssen, Inc v M/V Markos* 1999 AMC 2515, 2518 (SDNY 1999) *aff'd sub nom Thyssen Inc v Calypso Shipping Corp SA* 310 F 3d 102 (2d Cir 2002) *cert denied* 123 SCt 1573, 155 L Ed 2d 312 (US 2003).

[298] See Section III.B.ii above.

[299] ibid.

[300] Özdel (n 113) 181–95.

[301] See Section I.B above.

[302] [2000] 2 Lloyd's Rep 319, 329 (CA).

[303] ibid.

binding upon the carrier and the shipper. In essence, the time charterer was held to have acted on behalf of the shipowner in making the verbal alterations on the mode of payment of the sub-charter freight. On this matter Rix LJ said:[304]

> In my judgment, when a shipowner contracts that his freight should be payable as per a charter-party, he intends, and it is common ground with his shipper that he does so, that, at any rate until he steps in to claim his freight upon the failure of his time charterer, the whole manner or mode of the collection of the freight should be delegated to the time charterer. If the time charterer changes his bank, or bank account, and asks his sub-charterer to pay freight to a different account from that mentioned in the sub-charter, it is of no interest to the shipowner. If the time charterer is willing to accept freight not only in the form of a direct payment to the nominated account, but also, for his convenience, in the form of cash disbursements to his shipping agents, or to the master, then I see no reason why the shipowner should consider that such arrangements, even if they are different from that contemplated in the original charter-party, are outside the scope of his delegated authority to his time charterer.

The idea that the shipowner has delegated to the time charterer the manner of collecting freight under the shipowner's bill of lading creates a commercial result. For this reason, Rix LJ's decision can be justified. However, the main problem, for present purposes, is how this theory can be reconciled with one rule of incorporation: oral terms cannot be incorporated into the bill of lading. In fact, the answer is simple. On the facts of the case, there was no need for the oral term as to the manner of payment to be incorporated into the bill of lading. As between the shipowner and the shipper, the bill of lading was only evidence of the contract of carriage.[305] Hence, the oral arrangement entered into between the time charterer, on behalf of the shipowner, and the shipper constituted part of the contract of carriage evidenced under the bill of lading.

On the application of the delegation theory, it is submitted that it should not be extended to cases where the bill of lading is in the hands of the holders, ie endorsees/consignees: to do so would mean that oral terms could be incorporated into the bill of lading and this would be in stark contrast to the well-established rule—which can operate both against or in favour of the holder—that oral arrangements cannot vary the bill of lading terms.[306]

On the other side of the Atlantic, US courts have traditionally been hostile to the variation of the bill of lading terms through verbal agreements.[307] For this reason, the bill of lading cannot incorporate oral amendments to the charterparty whether or not the bill of lading is in the hands of the shipper. Just as with the position under English law, this does not mean that the shipper and the carrier cannot be bound by some oral terms. They may be bound by such terms precisely because the bill of lading in these cases is only evidence of contract of carriage.[308]

[304] ibid. See Section II.C above, where this reasoning is referred to as 'the delegation theory'.
[305] See n 3 above.
[306] See *Leduc v Ward* (1888) 20 QBD 475. See also Treitel and Reynolds (n 142) para 3-010.
[307] See *The Delaware* 81 US 579 (US 1872).
[308] ibid. See n 187 above.

ii. Time of Making the Amendments

Having discussed the required form of amendments, it is timely to ask when the amendments to the charterparty need to be made for incorporation. Under English law, no special incorporation language is required in the bill of lading in order to incorporate the amendments that have been made by the time the bill of lading is issued.[309] Amendments made after the issue date of the bill of lading cannot be incorporated merely because the holder has actual knowledge of these variations. The English rules of incorporation are not founded on notice.[310]

What is not clear is whether future amendments to the charterparty referred to can be incorporated through special incorporation language in the bill of lading. If the intention to incorporate is clear from the special incorporation language, it is likely that the courts will give effect to this intention.[311] However, it is difficult to argue that special incorporation language can easily succeed in the incorporation of such amendments. The courts will be slow to read an incorporation clause in such a way that the clause can incorporate future amendments: the courts have shown reluctance to read contract terms in a way that produces unreasonable and uncommercial results.[312] The salutary effects of treating incorporation clauses as capable of incorporating only those existing amendments at the issue date of the bill of lading are well known: a firm contractual position under bills of lading is desirable from the standpoint of the holders, and it is also essential to maintain the reliability and transferability of these instruments in international trade.

Under US law, the view taken towards this issue is the same as that of English law, unless the holder is not a 'stranger' to the charterparty.[313] Thus, where the holder is a 'stranger' within the meaning of the US rules of incorporation, only those charterparty provisions that have been altered before the bill of lading is issued can be incorporated.[314] Incorporation of such amendments does not entail any special wording.[315] However, the amendments that do not exist at the issue date of the bill of lading can hardly ever be incorporated into the bill of lading, regardless of any special language to that effect. This is best explained by the rule that the bill of lading must unmistakably refer to an existing charterparty for incorporation. Evidently, these barriers will disappear in the presence of a holder who is not a 'stranger' to the charterparty referred to. As the decision in *Lamb v Emhart* suggests, carriers will be able to introduce future alterations into the bill

[309] See *Fidelitas Shipping Co v V/O Exportchleb* [1963] 2 Lloyd's Rep 113 (CA).

[310] See n 113 above. See also, *Siboti K/S v BP France SA* [2003] 2 Lloyd's Rep 364, 368; *The Heidberg* [1994] 2 Lloyd's Rep 287, 313.

[311] See *The Northern Progress* [1996] 2 Lloyd's Rep 319 at 329. See also *Credit Lyonnais Bank Nederland NV v Export Credits Guarantee Department* [1998] 1 Lloyd's Rep 19, 38 (CA).

[312] In the context of bills of lading, see *The Miramar* [1984] 2 Lloyd's Rep 129 (HL). From a general contract law perspective, see *Schuler v Wickman Machine Tool Sales Ltd* [1974] AC 235.

[313] *Lamb v Emhart Corp* 47 F 3d 551 (2d Cir 1995).

[314] For US law, see *Japan Sun Oil Co Ltd v The M/V Maasdijk* 1995 AMC 726 (EDLa 1994).

[315] ibid.

of lading against such holders insofar as there is incorporation language to that effect.[316]

iii. Incorporation of Rectified Charterparties

Having concluded that amendments to charterparties may in principle be incorporated into the bill of lading, a further question, of some difficulty, is: could a charterparty be qualified for incorporation, even though it has been reformed by the courts under the remedy of rectification? As can be gleaned from US and English case law, the courts have been extremely cautious in exercising their discretion to grant rectification, so as not to damage certainty in commercial contracts.[317] Perhaps with a view to preventing parties from sidestepping their contractual obligations, the courts rectify a written contract only where the actual intention of the parties is not reflected accurately in the contract by reason of a mutual mistake.[318] Where there is a unilateral mistake caused by fraud or misrepresentation, or unfair dealing, the courts could also grant rectification.[319] Regardless of its limited scope of application, rectification is a 'drastic'[320] remedy, for the inquiry on mutual mistake or fraud is not confined to the contract wording, and extrinsic evidence is, therefore, admissible for this purpose.[321]

Limited availability of this equitable relief clearly signals the hostility of the courts towards making or rewriting the contracts for parties.[322] As the English and US authorities attest, imperfect contracts have frequently been cured by way of their construction as a whole.[323] In this respect, construction of the document is

[316] See Section III.C.ii above.

[317] For English law, see *The Olympic Pride* [1980] 2 Lloyd's Rep 67, 73. For US law, see *Snell v Insurance Company* 98 US 85, 89–90 (US 1878); *Backer Management Corp v Acme Quilting Co* 385 NE 2d 1062, 1066 (NY 1978); *Chimart Associates v David Paul* 66 NY 2d 570 (NY 1986). Under US law this equitable remedy is widely known as 'reformation' instead of rectification, see Restatement (Second) On Contracts, §155.

[318] For US law, see *Backer Management Corp*; *Winmar Co Inc v Teachers Insurance and Annuity Association of America* 870 F Supp 524, 535 (SDNY 1994); *Manufacturers' Finance Co v McKey* 294 US 442 (US 1935); *American President Lines Ltd v United States* 821 F 2d 1571, 1582 (Fed Cir 1987); *Mutual of Omaha Insurance Co v Russell* 402 F 2d 339, 344 (10th Cir 1968) *cert denied*, 394 US 973 (US 1969). See also Lord (n 185) §70:25. For English law, *Murray v Parker* (1854) 19 Beav 305 and *Burroughs v Abbott* [1922] 1 Ch 86 quoted in HG Beale, *Chitty on Contracts*, 31st edn (London, Sweet & Maxwell, 2011) para 5-111 fnn 471 and 473. See also *Chartbrook Ltd v Persimmon Homes Ltd* [2009] UKHL 38, para 48 (HL).

[319] For English law, see *Wood v Scarth* (1855) 2 K & J 33; *May v Platt* [1900] 1 Ch 616; *McCausland v Young* [1949] NI 49 quoted in Beale (n 318) at para 5-122 fn 535. For US law, see Restatement (Second) On Contracts, §155 para (b).

[320] D McLauchlan, 'The "Drastic" Remedy of Rectification for Unilateral Mistake' (2008) 124 *Law Quarterly Review* 608.

[321] For English law, see *Investors Compensation Scheme Ltd v West Bromwich Building Society (No 1)* [1998] 1 WLR 896, 912. See also K Lewison, *The Interpretation of Contracts* (London Sweet & Maxwell, 2007) 347. For US law, see *Snell v Insurance Company* 98 US 85, 89–90 (US 1878).

[322] For English law, see *The Starsin* [2004] 1 AC 715, 740, per Lord Bingham (HL). For US law, see *Cruden v Bank of New York* 957 F 2d 961, 976 (2d Cir 1992).

[323] For US law, see Restatement (Second) On Contracts, §202(d). For English law, see *The Nerano* [1996] 1 Lloyd's Rep 1.

made pursuant to the intention of the parties that can be reasonably ascertained both from the words used therein[324] and from the objective purpose of the contract.[325]

Given that, unlike contract construction, rectification entails reframing the contract pursuant to the actual intention of the parties, could it be said that a rectified charterparty can be incorporated and be binding upon a third-party holder? It is a well-recognised proposition of general contract law in both jurisdictions that a contract cannot be rectified to the detriment of a third party, where the third party has relied on the contract provisions in good faith and without notice of the mistake.[326] Having endorsed this reasoning in bill of lading cases, both English and US courts have taken the view that bill of lading terms can only be rectified vis-à-vis the original parties to the bill of lading.[327] Consequently, they have refused to grant rectification where the bill of lading has been negotiated with a third party.[328]

On the question of incorporation, it is difficult to argue that rectified charterparties can be taken as inapt for incorporation merely because their terms have been reformed by the courts. For incorporation purposes, the key question should be: when has the charterparty been rectified? Just as with the amendments to a charterparty, the rectified provisions should only be incorporated if the provisions have been rectified by the time the bill of lading is issued. Where a court reforms the charterparty after the bill of lading has been issued, the rectification should not be binding upon the holders. This conclusion should also follow in cases where the bill of lading is in the hands of the shipper who is also the charterer of the charterparty referred to. There are two main grounds in support of the latter proposition. First, the English rules of incorporation—which are peculiar to maritime law[329]—are not based on notice. Secondly, the cases on incorporation clearly show that the aim of the courts has been to create a firm contractual

[324] For US law, see *RJE Corp v Northville Industries Corp* 329 F 3d 310, 314 (2d Cir 2003); *Law Debenture Trust Co of New York v Maverick Tube Corp* 595 F 3d 458 (2d Cir 2010). For English law, see *Adamastos Shipping Co Ltd v Anglo-Saxon Petroleum Co Ltd* [1959] AC 133, 176 (HL).

[325] For English law, see *Prenn v Simmonds* [1971] 1 WLR 1381, 1385, per Lord Wilberforce (HL), where reference was made to 'genesis and aim of the transaction'. See also *Reardon Smith Line Ltd v Yngvar Hansen-Tangen* [1976] 1 WLR 989 (HL); *Investors Compensation Scheme Ltd v West Bromwich Building Society (No 1)* [1998] 1 WLR 896 (HL); *L Schuler AG v Wickman Machine Tool Sales Ltd* [1974] AC 235, 251 (HL). For US law, see Restatement (Second) On Contracts, §155.

[326] For English law, see *Bell v Cundall* (1750) Amb 101; *Smith v Jones* [1954] 1 WLR 1089; *Lyme Valley Squash Club Ltd v Newcastle-under-Lyme BC* [1985] 2 All ER 405, 413, quoted in Beale (n 318) para 5-139 fn 609. See also the *obiter dictum* of Steyn J in *The Cebu* [1993] QB 1, 15. For US law, see *Bolduc v Beal Bank, SSB*, 167 F 3d 667, 669, 674 (1st Cir 1999); *Fidelity Bank v Lutheran Mutual Life Insurance Co*, 465 F 2d 211, 214 (10th Cir 1972); *Great Atlantic Insurance Co v Liberty Mutual Insurance Co*, 773 F 2d 976, 980–81 (8th Cir 1985). See also Restatement (Second) On Contracts, §155 para (f).

[327] For US law, see *Baxter v Leland* 1 Abb Adm 348, 2 F Cas 1048, No 1124 (DCNY 1848). For English law, see *The Merak* [1965] P 223. See also the *obiter dictum* of Steyn J in *The Cebu* [1993] QB 1, 15.

[328] For English law, see *The Merak* [1965] P 223. For US law, see *Bradstreet v Heran* 2 Blatchf 116, 3 F Cas 1183, No 1792A (CCNY 1849); Restatement (Second) On Contracts, §155.

[329] See n 113 above.

position under the bill of lading as from the time it is issued. For this reason, the cases on the time of making amendments to the charterparty for incorporation should also be applied here by way of analogy. On the other side of the Atlantic, a holder may be bound by rectified charterparty provisions, regardless of the time of rectification, if the holder is not a 'stranger' within the meaning of the US rules of incorporation.

Having discussed the extent to which variations to the charterparty referred to can be carried across to the bill of lading, a further question will be whether a rescinded, terminated or invalidated charterparty can be incorporated.

E. Charterparties Rescinded, Terminated or Invalidated

When a charterparty is rescinded, terminated or invalidated, a holder may take the view that this fact is of itself sufficient to defeat its incorporation into the bill of lading, since such a charterparty is not even in force between its original parties. In such circumstances, a shipowner whose charterparty has ceased to be in force would perhaps be even more willing to have the charterparty incorporated into the bill of lading. To recover the charges arising under the charterparty from the respective holders, it is therefore likely that the shipowner, as the carrier under the bill of lading, will favour the incorporation of the charterparty. The issue of whether the contractual status of charterparties has any effect on their incorporation into bills of lading boils down to the question: is the incorporation of a charterparty treated as incorporation of provisions alone, or is it the incorporation of a contract that is in force between its original parties?

In US law, the dominant view has been to treat incorporation as no more than incorporating a set of terms that do not necessarily have to originate from a contract.[330] Thus, a charterparty can be incorporated into a bill of lading, irrespective of the fact that it is no longer binding between its original parties due to its being rescinded, repudiated or invalidated. Similarly, under English law, the mere fact that the relevant charterparty is repudiated will not itself debar incorporation.[331] Moreover, the weight of English authorities further suggests that the existence of a mistake, misrepresentation, non-disclosure, fraud or *ultra vires* on the part of the agent[332] whilst concluding the charterparty on behalf of the principal, should also not prevent incorporation.[333]

However, it is clear in both jurisdictions that the courts will not endorse such a receptive approach towards incorporation in cases where the incorporation clause

[330] *Shaw v Regents of University of California* 58 Cal App 4th 44, 67 Cal Rptr 2d 850, 121 Ed Law Rep 261 (3rd Dist 1997), quoted in PM Coltoff et al, *Corpus Juris Secundum* (St Paul, MN: Thomson West, 2010), 17A CJS Contracts §316.

[331] See *Akt Ocean v Harding* [1928] 2 KB 371. See also C Debattista, *Halsbury's Laws of England*, vol 7, 5th edn (London, Lexis Nexis, 2008) s 360.

[332] See *Akt Ocean v Harding* [1928] 2 KB 371. See also Treitel and Reynolds (n 142) para 3-030.

[333] *Akt Ocean v Harding* [1928] 2 KB 371 at 393–94.

expressly contemplates the charterparties that are effective between its original parties.[334] However, the contractual status of the charterparty referred to has no bearing on the question of incorporation in the absence of special incorporation language to that effect.

Treating incorporation of charterparties merely as an importation of their provisions is sound and persuasive. If the contrary were assumed, deciding on incorporation would involve a more complicated assessment, with courts having to examine whether the charterparty referred to is valid and enforceable between its original parties. Such an inquiry would put a strain on the resolution of this issue, especially in cases where the charterparty referred to and bills of lading are governed by different applicable laws. Even if the applicable laws of both contracts are the same, examining the existence of a material mistake, fraud, illegality or incapacity under the charterparty would undoubtedly bring an evidential burden. Most importantly, the view adopted in both jurisdictions is also conducive to making an unvarying representation under these transferable instruments. Had these contracts been made vulnerable to the status of a charterparty, this would have created serious uncertainties due to the possibility that charterparties may become inoperative between their original parties after the bill of lading is issued.

IV. Conclusion

The cardinal rules of contract law, which suggest that parties can only be bound by the terms which they have seen and agreed to, have no application to incorporation of charterparty clauses into bills of lading. Accordingly, what cargo interests need to be concerned about is an unseen charterparty, which may be a part of their contract of carriage if it overcomes the hurdles of the rules of incorporation. This chapter identified the first-step rules of incorporation, to which cargo interests should pay particular attention before seeking a copy of the charterparty referred to, as these rules may render either the bills of lading or the charterparty inapt for incorporation.

The analysis and discussion made thus far lead to the conclusion that both carriers and cargo interests should be mindful of the striking differences between US and English law regarding this issue. In particular, they need to bear in mind that English law sets the rules without considering the position or the knowledge of bill of lading holders, while US law adopts variable rules of incorporation that are mainly founded on the position of the bill of lading holder. A key point under US law is that this approach makes it possible for a bill of lading to provide a different contract for each subsequent bill of lading holder, from the shipper through

[334] For English law, see *Akt Ocean v Harding* [1928] 2 KB 371 at 383–84. For US law, see *The Michael Thanasis* 311 F Supp 170, 175 (DC Cal 1970) quoted in Coltoff (n 330) 17A CJS Contracts §316.

to the ultimate holder. While this unstable contractual position, created under these transferable instruments, is open to criticism, the US approach causes the incorporation issue to be more than a mere technical inquiry. On that basis, the US formulation could be taken to provide fairness to the parties.

While paying particular attention to these differences, both carriers and bill of lading holders must consider one key point: the rules outlined so far are only decisive in determining whether the charterparty referred to or the bill of lading is appropriate for incorporation. Consequently, they are not decisive with respect to which charterparty terms may be included in the bill of lading through the incorporation language. The next chapter will examine and discuss which charterparty provisions can be introduced through the incorporation clause.

3

Giving Effect to the Words of Incorporation

In international trade where CIF sellers enter into a voyage charterparty as required under their sale contracts, typically they would wish no longer to be bound by charterparty obligations after the shipment of the cargo. The reason for this is that CIF sellers who are also charterers lose their interest in the goods, and hence in the charterparty under which the goods are carried, from the moment of selling them to the respective buyers.[1] To meet the expectations of these parties, some standard-form voyage charterparties introduce cesser clauses, which purport to end the charterer's liability when the cargo is shipped on board and payment of freight and other charges, if any, incurred under the charterparty, are fully paid.[2] In consideration of the cessation of liability, cesser clauses also provide a right of lien for the benefit of the shipowners to secure the payment of the sums—such as dead freight, demurrage and damages for detention—due under the charterparty.[3]

With regard to the application of cesser clauses, the prevailing approach of English and US courts has been to proceed upon one key premise: shipowners could not reasonably be expected to release charterers from liability without obtaining an effective remedy in exchange.[4] Hence, unless the cesser clause clearly states otherwise,[5] these provisions are construed as being applicable only when the cessation of liability is conditional upon, and co-extensive with, an effective right of lien on the cargo.[6] With the rationale behind this approach being to provide a safety net for shipowners, the courts have allowed charterers to rely

[1] For this issue, see also MA Miller, 'Cesser Clauses' (2001) 26 *Tulane Maritime Law Journal* 71.

[2] See Art 8 of 'Gencon' Charter, as revised in 1922 and in 1976.

[3] For English law see *Fidelitas Shipping Co v V/O Exportchleb* [1963] 2 Lloyd's Rep 113 (CA). For US law, see *Yone Suzuki v Central Argentine Railway Limited* 1928 AMC 1521 (2d Cir 1928) *cert denied*, 278 US 652 (US 1929).

[4] For US law, see *Crossman v Burrill* 179 US 100 (US 1900). For English law, see *Clink v Radford & Co* [1891] 1 QB 625, 627–28; *The Sinoe* [1972] 1 Lloyd's Rep 201.

[5] For English law, see *The Aegis Britannic* [1987] 1 Lloyd's Rep 119, and for US law, see *Crossman v Burrill* 179 US 100 (US 1900).

[6] For English law, see *Fidelitas Shipping Co v V/O Exportchleb* [1963] 2 Lloyd's Rep 113, 120–21 (CA); *Hansen v Harrold Brothers* [1894] 1 QB 612, 618. For US law, see *Crossman v Burrill* 179 US 100 (US 1900) 1809–10.

on cesser clauses to the extent that shipowners have a commensurate remedy to retrieve their losses and payments due under the charterparty.[7]

Despite these precautionary measures to balance the interests of parties, the position of shipowners towards charterers is, nevertheless, weakened when the bill of lading that relates to the cargo is negotiated to a third party. The fragility derives from the rule of privity of contract,[8] which hinders the shipowners in their attempts to invoke lien and other rights arising under the charterparty against a third-party holder. The practical impact of this barrier is evident: upon the transfer of a shipowner's bill of lading to a third party, the shipowner would naturally wish to lien the cargo of the third-party bill of lading holder in the case of unpaid charges due under the charterparty. Exercising a lien on the cargo stands out as the most effective option for the shipowner, given that the holder has the ultimate interest in the cargo and will thus claim the delivery of cargo at the port of discharge. Nonetheless, due to the rule of privity of contract, shipowners cannot turn to and face the holder on the same terms as the charterparty. To put it another way, the shipowner will be debarred from relying on various favourable charterparty provisions against the holder, unless the bill of lading effectively incorporates the charterparty. Included in those provisions is the lien clause covering claims, inter alia, for demurrage and dead freight under the charterparty.

On the question of how the privity rule operates in respect of the owner's right of lien over the third-party holder's cargo, a closer look must be taken at the legal position in both jurisdictions. Under US general maritime law, the shipowner can exercise lien for the unpaid freight over the third-party holder's cargo.[9] The shipowner's right of lien is, however, limited to the amount of freight due under the bill of lading.[10] Thus, for the shipowner to exercise lien for the freight over the third-party holder's cargo on the same terms as the charterparty, the bill of lading must incorporate the freight provision in the charterparty.[11] Just as with freight, the shipowner, as carrier under the bill of lading, is entitled by the general maritime law to exercise lien over the holder's cargo for demurrage.[12] On the charterer's default in payment of any type of sums due under the charterparty,

[7] ibid. Some judicial decisions clearly convey the impression that the existence of an *in personam* liability of the consignee for the payment of relevant charges could be relevant in resolving the charterer's cessation of liability under the cesser clause. For US law, see *Crossman v Burrill* 179 US 100 (US 1900) and for English law, see *The Aegis Britannic* [1987] 1 Lloyd's Rep 119 and J Cooke et al, *Voyage Charters*, 3rd edn (London, Informa Law from Routledge, 2007) para 17.3.

[8] For US law, see *Trans-Asiatic Oil Ltd SA v Apex Oil Company* 1987 AMC 1115 (1st Cir 1986). For English law, see *Dunlop Pneumatic Tyre Co Ltd v Selfridge & Co Ltd* [1915] AC 847.

[9] *Jebsen v A Cargo of Hemp* 228 F 143, 146 (D Mass 1915) quoted in Cooke et al (n 7) para 17-62. See also *Bieghl & Co Inc v Apollonia Holding Inc* 693 F Supp 457, 465 (EDLa 1988); *The Bird Paradise* 72 US 545 (US 1866).

[10] See *Goodpasture Inc v The Pollux* 602 F 2d 84 (5th Cir 1979).

[11] Note, however, that a freight-prepaid stamp on the bill of lading will prevent the exercise of lien over the holder's cargo for the unpaid freight. See Cooke et al (n 7) para 17-80.

[12] See *Atlantic Richfield Co v Good Hope Refineries*, 604 F 2d 865, 872 (5th Cir 1979). See also G Blum et al, *American Jurisprudence*, 2nd edn (Eagan, MN, Thomson Reuters, 2014) §494. See also 49 USCA §80109(1).

the shipowner would naturally wish to exercise lien over the holder's cargo. Once this is recognised, it follows that the right to lien under the general maritime law cannot fulfil the shipowner's expectations. For the shipowner, the best solution is thus to incorporate into the bill of lading the charterparty lien clause, which typically covers a wide variety of claims, such as those for dead freight and damages for detention.

Under English law, the common law lien covers freight, general average and expenses of preserving goods. As carrier under the bill of lading, the shipowner can thus exercise lien on the holder's cargo in respect of these sums.[13] Given the narrow scope of the common law lien and the need to secure the sums due under the charterparty, contractual lien is also desirable under English law. In order for the shipowner to exercise lien vis-à-vis the holder on the same terms as the charterparty, the charterparty lien clause should be carried across to the bill of lading by way of incorporation. English courts have repeatedly held that shipowners are entitled to lien the cargo of third-party holders for the charges under the charterparty where there is a lien clause expressly stipulated under or incorporated into bills of lading.[14] In *The Miramar*, the shipowner was justified for exercising a lien against the holder's cargo for the unpaid demurrage arising from the charterparty.[15] There, the holder was held to be not personally liable for the demurrage on the grounds that the charterparty demurrage clause was not incorporated. Regardless of this finding, the shipowners were allowed to avail themselves of the incorporated charterparty lien clause for the unpaid demurrage. The case stands as authority for the proposition that personal liability is not a quid pro quo for the exercise of lien. However, in respect of the shipowner's right of lien over the holder's cargo for the unpaid freight, the courts would appear to require that the holder is personally liable for the freight under the bill of lading. In *Gardner v Trenchmann*, the bill of lading incorporating the charterparty lien clause was of limited use to the shipowners, for they were not entitled to exercise lien in excess of the bill of lading freight.[16] In a similar vein, a freight-prepaid stamp prevents the shipowner from exercising lien over the holder's cargo for the unpaid freight, where the holder does not actually know that the freight is unpaid.[17]

Leaving aside the right of lien over the cargo, the shipowner can have a right of lien on sub-freights, if the charterparty lien clause so provides.[18] In the case of such a lien clause in the charterparty, the shipowner will be entitled to intercept the sub-charterer's payment of his/her sub-freight to the charterer, where the

[13] See Cooke et al (n 7) para 17.15. See also *Hingston v Wendt* (1876) 1 QBD 367, 372–73; *Crooks v Allan* (1979) 5 QBD 38; and *Dakin v Oxley* (1864) 15 CB 646, 664.

[14] For English law, see *The Spiros C* [2000] 2 Lloyd's Rep 319 (CA); *The Agios Giorgis* [1976] 2 Lloyd's Rep 192.

[15] *The Miramar* [1983] 2 Lloyd's Rep 319 (HL).

[16] *Gardner v Trenchmann* (1884) 15 QBD 154. See also *Fry v Merchantile Bank of India* (1866) LR 1 CP 689.

[17] *The Indian Reliance* [1997] 1 Lloyd's Rep 52.

[18] See *The Cebu* [1993] QB 1, 15; *The Spiros C* [2000] 2 Lloyd's Rep 319 (CA); *Samsun Logix Corp v Oceantrade Corp* [2008] 1 Lloyd's Rep 450.

charterer fails to pay the charter hire or freight.[19] The same is also true under US law: where the charterparty gives the shipowner the right to lien on the sub-freights, the shipowner will be entitled, as a 'subrogee', to claim these sums, where the charterer is in default of its payment of freight or hire under the charterparty.[20] In both jurisdictions, the shipowners will have no right to claim the sub-freight from the sub-charterer if the sub-charterer has already made payment in good faith to the charterer before receiving notice of the lien.[21]

Although the interception of the payment of sub-freight can be exercised against a bill of lading holder who is also the sub-charterer, it does not create the same practical advantages as retaining the possession of the cargo to secure the unpaid charterparty charges. For this reason, it is in the best interests of shipowners to make sure that their respective charterparty lien clauses are incorporated into the bill of lading, with the effect that they could lien the cargo of the holders for the sums due under the charterparty. As far as US law is concerned, similar practical benefits arise from the use of incorporation clauses.

Incorporation of charterparties also has practical significance for charterers when they seek to relieve themselves of liability pursuant to the cesser clause. The cesser clauses are treated as co-extensive with the lien provided in the charterparty.[22] When the bill of lading is negotiated to a third party, the cesser clause will not be available to the charterer to the extent that the charterparty lien clause is ineffective vis-à-vis the bill of lading holder.[23] For the bill of lading holder to be subject to the charterparty lien clause, it has to be incorporated into the bill of lading.

Above all, the incorporation of a charterparty into the bill of lading is essential given that the only security for shipowners to enforce their contractual rights under the charterparty lies with the goods that they carry. For this reason, shipowners need to ensure that the goods remain their security for the charges and rights arising under the charterparty, even though the bill of lading covering the goods is negotiated to a third party.

The observations above underline the fact that incorporation of charterparty terms into the bill of lading becomes desirable both for shipowners and charterers. For these parties, who would obviously wish to overcome the barriers of incorporation, this chapter provides the second-step guidelines. The parties have a stake in knowing these rules on the grounds that, even after having complied with the prerequisites for incorporation as spelled out in the first chapter, they need to consider one further issue: the extent to which the incorporation clause

[19] See *Cornish Shipping Ltd v International Nederlanden Bank NV* 53 F 3d 499, 504 (2d Cir 1995).

[20] See ibid. See also Cooke et al (n 7) para 17.70.

[21] For English law, see *The Bulk Chile* [2013] 2 Lloyd's Rep 38 (CA). For US law, see *Cornish Shipping Ltd v International Nederlanden Bank NV* 53 F 3d 499, 504 (2d Cir 1995).

[22] For US law, see *Crossman v Burrill* 179 US 100 (US 1900); *The Arizpa* 1933 AMC 224 (4th Cir 1933). For English law, see *Fidelitas Shipping Co v V/O Exportchleb* [1963] 2 Lloyd's Rep 113, 120–21 (CA).

[23] For US law, see *Crossman v Burrill* 179 US 100 (US 1900) and *The Arizpa* 1933 AMC 224 (4th Cir 1933). For English Law, see *The Aegis Britannic* [1987] 1 Lloyd's Rep 119, 121–22; *The Sinoe* [1972] 1 Lloyd's Rep 201; *Fidelitas Shipping Co v V/O Exportchleb* [1963] 2 Lloyd's Rep 113, 120–21 (CA).

can carry across the charterparty clauses to the bill of lading. When the different nature of the various charterparty clauses is taken into account, it is far too unrealistic to assume that all charterparty terms can be introduced into the bill of lading, irrespective of the wording of the incorporation clause. Given that the parties need to ensure incorporation of some specific charterparty clauses, such as those relating to lien, demurrage, forum selection and freight, they must find the answer to one critical question: what words of incorporation should be used in order to incorporate particular charterparty provisions?

Despite a clearly drafted incorporation clause with sufficient breadth to introduce the desired charterparty provisions, a further problem usually arises due to the wording of the charterparty clauses which, for instance, simply refer to the charterer. If one instinctively reads these terms *in haec verba* under the bill of lading, these provisions will surely be viewed as neither relevant nor applicable to the holder.[24] However, a pro-shipowner approach could suggest transforming the word 'the charterers' to 'the receivers', for instance, in order to adapt this wording into the bill of lading and make the holder bound by these terms.

With a view to striking a balance between these conflicting interests of the carriers and the holders, both US and English courts exercise caution in employing the method of so-called 'verbal manipulation'.[25] The reason for their vigilance is to provide a certain level of protection to holders, who seldom have the right and the chance to see the charterparty referred to, including its various provisions drafted solely for the benefit of carriers.[26] Nevertheless, in order to give effect to the incorporation clause, the courts resort to this method and therefore adapt the imported charterparty provisions into the bill of lading to the extent possible. When the issue of 'manipulation' is viewed in that light, it becomes necessary to ask one question: to what extent should it be permissible to 'manipulate'[27] the incorporated charterparty wording, knowing that doing so leaves the holder exposed to unforeseeable liabilities towards the carriers?

In this chapter, the focus will first be on the issue of what words of incorporation are apt to describe and refer to which charterparty terms. Moving on from the interpretation of the words of incorporation, the chapter will then go on to consider the extent to which the courts could allow verbal manipulation.

I. What Words of Incorporation are Apt to Incorporate?

Anyone examining the widely used Congenbill 2007 standard-form bill of lading cannot fail to see the incorporation clause on its reverse side, which reads 'all

[24] See *Hamilton & Co v Mackie Sons* (1889) 5 TLR 677.
[25] See *The Merak* [1965] P 223, 260.
[26] See Section II below.
[27] Russell LJ in *The Merak* [1965] P 223, 260.

terms, conditions and exceptions as per charterparty including law and arbitration clause'. Evidently, this or a similar incorporation language is employed so as to carry across the widest possible range of charterparty provisions to the bill of lading. However, one may wonder the reason for this long wording under the incorporation clause, since the words 'all terms as per charterparty' would appear to be perfectly sufficient to achieve the objective.

The reason for this language can simply be explained by the drastic change in the incorporation clause over the years. In the early days it simply read 'paying for the said goods as per charterparty'[28] or 'paying freight and all conditions as per charterparty'.[29] It can easily be inferred from the change over the years that the recognised construction method for incorporation clauses is very different from giving the words their sole literal meaning. This being so, it is vital to analyse what incorporation words could aptly describe the particular charterparty clauses that they wish to bring into the bill of lading.

In a fluctuating freight market, shipowners who seek to compel their respective holders to pay the freight as per the charterparty rate may find it safer to expressly identify the charterparty freight in the incorporation clause. However, coupled with the freight provisions of the charterparty, they can also be anxious about incorporation of other terms such as those relating to demurrage, lien and forum selection. This situation raises a number of questions: is it possible to achieve the incorporation of all charterparty provisions if the express reference to 'freight' is juxtaposed with the words 'and all other conditions'? In the case of such an incorporation clause, does a specific reference to 'freight' lead to the incorporation of only the terms that are *ejusdem generis* with the provisions as to freight, or will they be effective to carry all other charter provisions? To defeat the application of the *ejusdem generis* rule, would a general reference to 'all terms and conditions whatsoever' of the charterparty be sufficient? Does the incorporation language, which points to 'all terms and conditions' of the charterparty, have a restrictive meaning in the absence of the word 'whatsoever'? Would use of the words 'conditions', 'terms', 'clauses', 'provisions' or similar phrases directly affect the breadth of the incorporating language?

Under both English and US law, there is a long series of judicial decisions where the costs of finding the solutions to all these issues were borne either by carriers or by the bill of lading holders. In accordance with the guidelines provided under the cases, carriers took further steps to effect incorporation of their desired charterparty terms by introducing new types of incorporation clauses that led to new discussions as to their construction. Nevertheless, all relevant US and English judicial decisions are aids to construction of which all concerned parties should be mindful, and which will be analysed in this section. For present purposes, the

[28] *Smith v Sieveking* (1855) E & B 589, 119 ER 600.

[29] *Russell and Others v Niemann* (1864) 17 CB (NS) 163; *Gray v Carr and Another* (1870–71) LR 6 QB 522; *Serraino v Campbell* [1891] 1 QB 298; *Wegener v Smith* (1854) 15 CBR 285; *Diederichsen v Farquharson Brothers* [1989] 1 QB 150.

initial question will be what words of incorporation can aptly carry across which charterparty provisions to the bill of lading. Thereafter, the incorporation of forum selection clauses will be analysed separately, given that this issue has been hotly disputed in courts and tribunals for more than a century.

A. How are the Charterparty Terms to be Described under a Bill of Lading?

In identifying what words of incorporation are apt to describe the desired charterparty provisions, the courts have suggested that the rules of construction are not constant: the manner of construing these words may vary according to the terms of the bills of lading.[30] Given that the main concern of carriers is to ensure the incorporation of the charterparty provisions that are of vital importance to them, the rules established under the key cases appear to have considerable influence on practice, and especially on the widely known standard-form bills of lading. To promote certainty, both English and US courts have shown a preference for following the established construction methods based on these bill of lading forms.[31]

i. Early Forms of Incorporation Wording

In the early years, the carriers' first attempts to bring all charterparty terms into the bill of lading were not successful where the clause simply read 'paying freight as per charterparty' or similar. Due to the reference being made to the charterparty freight, this language was held to be sufficient to bring into the bill of lading merely those charterparty provisions relating to freight.[32] Hence, in *Fry v Chartered Mercantile Bank of India, London and China*, the bill of lading provision stipulating that freight be payable as per charterparty was taken as competent to import the charterparty lien clause relating to freight.[33] In line with this reasoning, English courts consistently refused to import charterparty demurrage clauses when the incorporation wording did no more than mention the charter freight.[34] Having been influenced by the English approach, the courts across the Atlantic took a similar view on this matter. The authority for this proposition is the US Supreme Court decision in *Crossman v Burrill*. There, the incorporation clause

[30] For English law, see *OK Petroleum AB v Vitol Energy SA* [1995] 2 Lloyd's Rep 160; *Siboti K/S v BP France SA* [2003] 2 Lloyd's Rep 364; *The Ethniki* [2000] CLC 446. For US law, G Gilmore and C Black, *Law of Admiralty*, 2nd edn (St Paul, MN, West Publishing Company, 2001) 220.

[31] For English law, see *The Annefield* [1971] P 168. For US law, see *Vimar Seguros y Reaseguros SA v M/V Sky Reefer* 515 US 528, 551–52 (US 1995).

[32] For US law, see *Crossman v Burrill* 2006 AMC 1803, 1809–10 (US 1900). See also W Poor, *American Law of Charterparties and Bills of Lading*, 5th edn (New York, NY, Matthew Bender, 1968) 72. For English law, see *Smith v Sieveking* (1855) 5 E & B 589, 119 ER 600. See also GD Keogh, 'The Shipowner's Lien for Freight' (1898) 14 *LQR* 153.

[33] See *Fry v Chartered Mercantile Bank of India, London and China* (1965–66) LR 1 CP 689.

[34] *Smith v Sieveking* (1855) E & B 589; *Chappel v Comfort* (1861) 10 CB (NS) 802.

in the bill of lading contained a mere reference to the charterparty freight and average under bill of lading terms.[35] Acknowledging that such restrictive wording cannot import any other charterparty clauses, the Court relieved the holder of liability for the demurrage incurred under the charterparty.[36]

Having seen that broader language must be employed in order to impose further charterparty obligations onto holders, carriers started to insert incorporation clauses containing general words with considerable breadth. However, contrary to their expectations, wording of these clauses was treated as too general and ambiguous to import all charterparty provisions into the bill of lading. As the explanations below will show, the restrictive interpretation of the incorporation language was preferred for three key reasons. First, narrow construction of the loose descriptions against carriers was desirable[37] on the grounds that application of the *contra proferentem* rule under bills of lading was—and still is—recognised.[38] Secondly, to give the general words their literal meaning and therefore to incorporate all charterparty terms, would be detrimental to the holders, who in almost all cases had no access to the charterparty referred to. Thirdly, this limitation was necessary for the purpose of saving the bills of lading from inconsistent charterparty provisions.[39]

Of the most significant construction methods to limit the scope of incorporation was the *ejusdem generis* rule, in cases where the incorporation clause read 'freight and all other conditions as per charterparty'. Due to the effect of the preceding word 'freight', the courts read the reference to 'all other conditions' as apt to incorporate only the conditions to be performed by the bill of lading holders to get delivery of the goods.[40] To put it another way, both US and English courts refused to construe the word 'conditions' in isolation from the word 'freight' because payment of freight in this incorporation language was immediately

[35] *Crossman v Burrill* 179 US 100, 109 (US 1900); *Dayton v Parke* 97 Sickels 391, 37 NE 642 (NY 1894).

[36] ibid. Nonetheless, it must be borne in mind that the courts could imply a term that the goods are to be discharged within a reasonable time. Such an obligation is likely to be imposed on the person who has presented the bill of lading for delivery of the goods. For English law, see *The Spiros C* [2000] 2 Lloyd's Rep 319, para 74. For US law, see *Dayton v Parke* 97 Sickels 391, 37 NE 642 (NY 1894) at 399.

[37] Consequently, unless the courts adopt a contrary approach for that particular clause, ambiguities in the contract provisions are resolved against the carrier. For US law, see *Centrosoyus-America v US* 30 F 2d 302 (DCNY 1928). A recent case supporting this proposition is *Royal Insurance Co v Orient Overseas Container Line Ltd* 2008 AMC 337, 341 (6th Cir 2008). For English Law, see *Serraino v Campbell* [1891] 1 QB 283, 297. For a more recent case, see *The KH Enterprise* [1994] 2 AC 324, 329 (PC).

[38] For English law, see *The Irbenskiy Proliv* [2005] 1 Lloyd's Rep 383, 386; *The Starsin* [2004] AC 715, 779 (HL). For US law, see *Royal Insurance Co v Orient Overseas Container Line Ltd* 2008 AMC 337, 341 (6th Cir 2008).

[39] For the rule of consistency see Chapter 5.

[40] For English law, see *Serraino & Sons v Campbell and Others* [1891] 1 QB 283, 289; *Diederichsen v Farquharson Brothers* [1898] 1 QB 150. See also TG Carver and RP Colinvaux, *Carver's Carriage by Sea*, vol 1, 13th edn (London: British Shipping Laws Series, 1982) para 720. For US law, see *Centrosoyus-America Inc v United States* 31 F 2d 610, 611 (SDNY 1929) quoting *Serraino & Sons v Campbell* [1891] 1 QB 283, 297. See also Poor (n 32) 72.

followed by the other conditions of the charter. They further took the view that the conditions in that sense merely point to the other payment obligations borne by the consignees for delivery of the cargo.[41] Consequently, while accepting that express reference to freight is capable of importing all charterparty clauses relating to freight,[42] the courts viewed the generic word 'condition' as capable of describing the charterparty demurrage provisions.[43] This wording was also effective to carry across charterparty lien clauses with respect to freight,[44] demurrage[45] and dead freight[46] to the bill of lading.

In early English cases, this incorporation wording was made subject to one further restriction: the word 'condition' was held to be insufficient to describe the provisions which, if applied, would have the effect of removing or lessening the carrier's liability vis-à-vis the holder for the carriage of goods.[47] Given these provisions would operate as an exemption clause, such provisions could only aptly be described with an express reference to 'exception' or 'negligence clause'[48] in the incorporation clause.[49] Hence, in *Diederichsen v Farquharson Brothers*, the charterparty clause exempting the shipowner of liability for deck carriage was not incorporated through the incorporation clause, which did not mention 'exceptions'.[50] The decision in *Serraino v Campbell* had the same effect, where the Court decided against incorporation of the charterparty clause, which would, if incorporated, strip the carrier of liability for the cargo loss occasioned by the negligence of the master.[51]

[41] *Serraino & Sons v Campbell and Others* [1891] 1 QB 283 and *Diederichsen v Farquharson Brothers* [1898] 1 QB 150. See also G Treitel and FMB Reynolds, *Carver on Bills of Lading*, 3rd edn (London, Sweet & Maxwell, 2011) para 30-020. For US law, see *Centrosoyus-America Inc v United States* 31 F 2d 610, 611 (SDNY 1929).

[42] This was held to include the lien for freight and mode of its payment. For US law, see *Crossman v Burrill* 179 US 100 (US 1900). For English law, see *Serraino & Sons v Campbell and Others* [1891] 1 QB 283 at 295; *Kern v Deslandes* (1861) 10 CB (NS) 205.

[43] For US law, see *Yone Suzuki v Central Argentine Railways* 27 F 2d 795, 801–02 (2d Cir 1928); *The Hans Maersk* 266 F 806 (2d Cir 1920). For English law, see *Porteus v Watney* (1877–78) LR 3 QBD 534; *Wegener v Smith* (1854) 15 CB 285. Where the charterparty demurrage clause is not confined to discharge port demurrage, the word 'condition' would probably not cover loading port demurrage, see *Steamship 'Country of Lancaster' Limited v Sharp & Co* (1889) 24 QBD 158. However, it is submitted that demurrage should be taken as another payment obligation to be performed by the consignee for delivery of the cargo. Consequently, the word must therefore be construed as such.

[44] For English law, see *Gardner & Sons v Trechmann* (1884–85) LR 15 QBD 154, where it was stated that the right to lien would nevertheless be limited to the bill of lading freight expressly provided thereunder. For US law, see *O'Connel v One Thousand & Two Bales of Sisal Hemp* 75 F 408–10 (SD Ala 1896), quoting *Gardner v Trechmann*.

[45] For English law, see *Porteus v Watney* (1877–78) LR 3 QBD 534, 541. For US law, see *O'Connel v One Thousand & Two Bales of Sisal Hemp* 75 F 408–10 (SD Ala 1896).

[46] For English law, see *Kish v Taylor* [1912] AC 604. See also Keogh (n 32) 144. For US law, see *O'Connel v One Thousand & Two Bales of Sisal Hemp* 75 F 408–10 (SD Ala 1896).

[47] See *Russell v Niemann* (1864) 17 CB (NS) 163.

[48] See *The Northumbria* [1906] P 292.

[49] ibid.

[50] [1898] 1 QB 150.

[51] [1891] 1 QB 283, 289–90.

The further consequence of these semantic considerations was clear: an incorporation clause which refers to the 'conditions' and 'exceptions' of the charterparty was deemed insufficient to incorporate the charterparty provisions that did not strictly fall within the meaning of these words.[52] On the issue of what meaning was ascribed to the word 'exception' in the incorporation clause, the main guidance is *Hogarth Shipping Company v Blyth, Greene, Jourdain & Co.*[53] There, the incorporation clause referred to both the conditions and exceptions of the charterparty. The relevant charterparty contained a conclusive evidence clause providing that the bill of lading would be deemed conclusive proof of the cargo shipped and its condition. In a cargo claim for short delivery, the holder sought to rely on this provision to prevent the shipowner from adducing evidence showing that all the cargo placed on board had been delivered. Holding against the incorporation of the conclusive evidence clause, the Court took the clause as neither a 'condition' nor an 'exception'. On this matter, Swinfen Eady LJ said:[54]

> The exceptions are provisions which limit the obligation of the shipowner or carrier to deliver the goods safely: he agrees to do this, unless prevented by excepted perils. The conclusive evidence clause is not an exception or qualification of the shipowner's liability, but an extension to it, it renders him liable for goods stated to have been shipped on board, whether actually shipped or not.

In the *Hogarth Shipping* decision, the conclusive evidence clause was stated to be a 'term' of the contract.[55] This, quite understandably, led to the addition of the word 'term' to the incorporation language. Thus, in *Fort Shipping Co v Pederson*, the incorporation language additionally referred to all 'terms' of the charterparty. The charterparty conclusive evidence clause—which had previously been held to be neither a condition nor an exception—was this time incorporated through the words of incorporation due to the additional word 'term' therein.[56]

Across the Atlantic, the courts also applied the *ejusdem generis* rule when interpreting words of incorporation that read 'freight and all other conditions as per charterparty'. Hence, they also did not find this wording sufficient to incorporate exceptions to liabilities in the charterparty.[57] On the issue of what meaning should be ascribed to the word 'exceptions' in the incorporation clauses, US courts followed a similar line of reasoning to that adopted in the *Hogarth Shipping* decision. In *Centrosoyus-America v US* the Court was concerned with the question of whether a 'liberty-to-deviate' clause could be incorporated through a reference to 'exceptions' in the incorporation clause.[58] When holding in favour of incorporation, the Court took the view that the clause had something to do with

[52] See *Hogarth Shipping Company Ltd v Blyth, Greene, Jourdain & Co Ltd* [1917] 2 KB 534.
[53] ibid.
[54] ibid, at 548–49.
[55] ibid, at 556.
[56] *Fort Shipping Co v Pederson* [1924] 19 Ll L Rep 26.
[57] See *Yone Suzuki v Central Argentine Railways* 27 F 2d 795, 801–02 (2d Cir 1928). See also Poor (n 32) 72.
[58] 31 F 2d 610 (SDNY 1929).

safe delivery and carriage of the cargo.[59] As an alternative ground, they further stated that the use of the words 'condition' and 'exception' would create the same effect as that arising from the reference to 'terms' in the incorporation clause. Put another way, the combined effect of the words 'conditions' and 'exceptions' was treated as that of the word 'term'. The latter ground was somewhat inconsistent with the reasoning given in the *Hogarth Shipping* decision, which suggested that the word 'term' would be needed to describe charterparty provisions that do not strictly come within the scope of conditions or exceptions.[60] Furthermore, it signalled the tendency of US courts to depart from rigid semantic considerations where necessary, considering that commercial men may not know the breadth of incorporating words assigned by the courts.[61]

ii. Modern Forms of Incorporation Wording

In the modern forms of incorporation clause, the word 'conditions' is not preceded by 'the payment of freight' to avoid application of the *ejusdem generis* rule. These days, it is commonly preceded by the word 'terms'.[62] It is also common to see the incorporation clauses containing more descriptive and comprehensive words such as 'all terms, conditions, exceptions and liberties' so that a wide range of charterparty provisions can be included.[63] Following these drastic changes in the incorporation language, both US and English courts have ascribed wider meaning to the word 'condition' given that in modern forms it is no longer juxtaposed with the word 'freight'. However, on the whole, their interpretation of this new wording differs considerably. For this reason, the legal positions under the English law and US law on this issue will be considered separately.

a. English Law

In almost all cases preceded by the word 'term', the word 'condition' has been redefined: it is now interpreted as apt to incorporate the conditions that are germane to shipment, carriage and discharge of the cargo.[64] Put another way, the general incorporation wording, which does not contain any specific reference to a charterparty provision, is taken to describe only those charterparty provisions relating to the subject matter of the bill of lading, as a contract of carriage.[65] With this

[59] ibid, at 611.

[60] [1917] 2 KB 534, 556.

[61] *Centrosoyus-America Inc v United States* 31 F 2d 610, 611 (SDNY 1929).

[62] As an example, see *The Fjord Wind* [2000] 2 Lloyd's Rep 191 and *The Sormovksiy* [1994] 2 Lloyd's Rep 266. In both cases the incorporation clause read 'all terms and conditions as per charterparty'.

[63] See *The Annefield* [1971] P 168; *The Njegos* [1936] 53 Ll L Rep 286.

[64] See *TW Thomas & Portsea Shipping Co Ltd* [1912] AC 1, 6 (HL); *The Annefield* [1971] P 168 at 175; *The Nerano* [1996] 1 Lloyd's Rep 1, 4; *The Delos* [2001] 1 Lloyd's Rep 703, 706; *The Njegos* [1936] 53 Ll L Rep 286 at 295; *The Phonizien* [1966] 1 Lloyd's Rep 150, 155; *The Spiros C* [2000] 2 Lloyd's Rep 319 at 335 (CA).

[65] See *OK Petroleum AB v Vitol Energy SA* [1995] 2 Lloyd's Rep 160, 165; *The Ethniki* [2000] CLC 446, 452; *The KH Enterprise* [1994] 2 AC 324, 346.

more liberal interpretation, the definition of the word 'conditions' was extended to comprise the obligations to be performed not only by the receivers of the cargo, but also by the carriers.[66] Consequently, through the word 'conditions', those charterparty provisions in relation to the responsibility of the shipowner for making the vessel seaworthy were incorporated,[67] as was a clause permitting discharge of the cargo against production of a bank guarantee.[68] On the incorporation of charterparty provisions as to loading and discharge operations, further guidance can be drawn from the decision in *The Jordan II.* The decision suggests that charterparty provisions releasing the shipowners from the risk and costs of loading and discharge operations can readily be incorporated through the word 'condition'.[69]

On the whole it is clear that English courts are now reluctant to rely on the *ejusdem generis* rule when construing incorporation clauses in bills of lading.[70] For this reason, the incorporation clauses which read 'freight and all other terms and conditions as per charterparty' should no longer be taken to be different from an incorporation clause that refers to 'all terms and conditions' of the charterparty.[71] This has its support from the decision in *The Varenna*, where the incorporation clause read 'all conditions and exceptions of [the] charterparty, including the negligence clause are deemed to be incorporated in [the] bill of lading'. Although the word 'conditions' was not preceded by 'terms' in the incorporation clause, the Court preferred not to treat the words 'all conditions' differently from 'all terms and conditions'.[72] Bringing both types of wording within the framework of the 'general words of incorporation', the Court took the view that they could only incorporate the charterparty provisions that were germane to shipment, carriage and discharge of the cargo.[73]

These observations should not be taken to mean that the slight variations between the meanings of 'condition', 'term' and 'clause' have not completely disappeared with the decision in *The Varenna.*[74] In this area of commerce, where clarity and certainty is of the utmost importance, the courts have preserved their early approach as to how the charterparty exemption clauses can aptly be described. Consequently, for these clauses to be incorporated, specific reference to 'exceptions' in the incorporation clause is still necessary,[75] unless the word 'term'[76] or a

[66] For a similar view, see Treitel and Reynolds (n 41) para 3-018.

[67] See *The Fjord Wind* [2000] 2 Lloyd's Rep 191.

[68] See *The Sormovksiy* [1994] 2 Lloyd's Rep 266.

[69] *The Jordan II* [2005] 1 Lloyd's Rep 57 (HL). See also *The Eems Solar* [2013] 2 Lloyd's Rep 487, where a similar view has been taken. Both cases show that general words of incorporation can aptly describe FIOST and similar charterparty provisions.

[70] See *The Varenna* [1984] QB 599, 617 (CA).

[71] ibid.

[72] ibid, at 620.

[73] ibid, at 620–21.

[74] ibid.

[75] For a similar view, see Cooke et al (n 7) para 18.52.

[76] See ibid and also *Fort Shipping v Pederson* [1924] 19 Ll L Rep 26.

word with the broadest possible meaning such as 'whatsoever' is inserted therein.[77] These semantic differences do not, however, have any effect on incorporation of demurrage, lien and freight clauses, given that even the early forms of incorporation clause were already adequate to achieve this purpose.[78] However, it will be recalled that the narrowest form of incorporation language—which merely refers to the charterparty freight—is not apt to incorporate to that extent. With respect to demurrage clauses, one further point must be made: since the *ejusdem generis* rule no longer comes into play under the modern incorporation wording, it is beyond any doubt that general words of incorporation are competent to import loading port demurrage precisely because it is germane to shipment of cargo.[79]

Regardless of their new extensive scope, general words of incorporation are, however, inoperative to cover charterparty provisions that are ancillary to the subject matter of the bill of lading, as a contract of carriage. In light of the consistent line of English authorities led by the famous decision in *Thomas v Portsea*, these terms can only aptly be described through special words of incorporation, that is to say, with an express reference to such provisions in the incorporation clause.[80] The incorporation clauses with a general reference to the charterparty thus fall short of describing such ancillary charterparty provisions, regardless of the scope of the general words of incorporation:[81] even though the word 'term' or 'clause' has a wider meaning than the word 'condition', and the word 'whatsoever' has much more width than the other general incorporating words,[82] these differences have no role to play when determining the incorporation of such provisions. Thus, in *Siboti K/S v BP France SA*, the inclusion of the word 'whatsoever' was held not apt to describe the exclusive jurisdiction clause,[83] and also in *The Delos*, where the same word was again considered as insufficient to incorporate the charterparty arbitration clause.[84] Unsurprisingly, in *The Varenna* the word 'term' was also inapt to incorporate a charterparty arbitration clause into the bill of lading.[85]

At this juncture, a question arises as to which charterparty provisions fall outside the subject matter of the contract of carriage contained in or evidenced by the

[77] *The Garbis* [1982] 2 Lloyd's Rep 283, 288, where it was held that the term 'whatsoever' was apt to import even those unusual charterparty provisions.

[78] However, it must be borne in mind that the narrowest form of incorporation language, which merely refers to the charterparty freight, does not have such force. See the explanations above.

[79] Provided, of course, the charterparty demurrage clause does not merely contemplate discharge port demurrage. See also *The Jordan II* [2005] 1 Lloyd's Rep 57, where a similar pattern of reasoning was adopted, and the FIOST clause was held to be incorporated through general words of incorporation.

[80] See *Thomas v Portsea Shipping Co Ltd* [1912] AC 1, 6 (HL).

[81] See ibid. See also *OK Petroleum AB v Vitol Energy SA* [1995] 2 Lloyd's Rep 160, 165.

[82] For a similar view, see Treitel and Reynolds (n 41) para 3-014.

[83] *Siboti K/S v BP France SA* [2003] Lloyd's Rep 364.

[84] *The Delos* [2001] 1 Lloyd's Rep 703, 706.

[85] See [1984] QB 592, 594. But see *The Merak* [1965] P 223, where the word 'clause' was treated as apt to describe a charterparty arbitration clause. For more discussion of the case see M Özdel, 'Incorporation of Charterparty Clauses into Bills of Lading: Peculiar to Maritime Law?' in M Clarke (ed), *Maritime Law Evolving* (Oxford, Hart Publishing, 2013) 181.

bill of lading. It is well established under case law that arbitration and jurisdiction clauses fall outside the scope. What is not so clear is what other types of charterparty provision are also ancillary. In particular, can general words of incorporation incorporate a choice-of-law clause or a time bar in the charterparty? On the nature of choice-of-law clauses, it is tempting to think that they are ancillary to the subject matter of the contract. This is supported to some extent by the severability of the choice-of-law clauses: in principle, a choice-of-law clause applies even to disputes as to the validity of the contract,[86] as with arbitration clauses.[87] The main difficulty with this view is evident: the choice-of-law clause governs the mode of parties' performance under the contract of carriage.[88] For this reason, the choice-of-law clause is probably one of the most suitable provisions for incorporation into the bill of lading. English courts have also looked favourably on the incorporation of the charterparty choice-of-law clauses through general words of incorporation.[89] At any rate, where the choice-of-law provision is within a clause that is specifically referred to in the incorporation clause, the clause in its entirety will be incorporated into the bill of lading.[90]

On the question of whether a charterparty time-bar clause can aptly be incorporated through general words of incorporation, the decision in *OK Petroleum Vitol Energy SA* is of some assistance.[91] There, a charterparty time-bar clause could not be incorporated into a sale contract that referred to 'demurrage as per charterparty'. Although exclusively applicable to claims for demurrage, the time-bar clause was held to be ancillary to the charterparty provisions on demurrage. In arriving at this conclusion, Colman J took specific account of the main purpose for the reference to demurrage in the sale contract, as well as the probable effects of the time-bar clause in the sale contract.

For present purposes, the decision must be treated with caution given that the cases on incorporation in the context of bills of lading are 'materially' different from those in the context of sale contracts.[92] Nonetheless, some useful guidance can be drawn from Colman J's approach in this case: it suggests that when evaluating the nature of the charterparty time-bar clause—to decide whether the clause is germane to the subject matter of the contract—it is essential to see how the clause operates in the charterparty, as well as its probable effects in the bill of lading when its incorporation is assumed. Given that a time-bar clause can come in various different shapes, much will turn on the nature of the relevant time-bar clause when deciding

[86] On this issue, see A Briggs, *Agreements on Jurisdiction and Choice of Law* (Oxford, Oxford University Press, 2008).

[87] See *Fiona Trust v Privalov* [2007] UKHL 40.

[88] See *Amin Rasheed Shipping Corp v Kuwait Insurance Co* [1984] AC 50 (CA).

[89] See *The San Nicholas* [1976] 1 Lloyd's Rep 8, 12 (CA), per Denning LJ, quoting *The Njegos* [1936] P 90, 105–07. For a recent decision of the High Court of Singapore on this issue see *The Dolphina* [2012] 1 Lloyd's Rep 304, where the Court held that the general words of incorporation can incorporate the charterparty choice-of-law clause into the bill of lading.

[90] See *The Oinousson Pride* [1991] 1 Lloyd's Rep 126, 130.

[91] [1995] 2 Lloyd's Rep 160.

[92] ibid, at 163–64, per Colman LJ.

whether general words can incorporate it. However, where the incorporation language makes a specific reference to a charterparty clause containing its time-bar provision, it is likely that the specified clause will be incorporated in its entirety.[93]

The need to have special words of incorporation to incorporate such ancillary charterparty provisions is clearly to the holders' benefit: the rule permits the incorporation of such provisions only to the extent that they have been brought to the holders' attention in the incorporation clause. However, this position raises the question of whether it is actually necessary to alert the holders about the incorporation of these provisions, some of which can be standard and customary. Despite the fact that their existence under the charterparty is unlikely to be surprising to many, the requirement of making a specific reference to such charterparty provisions must nevertheless be maintained under English law. Established by a long line of cases, this rule of incorporation now lies at the heart of the English rules of incorporation. It is unlikely that the courts will depart from this well-established interpretation of the general words of incorporation, given their reluctance to disturb rooted interpretations of standard clauses.[94]

b. US Law

US courts adopt a more receptive approach to the issue of what charterparty provisions can be incorporated through general words of incorporation. In this respect, they have repeatedly held that general words of incorporation can carry across all charterparty provisions, insofar as there is an incorporation clause clearly demonstrating the intention to achieve this result.[95] However, the courts have refused to take the view that those charterparty terms whose nature is repugnant to bills of lading can be incorporated, regardless of the intention that can objectively be ascertained under the bill of lading.[96] Consequently, for the purposes of manifesting the intention to incorporate to the widest possible extent, carriers are encouraged to use expansive language in the incorporation clause.[97]

On the question of what particular form of incorporation wording is deemed to demonstrate the required intention, the main guidance is the decision in *Continental UK Ltd v Anagel Confidence Compania Naviera*, which contained an incorporation clause that read 'all terms, conditions and exceptions of the charterparty'.[98] There, the highlighted phraseology was treated as a 'catch-all'

[93] *Denny, Mott & Dickson Ltd and Others v Lynn Shipping Company Ltd* [1963] 1 Lloyd's Rep 339.

[94] See *The Annefield* [1971] P 168. See also *The Jordan II* [2005] 1 Lloyd's Rep 57 (CA), where this line of reasoning was adopted.

[95] See *Son Shipping Co Inc v De Fosse & Tanghe* 1952 AMC 1931, 1933 (2d Cir 1952). Also see for US law, G Gilmore and C Black, *Law of Admiralty*, 2nd edn (Mineola, NY, West Publishing Company, 2001) 220.

[96] *O'Connel v One Thousand and Two Bales of Sisal Hemp* 75 F 410 (DC Ala 1896).

[97] See *Energy of Transport Ltd v M/V San Sebastian* 348 FSupp2d 186, (SDNY 2004). This liberal perspective of the courts is also adopted by New York Arbitrators, see *In Re Arbitration Between Alpine Shipping Company of Monrovia and Palm Shipping Co SMA No 1485 (October 22, 1980)* where the general words of incorporation were treated as apt to import the charterparty choice of law clause.

[98] *Continental UK Ltd v Anagel Confidence Compania Naviera* 1987 AMC 2012, 2017 (SDNY 1987).

clause, and it was taken to incorporate the arbitration clause. This decision should not be taken to mean that the semantic considerations have no relevance whatsoever: with respect to the incorporation of 'negligence' and 'liberty-to-deviate' clauses, it is evident that the position is similar to that under English law. For these provisions to be carried across to the bill of lading, the courts require that incorporation clauses contain either an express reference to exceptions or expansive language with the widest possible scope, such as 'all terms whatsoever' of the charterparty.[99]

Having briefly discussed the US law position with regard to this issue, one of its key features must be stressed: unlike English law, no categorisation is made among charterparty provisions for the purposes of their incorporation. Instead, all those provisions in the charterparty are taken as 'any other contract' provisions,[100] which can be appropriately described with general words of incorporation.[101] It naturally flows from this approach that carriers are merely expected to use comprehensive words of incorporation manifesting the intention to import all charterparty provisions. Leaving aside this key difference between the US and English approaches, it is common to both jurisdictions that little effort is expected from carriers to incorporate the provisions which are germane to shipment, carriage and the discharge of goods.[102]

This expedient method for incorporation may raise criticism from the holders, with the rules facilitating incorporation of many unfavourable charterparty provisions: demurrage clauses,[103] FIOST and similar clauses.[104] Nonetheless, the holders' position is not actually as hopeless as it seems. Even if these charterparty terms can be introduced into bills of lading through general words of incorporation, this does not necessarily mean that they will be applicable to the bill of lading holders:[105] in both jurisdictions the decision on incorporation is made prior to determining applicability of the incorporated charterparty clauses for the holders. Consequently, following the further rules of incorporation, many of the incorporated provisions, including those identified, may turn out to be inapplicable to the bill of lading holder.

[99] As a result of this line of thinking, the word 'exception' was held sufficient to describe a liberty to deviate clause, *Centrosoyus-America Inc v United States* 1929 AMC 289 (SDNY 1929); *Son Shipping Co Inc v De Fosse & Tanghe* 1952 AMC 1931, 1933 (2d Cir 1952); *Southwestern Sugar & Molasses Co v Eliza Jane Nicholson* 1955 AMC 746 (SDNY 1954).

[100] See *Son Shipping Co Inc v De Fosse & Tanghe* 1952 AMC 1931, 1933 (2d Cir 1952).

[101] ibid.

[102] For US law, see ibid. See also JW McKearn, 'Shipowner Denied Lien Against Third Party's Cargo For Charterer's Unpaid Charter Hire' (1980) 26 *Loyola Law Review* 416, 418. For English law, see *The Miramar* [1984] AC 617 (HL).

[103] For the views highlighting the unfairness of holding the endorsees liable for loading port demurrage, see Miller (n 1) 86–87.

[104] For US law, see *Associated Metals & Minerals Corp v M/V Arktis Sky* 1993 AMC 509 (2d Cir 1992). For English law, see *The Jordan II* [2005] 1 Lloyd's Rep 57 (HL); *The Coral* [1993] 1 Lloyd's Rep 1, 5. For discussions as to whether they are applicable to bill of lading holders and whether they are in line with the Hague and the Hague-Visby Rules, see Chapter 5.

[105] See, for instance, *Andreas Vergottis v Robinson David & Co Ltd* [1928] 31 Ll L Rep 23, 27.

Among the charterparty provisions that are not directly germane to shipment, carriage and discharge of goods, the incorporation of forum selection clauses has been hotly debated for at least a century. Due to its significance to the parties to bills of lading, this issue deserves separate treatment.

B. Incorporating the Charterparty Forum Selection Clauses

i. Overview

From a purely practical perspective, parties to the bill of lading would naturally seek to bring their dispute before the forum they believed most convenient and that would be conducive to a favourable outcome. For this reason, it is not uncommon for parties to make their choice by way of an evaluation of the respective mandatory and procedural rules of the available fora.[106] In broad terms, the rationale behind weighing up the matters of procedure is twofold. First, these issues have a direct impact on efficiency of the dispute settlement procedures, especially in terms of cost and duration.[107] Secondly, the rules of procedure can impair the substantive rights of the parties.[108]

The effects of the rules of procedure can best be illustrated through an analysis of the challenges made against arbitration awards under English and US law. It is plain that the English Arbitration Act ('the 1996 Act') governs this issue where the seat of the arbitration is in England, Wales or Northern Ireland,[109] and that the US Federal Arbitration Act ('the 1925 Act') comes into play where a tribunal sits in the United States.[110] Both statutes envisage limited grounds for judicial review of arbitration awards in order for the awards to be finalised in a timely and cost-efficient manner.[111]

This objective seems to have been further prioritised under US law on the grounds that, unlike English law, the awards are not in principle subject to judicial review for error of law.[112] *Vacatur* or modification of arbitration awards can only

[106] See AS Bell, *Forum Shopping and Venue in Transnational Litigation* (Oxford, Oxford University Press, 2003) para 2.09.

[107] ibid, at para 2.04.

[108] ibid, at para 2.09.

[109] See s 2 of the 1996 Act.

[110] See 9 USC §9, §10(a). The provisions with regard to the challenge of arbitration awards are equally applicable to those cases where the arbitration agreement comes under (a) Chapter II of the 1925 Act, which implements the New York Convention and sets out provisions in relation to agreements and awards under the Convention, and (b) Chapter III, which implements the Inter-American Convention in International Commercial Arbitration.

[111] For US law, see 9 USC §10 and §11. For English law, see ss 67, 68 and 69 of the 1996 Act.

[112] See *Bowen v Amoco Pipeline Co* 254 F 3d 925, 931 (10th Cir 2001). On certain grounds, it can be argued that this objective is equally of the highest importance under the 1996 Act, see s 70(2)(b), which provides that before taking any judiciary action for challenge of the award, parties must exhaust any available arbitral process available. Moreover, see s 70(3) of the same act, where a 28-day time bar is envisaged for challenge of the award. On this matter, the time bar in the United States is three months, see 9 USC §12.

be made pursuant to the grounds set out under 9 USC §10 and §11, which do not set error of law as a ground for challenge. With the recent US Supreme Court decision in *Hall Associates v Mattel*, it is now also clear that the statutory grounds for challenge are exclusive,[113] and parties are thus not permitted to extend or restrict them in their arbitration agreements.[114] The practical effect of this is evident: where the chosen seat of arbitration is in the United States, parties may not ask the court to reconsider the award on a point of law, regardless of the fact that there is an express provision in their arbitration agreements to that effect.[115]

The only possible exception to this rigidity arises in cases where the arbitrator intentionally refuses to apply the law and reaches an erroneous result on a point of law:[116] this ground, which is labelled as 'manifest disregard of law', still survives the decision in *Hall Associates v Mattel.* Although this ground is in essence non-statutory, it can be raised under the guise of either of the two statutory grounds: 'acting in excess of powers'[117] and 'acting in wilful misconduct'.[118] Parties in those cases are entitled to move for *vacatur* of the award on the grounds that such an arbitrator can either be taken to have exceeded his or her powers,[119] or be deemed guilty of wilful misconduct.[120]

While the 1925 Act does not permit reconsideration of awards on the merits, the 1996 Act expressly provides for appeal of awards for error of law. English courts can thus review the award on a point of English law,[121] provided that the parties have not, in their arbitration agreements, contracted out of the right to appeal expressly or by implication.[122] Due to the importance of the finality of awards, the 1996 Act does not grant leave to appeal[123] an award for error of law,

[113] *Hall Street Associates v Mattel Inc* 128 SCt 1396 (US 2008).

[114] ibid.

[115] ibid.

[116] It is important to note that mere error of law on the part of the arbitrator is not taken as manifest disregard of law, see *Duferco Steel Trading v T Klaveness Shipping A/S*, 333 F 3d 383, 389 (2d Cir 2003); *Bowen v Amoco Pipeline Co* 254 F 3d 925 (10th Cir 1995). For a contrary view, see *Citigroup Global Markets Inc v Bacon* 562 F 3d 349, 355 (5th Cir 2009), *Grain v Trinity Health, Mercy Health Services Inc* 551 F 3d 374 (6th Cir 2008).

[117] See 9 USC §10(a)(4).

[118] 9 USC §10(a)(3). See *Stolt-Nielsen SA v Animal Feeds International Corp* 548 F 3d 85, 94 (2d Cir 2008) *cert granted*, 129 SCt 2793 (2009).

[119] See 9 USC §10(a)(4).

[120] 9 USC §10(a)(3).

[121] There is no right to appeal where the governing law of the dispute is not English law, see *Reliance Industries Ltd v Enron Oil & Gas India Ltd* [2002] 1 All ER (Comm) 59. Under English procedural law, the law chosen by the parties is presumed to be the same as English law, where the contrary is not proved, see L Collins, *Dicey, Morris & Collins on the Conflict of Laws*, 15th edn (London, Sweet & Maxwell, 2012) para 9-025. Where an arbitrator uses English law principles in such circumstances as a matter of procedural law, this does not mean that the arbitrator applies English law to the dispute. See *Reliance Industries* above.

[122] As regards contracting out of the right to appeal by implication see s 69(1) of the 1996 Act, which, inter alia, talks of agreements to dispense with reasons in the award. For express agreements to dispense with the right to appeal, see Art 34(6) of the ICC Rules of Arbitration 2012. See also *Sanghi Polyesters Ltd (India) v International Investor (KCFC) (Kuwait)* [2000] 1 Lloyd's Rep 480.

[123] See s 69(2), which states that an appeal cannot be brought except with the agreement of all the other parties to the proceedings, or with the leave of the court.

unless the decision of the tribunal on the question that the tribunal was asked to determine is obviously wrong.[124] Where the question is one of general public importance,[125] leave to appeal may be given if the decision of the tribunal is 'at least open to serious doubt'.[126]

As these explanations suggest, there is much that hinges on the choice of seat of the arbitration. Assuming that the seat of the arbitration is in London and the governing law of the dispute is English law, it is possible for the losing party to obtain leave to appeal for error of law. However, were the seat of the arbitration to be New York, the losing party would not in principle have the right to appeal for error of law. This situation clearly illustrates that procedural rules indeed considerably affect the substantive rights of parties, as well as the efficiency of the settlement of disputes. It here proves valuable to note that these observations illustrate only some of the reasons for long and fierce jurisdictional battles. There are evidently a number of other factors leading to such battles. Included in these factors is the nature of international carriage of goods by sea: there is usually more than one forum before which the parties could bring their claims, and it is not uncommon for each party to favour a different forum.

With carriers entering into contracts of carriage with many cargo interests located in various jurisdictions, they are typically concerned about the likelihood of battles over jurisdiction. To prevent the bill of lading holders from forum shopping, carriers in almost all cases insert or seek to incorporate forum selection clauses into bills of lading. Irrespective of the forum designated in the forum selection clause, it is not an unlikely eventuality for bill of lading holders to prefer to bring a claim against the carrier before the courts located in their principle place of business. The carrier will naturally seek to enforce the forum selection clause against a holder that has brought proceedings before these courts. If the forum selection clause is sought to be incorporated, it is not news that the holder is likely to challenge the incorporation of the forum selection clause.

On the incorporation and enforcement of the forum selection clauses in bills of lading, a long line of US and English authorities show that the courts have repeatedly considered three key facts in establishing their positions: the cargo interests' possible mistrust of foreign arbitration and litigation,[127] the nature of forum

[124] See s 69(3) of the 1996 Act.

[125] Interpretation of a provision in a standard-form contract is not necessarily considered of general public importance, see *The Northern Pioneer* [2002] EWCA (Civ) 1878.

[126] See s 69(3) of the 1996 Act. In a case, the difference of view between experienced arbitrators on the question that the arbitrators were asked to determine can of itself be sufficient to meet this criterion, see *The Northern Pioneer* [2002] EWCA (Civ) 1878 at para 64 (CA).

[127] For English law, see *Thomas v Portsea* [1912] AC 1, 8–9 (HL). For US law, see *Siderius Inc v M/V Ida Prima* 613 F Supp 916, 921 (SDNY 1985).

selection clauses,[128] and the fact that the holders seldom have the chance and the right to have sight of the charterparty referred to.[129]

Before we become immersed in the current legal position, some of the prime reasons for the hostile approaches towards foreign forum selection clauses must be discussed. For the holders, foreign litigation or arbitration can seem expensive to carry out in comparison to bringing an action in their own jurisdiction. Moreover, it can also be a time-wasting practice in terms of obtaining representation and following proceedings in a distant place. Under US law, similar arguments were raised notably in *Indussa Corporation v SS Ranborg.*[130] Refusing to enforce the forum selection clause in the bill of lading, which provided for litigation in Norway, the Court took the view that:

> From a practical standpoint, to require an American plaintiff to assert his claim only in a distant court lessens the liability of the carrier quite substantially when the claim is small. Such a clause puts 'a high hurdle' in the way of enforcing liability.[131]

English courts, too, have acknowledged the similar effects of forum selection clauses, In *Thomas v Portsea*, the House of Lords underlined similar practical problems arising from foreign forum selection clauses while deciding the incorporation of a charterparty clause providing for arbitration in the port where the dispute occurred.[132] In particular, they underlined the practical difficulty facing the holders in the case of a binding forum selection clause obliging these parties to arbitrate the dispute in a place with which they had no connection.[133]

Above all, the early US cases reveal scepticism over the ability of foreign fora to afford adequate protection to cargo interests. This antiquated reason for the mistrust of foreign courts was well reflected in the famous *Indussa* decision. There, the Court doubted whether foreign courts would safeguard cargo interests in the same way as a US court would.[134] Thus, they refused to strip the cargo interests of the right to resort to US courts, regardless of the fact that the foreign courts would also apply the Hague Rules, or other uniform rules.[135] At the root of this

[128] More specifically the question has been whether forum selection clauses must be treated as ancillary to the subject matter of the contract or just as any other contract provisions. For English law, see *Thomas v Portsea* [1912] AC 1, 8–9 (HL). For US law, see *Son Shipping Co Inc v De Fosse & Tanghe* 1952 AMC 1931 (2d Cir 1952).

[129] For US law, see *Thyssen Inc M/V/Markos N* 1999 AMC 2515 (SDNY 1999) *aff'd sub nom Thyssen Inc v Calypso Shipping Corp SA* 310 F 3d 102 (2d Cir 2002) *cert denied* 123 SCt 1573, 155 L Ed 2d 312 (US 2003); for English law, see *The Federal Bulker* [1989] 1 Lloyd's Rep 103.

[130] *Indussa Corporation v SS Ranborg* 1967 AMC 589, 597 (2d Cir 1967).

[131] ibid. A similar view was taken in *State Establishment for Agricultural Product Trading v M/V Wesermunde*, which involved a forum selection clause providing for London Arbitration, see 988 AMC 1988 (11th Cir 1988). This ruling was then overruled in *Vimar Seguros v Reaseguros SA v M/V Sky Reefer* 515 US 528 (US 1995). Due to the reasoning of the Court in *Sky Reefer*, the decision in *Indussa* must be considered as tacitly overruled, see the Court of Appeal ruling in *Sky Reefer* 1994 AMC 2513, 2518 (1st Cir 1994).

[132] See [1912] AC 1, 8–9.

[133] ibid.

[134] 1967 AMC 589, 597 (2d Cir 1967).

[135] ibid.

approach there was another archaic understanding: the right of a US citizen to receive justice from the courts was understood to comprise part of their substantial rights.[136] As a result of this line of thinking, parties were not deemed entitled to contract out of the power of the courts of competent jurisdiction to adjudicate the disputes.[137]

So far as the probable grounds for mistrust of arbitration are concerned, the decision in *Organes Enterprises Inc v M/J Khalij Frost* is illustrative.[138] There, the Court expressed their mistrust of arbitration on two main points when refusing to enforce the arbitration clause under the bills of lading. First, there are strictly limited grounds for any challenge of an arbitration award,[139] and secondly, arbitrators rarely provide an explanation of the reasons for their decision.[140] In fact, the advantages of arbitration come down more heavily in favour of arbitration. The restrictions to the grounds for challenge of arbitration awards are usually taken as beneficial, precisely because they may reduce litigation costs and unnecessary delays.[141] Arbitration is also a flexible procedure, given that if the parties wish to ensure the legal accuracy of the award, they are in principle entitled by the 1996 Act to challenge an award for error of law, where the dispute is governed by English law.[142]

Moreover, unlike the view of the US Court in *Organes Enterprises*, almost all the institutional arbitration rules provide that parties may require the arbitrators to give reasons for the award.[143] In this respect, the same flexibility in the form of arbitration awards is also envisaged under the 1996 Act.[144] The other obvious advantages include the ability to bring the dispute before a neutral forum[145] and to choose arbitrators who are experts in the subject matter.[146] Arbitration could also be viewed as a better alternative because it can be kept confidential for the benefit of parties seeking to avoid publicity.[147]

[136] See *Home Insurance Co of New York v Morse* 87 US 445 (US 1874).

[137] *Nashua River Paper Co v Hammermill Paper Co* 223 Mass 8, 111 NE 678, 680 (Mass 1916).

[138] *Organes Enterprises Inc v M/J Khalij Frost* 1989 AMC 1460 (SDNY 1989).

[139] See the explanations above in this section.

[140] See *Organes Enterprises Inc v M/J Khalij Frost* 1989 AMC 1460 (SDNY 1989) at 1462–63.

[141] See ML Moses, *International Commercial Arbitration* (Cambridge, Cambridge University Press, 2008) 4.

[142] See s 69(1) of the 1996 Act. As regards the 1925 Act, it does not allow parties to extend or reduce the grounds for challenge, see *Hall Street Associates v Mattel Inc* 128 SCt 1396 (US 2008).

[143] See Art 22 of the London Maritime Arbitrators Association (LMAA) Terms. See also Art 29 of the Society of Maritime Arbitrators (SMA) Rules, where it is expressly required that an award be given with reasons. This provision must be read together with Art 1 of the Rules, which provides that the parties could alter the terms. Similarly, see Art 32 of the UNCITRAL Arbitration Rules and Art 31(2) of the ICC Rules of Arbitration 2012.

[144] See s 52 of the 1996 Act. See also para 247 of the DAC Report.

[145] See Moses (n 141) 3.

[146] Also raised in R Merkin, *Arbitration Law* (London, Informa, 2004) at para 1.2. See also *Mitsubishi Motors Corp v Soler Chrysler-Plymouth Inc* 473 US 614, 633 (US 1985). See also *M/S Bremen v Zapata Off-Shore Co* 407 US 1, 12 (US 1972).

[147] See Y Baatz, *Maritime Law*, 2nd edn (London, Sweet & Maxwell, 2011) 4.

Probably due to these advantages, judicial hostility towards arbitration clauses no longer survives under US law.[148] It also seems that both the change in the approach and the strong federal policy in favour of arbitration, which is enshrined under the FAA, have been recognised in order to facilitate the competition of American businesses in global markets.[149] This objective can equally be considered as the rationale for US courts to hold parties to their bargain in the case of choice-of-court agreements. This proposition receives support from the leading US Supreme Court decision in *Bremen v Zapata Off-Shore Co* where the Court stated that 'The expansion of American business and industry will hardly be encouraged if, notwithstanding solemn contracts, we insist on a parochial concept that all disputes must be resolved under our laws and in our courts'.[150]

With regard to the perspective of English courts, it is clear that they have always been inclined to enforce forum selection clauses unless there is a good reason for not doing so.[151] In particular, the courts have exhibited a receptive approach towards arbitration.[152] Nevertheless, as the explanations below will show, their stance must not be taken so far as to convey the impression that the incorporation of forum selection clauses is treated just as any other charterparty provisions. With all this relevant background, the next section will examine how both English and US courts interpret the words of incorporation with a view to deciding whether a forum selection clause can be carried across to the bill of lading.

ii. What Words are Operative for the Incorporation of Forum Selection Clauses?

Considering the position of the holders who have no means of knowing the charterparty provisions, English courts take a vigilant approach towards the incorporation of forum selection clauses. As the explanations below will show, the approach of US courts is diametrically opposed to that of English law. For this reason, the legal positions in these jurisdictions will be dealt with separately.

a. English Law

English courts require an express reference to the choice-of-forum clause in bills of lading for the purposes of their incorporation. The courts thus call for a clear notice to be given to the bill of lading holders in order to alert these parties regarding the incorporation of a charterparty arbitration clause or jurisdiction clause. The leading authority for these propositions is *Thomas v Portsea*, where

[148] See *Vimar Seguros v Reaseguros SA v M/V Sky Reefer* 515 US 528 (US 1995).

[149] See *Mitsubishi Motors Corp v Soler Chyrsler-Plymouth Inc* 473 US 614 (US 1985).

[150] *Bremen v Zapata Off-Shore Co* 407 US 1, 9 (US 1972). To the same effect is another US Supreme Court ruling in *Carnival Cruise Lines v Shute* 499 US 585 (US 1991).

[151] See *Donohue v Armco* [2002] CLC 440, 449, per Lord Bingham (HL). See also *The Eleftheria* [1969] 1 Lloyd's Rep 237. See also SM Denning, 'Choice of Forum Clauses in Bills of Lading' (1970–71) 2 *Journal of Maritime Law and Commerce* 17, 38.

[152] *The Varenna* [1984] QB 599, 604 (HL).

the incorporation clause was held to be inapt to describe and incorporate the charterparty arbitration clause in the absence of an express reference to such a clause.[153] Following this rationale, the Court in *Siboti K/S v BP France SA* took the view that a charterparty exclusive jurisdiction clause should also not be incorporated without any specific reference.[154]

The rule that general words of incorporation are not apt to describe forum selection clauses is justified in two ways. With the commonly used incorporation language pointing to the conditions and exceptions of the charterparty, the first argument is a semantic one, according to which the courts refuse to hold such provisions as either a condition or an exception.[155] Accordingly, in *The Varenna*, where the incorporation clause read 'all conditions and exceptions of which charterparty, including the negligence clause, are deemed to be incorporated in bill of lading',[156] the Court largely relied on this argument in holding against incorporation of the arbitration clause. The second reason is that forum selection clauses are ancillary to the subject matter of the contract of carriage contained in or evidenced by bills of lading. In other words, they are not directly germane to shipment, carriage and discharge of the cargo.[157] This reasoning underpins the suggestion that even words of incorporation of a wider breadth such as provisions, clauses, and terms[158] are inapt for incorporation of charterparty forum selection clauses, despite the fact that their purely literal meaning may suggest the contrary. As a result of this line of thinking, the famous *Siboti* decision further clarified that general words of incorporation are not apt to carry across such provisions, even where the word with the broadest scope of meaning, 'whatsoever', is inserted into the incorporation clause.[159]

A Confusing Twist in the Application of the Description Test—The Merak

Until recently, there was only one English case, *The Merak*,[160] which could hardly be reconciled with the rule that special words are needed to incorporate forum selection clauses.[161] Contrary to this rule, in *The Merak*, the words 'all terms, conditions, clauses and exceptions' were found to be apt to describe the arbitration clause in two respects. First, comprehensiveness of the word 'clause' in the incorporation clause led the Court to hold that the incorporating language was sufficient to import, inter alia, the charterparty arbitration clause.[162] One may

[153] [1912] AC 1 (HL). Similarly *The Nerano* [1996] 1 Lloyd's Rep 1 (CA).
[154] [2003] 2 Lloyd's Rep 364.
[155] See *The Varenna* [1984] QB 592.
[156] ibid.
[157] *TW Thomas & Portsea Shipping Co Ltd* [1912] AC 1, 10 (HL).
[158] ibid, at 8.
[159] [2003] 2 Lloyd's Rep 364.
[160] [1965] P 223.
[161] For a similar view, see *Habas Sinai ve Tibbi Gazlar Isthisal Endustri AS v Sometal SAL* [2010] EWHC 29.
[162] See *The Merak* [1965] P 223 at 253. See also *The Federal Bulker* [1989] 1 Lloyd's Rep 103, where *The Merak* was distinguished, for the incorporation clause was devoid of the word 'clause'.

find this particular reasoning somewhat consistent with the decisions in *Thomas v Portsea* and *The Varenna* where the 'conditions' of the charterparty were expressly stipulated in the incorporation clause without the word 'terms'.[163] Even though the breadth of the word 'clauses' is broader than that of 'conditions', and both *The Varenna* and *Thomas v Portsea* can be distinguished on that basis, this reasoning is not persuasive, given the decision in *Siboti*.[164] The incorporation clause in *The Merak* was narrower in scope than that in *Siboti*, where a wider form of general incorporation wording, which contained the all-encompassing word 'whatsoever', was not held to qualify for this purpose.

Secondly, in *The Merak*, the Court took specific account of the charterparty arbitration clause covering the disputes arising under bills of lading.[165] This justification, which is that the charterparty wording may be relevant in resolving this matter, was initially heard in *Thomas v Portsea*:[166] whilst standing against the incorporation of the arbitration clause, as an alternative argument, the House of Lords decision in *Thomas v Portsea* hinged on the wording of the arbitration provision, which merely pointed to the disputes arising out of the conditions of the charterparty.[167] In so doing, it suggested *obiter* that charterparty arbitration clauses contemplating disputes under bills of lading be incorporated, despite general words of incorporation already being stated therein.[168] Thereafter, this view was favoured in well-recognised cases such as *The Annefield*[169] and *The Rena K*.[170] Additionally, even the Court in *The Varenna*[171]—which established the rule that the bill of lading was the primary document to be considered[172]—appeared to confirm the possibility of introducing arbitration clauses with such wording in the absence of a specific reference to arbitration in the bills of lading.[173]

This approach contains serious flaws when the chain of English incorporation rules is evaluated in its entirety. Having accepted that the bill of lading is the

[163] See *Thomas v Portsea* [1912] AC 1, 10 (HL) and [1984] QB 592 (HL).

[164] [2003] 2 Lloyd's Rep 364.

[165] See [1965] P 223, 259. See also *The Varenna*, where *The Merak* was not applied on the basis that the arbitration clause solely provided for arbitration of disputes arising 'under this charter', instead of referring to the disputes 'under bills of lading'. See the London arbitration award no 22/00, where the arbitrators followed this reasoning adopted in *The Merak*, when holding in favour of the incorporation of a charterparty arbitration clause through general words of incorporation, see 22/10 *Lloyd's Maritime Law Newsletter*.

[166] [1912] AC 1.

[167] ibid, at 5–6 and 9. Somewhat contradictorily, there it was also stated that the bill of lading was the primary document to be considered, see page 8.

[168] See *The Annefield* [1971] P 168, 184 (CA); *The Rena K* [1979] QB 377, 389–90. For arguments giving weight to the charterparty wording before the incorporation of the charterparty terms into the bills of lading, see *The Delos* [2001] 1 Lloyd's Rep 703, 706; *The Phonizien* [1966] 1 Lloyd's Rep 150.

[169] [1971] P 168.

[170] [1979] QB 377.

[171] [1984] QB 592.

[172] ibid, at 596.

[173] ibid, at 598–99. Some English authorities suggest that the wording of the charterparty arbitration clause, which refers to the disputes 'under bills of lading', is sufficient to incorporate the arbitration clause despite the general words of incorporation under bills of lading. See Cooke et al (n 7) para 18.51. For a contrary view, see Treitel and Reynolds (n 41) para 3-032.

primary document to be taken into account, there are no logical reasons for giving the charterparty wording the effect of determining what words of incorporation are apt to describe the charterparty provisions. The result of accepting the aforesaid is that charterparty provisions should only be taken into consideration after their incorporation is achieved by the incorporation clause under the bills of lading.[174] Moreover, allowing incorporation of arbitration clauses, just because of the charterparty wording, cannot be reconciled with the well-established rule that is at the heart of the English rules of incorporation: in the case of two-contract cases,[175] the incorporation of ancillary provisions requires a specific reference to be made in the incorporating contract.[176]

Another reason for the Court in *The Merak* to decide in favour of incorporation of the arbitration clause was a mistaken reference in the incorporation clause. Instead of clause 30 of the charterparty, which was the arbitration clause, the reference therein was to clause 32 of the charterparty. Observing the principle of general contract law that a contract cannot be rectified to the detriment of a third party, the Court stood against rectification of the mistaken reference. Since the holder was not the original party to the bill of lading, the reference was considered as merely superfluous and was discarded. Notably, the bill of lading holder was also the charterer of the charterparty that the bill of lading sought to incorporate. When holding in favour of incorporation and treating the mistake *nihil ad rem*, the knowledge of the holders, which they happened to have because they were also the charterer, was given no weight by the majority. Instead, they relied on the two main underpinnings which are, with respect, contrary to the settled principles of incorporation. Unlike the majority, Davies J said:[177]

> Whatever might have been the position if this bill were in the hands of a stranger to the charterparty of April 21, these plaintiffs were parties to it and therefore must be taken to have had knowledge of all its terms. They knew therefore that clause 30 was nihil ad rem. They knew that by clause 32 arbitration was provided for not only for disputes arising out of the charterparty but also for those arising out of any bill of lading issue thereunder … In light to all these circumstances, it is impossible to hold that clause 32 was not incorporated into the bill of lading.

Considering the long line of authorities regarding incorporation in bill of lading cases, it is prudent not to place too strong a reliance on this statement of Davies J. Throughout the discussions, we have seen that the words of incorporation and certainly not the actual knowledge of the bill of lading holder are decisive when choosing which particular charterparty provisions can be carried across to the bill of lading. Perhaps for these reasons, the Court in *The Federal Bulker* treated

[174] See *Siboti K/S v BP France SA* [2003] 2 Lloyd's Rep 364, 369; *The Coral* [1993] 1 Lloyd's Rep 1, 6.

[175] See *Habas Sinai ve Tibbi Gazlar Isthisal Endustri AS v Sometal SAL* [2010] 1 Lloyd's Rep 661 and *The Athena* [2007] 1 Lloyd's Rep 280.

[176] *OK Petroleum AB v Vitol Energy SA* [1995] 2 Lloyd's Rep 160, 168; *The Federal Bulker* [1989] 1 Lloyd's Rep 103, 105.

[177] [1965] P 223, 255–56.

the facts of *The Merak* as unique and unusual, suggesting that this ruling would be of limited application. On the whole, the requirement of making explicit reference to arbitration under the incorporation clause is likely to be predominantly applicable under English law for the benefit of cargo interests. Consequently, no matter how broad the general words of incorporation are, under English law, carriers' chances of incorporating the charterparty arbitration clause pointing to the dispute arising under bills of lading remain rather low.

Relaxation of the Description Test—Recent Decisions

What happens when the incorporation clause shows an intention to incorporate a dispute resolution clause, but fails to specify correctly whether an arbitration clause or a jurisdiction clause is intended? The first decision to consider is *YM Mars Tankers Ltd v Shield Petroleum (Nigeria) Ltd.*[178] The case involved a bill of lading on the Congenbill form, which provided for the incorporation of, inter alia, the 'Law and Arbitration clause' of the charterparty. The relevant charterparty contained a clause headed 'Law and Litigation' under which a two-tiered dispute resolution was provided: small claims as defined under the clause were to be referred to arbitration, and English courts were designated for larger claims. Gloster J found in favour of the incorporation of the dispute resolution clause, particularly since it was 'uncommercial' and 'absurd' to sever the dispute resolution clause and only to incorporate the provisions on arbitration. In *The Channel Ranger*, the reference in the bill of lading was again to the 'Law and Arbitration' clause of the charterparty, although this time the charterparty provided for English law and jurisdiction.[179] Thus, the facts in *The Channel Ranger* were different from those of *YM Mars Tankers Ltd*. Nonetheless Males J relied on the decision of Gloster J to support the proposition that[180]

> the question for decision is a question of construction of the bill of lading and that at least in some circumstances a reference to 'arbitration' in the bill of lading may properly be read as providing for court jurisdiction—indeed, it goes further by saying that in some circumstances any other conclusion would be 'uncommercial' and 'absurd'.

Both decisions suggest that the courts can be flexible about the degree of specificity in the reference to the dispute resolution clause of the charterparty. The flexibility introduced by Gloster J's decision is obviously judicious, given the wide use of multi-tiered dispute resolution clauses.[181] The decision of Males J goes further than that of Gloster J in *YM Mars Tankers Ltd*: it suggests that as long as the reference in the bill of lading alerts the holder as to the possible incorporation of at least one kind of dispute resolution clause, it can be read as extending to the

[178] *YM Mars Tankers Ltd v Shield Petroleum (Nigeria) Ltd* [2012] EWHC 2652 (Comm).

[179] [2010] 1 Lloyd's Rep 337.

[180] ibid, at 345.

[181] Perhaps for this reason, the words of incorporation in the Congenbill 2007 form read 'all terms and conditions, liberties and exceptions of the Charterparty, dated as overleaf, including the Law and Arbitration Clause/Dispute Resolution clause, are herewith incorporated'.

other type of dispute resolution clause in the charterparty. In *The Channel Ranger*, a reference to 'arbitration' was read as providing for jurisdiction. If this line of reasoning were followed, a reference to 'litigation' should equally be treated as a reference to arbitration. This flexibility is perhaps necessary given that the particular dispute resolution method provided in the relevant charterparty may not coincide with the reference in the incorporation clause. If this is the way forward, English rules of incorporation can be treated as one step closer to the US rules of incorporation, which will be discussed below.

b. US Law

When compared with the identified rules of incorporation under English law, it is clear that US courts take a diametrically opposed view on incorporation of forum selection clauses. This contrast derives from the fact that, under US law, arbitration and jurisdiction clauses are taken just as any other charterparty provisions.[182] Consequently, all charterparty provisions, including the arbitration, exclusive jurisdiction and time-bar clauses, can be incorporated through general words of incorporation provided that the wording of the incorporation clause has sufficient breadth to manifest the intention to incorporate to that extent.[183] General words of incorporation are thus given the force to effectively incorporate arbitration, exclusive jurisdiction and time-bar clauses,[184] making any specific reference redundant.[185]

As regards the incorporation of arbitration clauses, there are mainly two reasons for the fact that they are not to be treated as different from those other charterparty provisions. First, with the enactment of the 1925 Act—which asserts a policy favouring arbitration—US courts no longer preserve the old judicial

[182] *Son Shipping Co Inc v De Fosse & Tanghe* 1952 AMC 1931, 1933 (2d Cir 1952); *Fairmont Shipping and Botelho Shipping Corp v Primary Industries Corp* F Supp 1988 WL 7805 (SDNY 1988); *Lowry & Co Inc v SS Le Moyne D'Iberville* 1966 AMC 2195 (SDNY 1966). But see *Siderius Inc v M/V Ida Prima* 613 F Supp 916 (SDNY 1985).

[183] ibid. See also *Energy of Transport Ltd v M/V San Sebastian* 348 F Supp 2d 186 (SDNY 2004). Conversely, see *State Establishment for Agricultural Product Trading v M/V Wesermunde* 1988 AMC 2328, 2337 (11th Cir 1988), where the Court declined to incorporate the arbitration clause, for there was no express reference to the clause in the bill of lading to alert the holder as to the possibility of the incorporation of the arbitration clause.

[184] See *Duferco Steel Inc v M/V Kalisti* 1998 AMC 171 (7th Cir 1997).

[185] See *Son Shipping Co Inc v De Fosse & Tanghe* 1952 AMC 1931, 1933 (2d Cir 1952); *Ibeto Petrochemical Industries Limited v M/T Beffen* 2007 AMC 213 (2d Cir 2007); *Continental Insurance Company v Polish Steamship Company* 2003 AMC 2718 (2d Cir 2003); *Continental Insurance Company v M/V Nikos N* 2002 AMC 1287 (SDNY 2002); *Chilean Nitrate Sales Corp v Steamship Nortuna* 1955 AMC 1576 (SDNY 1955); *Cia Platamon v Empresa Colombiana* 1980 AMC 538, 540 (SDNY 1979); *Henkel KG v M/T Stolt Hipo* 1980 AMC 2618 (SDNY 1980); *Midland Tar Distillers Inc v M/L Lotos* 362 F Supp 1311, 1312 (SDNY 1973); *State Trading Corp of India Ltd v Grunstad Shipping Corp (Belgium) N/V* 582 F Supp 1523 (SDNY 1984). However, it should be noted that if the language in the incorporation clause is not expansive and if it brings *ejusdem generis* considerations to the fore, the arbitration clause will not be carried into the bill of lading, see Poor (n 32) 72.

hostility towards arbitration.[186] This liberal policy, which is enshrined in the 1925 Act, requires that the courts construe and resolve the ambiguity in favour of arbitration.[187] In line with this policy, US courts afford general incorporation wording a considerable breadth of meaning as operative to introduce charterparty arbitration clauses. Secondly, given the frequent use of arbitration clauses in charterparties, US courts tend to take the view that the existence of these clauses under charterparties should be anticipated by the holders, who are treated as sophisticated parties.[188] Evidently, this view also justifies the incorporation of exclusive jurisdiction clauses through general incorporation wording, given that such clauses are also commonplace in charterparties.

The impression thus created under US law suggests that carriers are able to incorporate arbitration clauses into bills of lading if the incorporation language in the bill of lading is expansive enough to manifest the intention to do so. In this context, they do not need to use extra care in the very wording of the incorporation clauses: even those provisions simply directing the holders to all conditions and exceptions of the charterparty achieve this purpose. In New York arbitration this well-established rule of incorporation has also been recognised.[189]

c. The Incorporation of Forum Selection Clauses from a General Perspective

In light of these observations, it is clear under US law that the general incorporation wording is capable of carrying with it all ancillary charterparty provisions, including forum selection clauses. In sharp contrast to this, under English law, incorporation of such provisions requires special words of incorporation. Restricting the reach of these clauses mainly finds support from the traditional English view: provisions of an ancillary nature can only be incorporated as long as they are expressly referred to in the incorporating contract. Although deeply rooted in the judicial decisions pertaining to incorporation of charterparties into bills of lading, this traditional view has also been applied to incorporation cases in general. A good example is the ruling in *OK Petroleum AB v Vitol Energy SA*, where the general incorporation language in the contract of sale was found insufficient to describe the time bar in the charterparty demurrage clause.[190] Similarly,

[186] See *Chevron USA Inc v Consol Edison Co of New York Inc* 872 F 2d 534, 537 (2d Cir 1989); *Paramedics Electromedicina Comercial Ltd v GE Med Sys Info Tech Inc* 369 F 3d 645, 654 (2d Cir 2004); *Moses H Cone Memorial Hospital v Mercury Construction Corp* 460 US 1, 24 (US 1983); *FD Import & Export Corp v M/V Reefer Sun* 2003 AMC 60, 63 (SDNY 2002); *Japan Sun Oil Co Ltd v The M/V Maasdijk* 1995 AMC 726 (EDLa 1995); *Michael v SS Thanasis* 311 F Supp 170, 178 (ND Cal 1970).

[187] See *Usinor Steel Corporation v M/V Koningsborg* 2004 AMC 438 (SDNY 2004); *Citrus Marketing Board of Israel and Agrexco Ltd v M/V Ecuadorian Reefer* 1991 AMC 1042 (DMass 1990); *Continental Insurance Company v M/V Nikos N* 2002 AMC 1287, 1290 (SDNY 2002); *Japan Sun Oil Co v M/V Maasdijk* 1995 AMC 726 (EDLa 1994).

[188] *Steel Warehouse Co v Abalone Shipping Ltd of Nicosai* 1998 AMC 2054 (5th Cir 1998).

[189] See *In Re Alpine Shipping Company of Monrovia and Fuel Oil Trading Co Geneva* SMA No 1485 (22 October 1980), and in *Re Arbitration Between Alimentos Precocidos Guayana CA and Her An Shipping SA* SMA No 3468 (14 August 1998).

[190] [1995] CLC 850.

the Privy Council in *The Mahkutai* adopted this approach for the construction of the Himalaya clause in the bill of lading.[191] There, the key question was whether the shipowner, who was not a party to the bill of lading, could benefit from the exclusive jurisdiction clause stipulated therein by reason of the Himalaya clause. Having found against the shipowner, the Privy Council preferred to read the Himalaya clause as not embracing the exclusive jurisdiction clause precisely because the clause was merely pointing to 'all exceptions, limitations, provisions, conditions and liberties' in the bill of lading.

Nonetheless, it can scarcely be argued that this well-rooted approach is equally applicable to all incorporation cases. As the judicial decisions suggest, different factual circumstances could lead the courts to take different courses of action. This is best illustrated with the ruling in *The Pioneer Container*, where the Privy Council held that the holder had consented to the exclusive jurisdiction clause in the feeder bill of lading because the bill of lading expressly stated that the carrier had authority to sub-contract the whole or part of the carriage of goods 'on any terms'.[192] As a result of this sub-bailment of the goods on any terms, the carrier under the feeder bill of lading was held to have the right to compel the holder to litigate pursuant to the exclusive jurisdiction clause. On taking the holder's goods, the carrier under the feeder bill of lading was taken to have assumed obligations vis-à-vis the holder pursuant to all the terms of the feeder bill of lading. On this matter, Lord Goff said[193] 'Where, as here, the consent is very wide in its terms, only terms which are so unusual or so unreasonable that they could not reasonably be understood to fall within such consent are likely to be excluded'.

Given that forum selection clauses are commonplace in bills of lading in container trade, the exclusive jurisdiction clause was not treated as unreasonable. A similar line was also taken in *Modern Building (Wales) Ltd v Limmer & Trinidad Co Ltd*, which contained a sub-contract agreement made for the construction of a building.[194] At the heart of the dispute was the question of whether the phrase 'in full accordance with the appropriate form for nominated Sub-Contracts (RIBA 1965 Edition)' could bring with it the arbitration clause in the identified standard terms. With a view to resolving this issue, the Court preferred to put arbitration clauses on an equal footing with other contract terms, regardless of the ancillary nature of these provisions. In so doing, it gave the general incorporation wording in the sub-contract agreement the effect of incorporating the arbitration clause.

These decisions obviously add layers of complexity in determining what incorporation words are competent to describe the forum selection clauses in general incorporation cases. More specifically, the difficulty is in identifying the

[191] *The Mahkutai* [1996] AC 650.
[192] *The Pioneer Container* [1994] 2 AC 324.
[193] ibid, at 346.
[194] *Modern Building (Wales) Ltd v Limmer & Trinidad Co Ltd* [1975] 2 Lloyd's Rep 318.

circumstances in which the traditional view established in *Thomas v Portsea* must be abandoned. Somewhat unexpectedly, the answer is now clear cut in light of the recent Commercial Court judgment in *Habas Sinai ve Tıbbi Gazlar Isthisal Endustri AS v Sometal SAL.*[195] The case hinged on whether the sale contract incorporated the arbitration clause stipulated in those other sale contracts previously made between the same parties. In this connection, Clarke J engaged in construction of the incorporation clause, which provided that 'all the rest will be the same as our previous contracts'. Regardless of these general words, he held in favour of incorporation. In support of this finding, he took the view that the case was different from those bill of lading cases, which he described as 'two-contract cases', where incorporation is concerned with the contracts made between different parties.[196] On this basis, Clarke J set the rule that has become of valuable guidance in incorporation cases. Unlike the 'two-contract cases', general words of incorporation are capable of incorporating choice-of-forum clauses in 'one-contract cases': cases where the contract refers to a set of standard terms or where the parties incorporate their previous contract.

Even though this formulation may not explain all judicial decisions on incorporation, such as the ruling in *The Pioneer Container*, it provides a sound basis to determine incorporation of not only the forum selection clauses. The reason is simply that the *Habas* formula places emphasis on the different contexts of incorporation cases, and this saves the rules of incorporation from being overly rigid and technical. Having observed at length the key rules of construing the incorporation wording, it is now timely to consider the practical consequences of the legal position under English law and US law.

d. What Should the Carriers Anticipate When Seeking to Incorporate?

In the absence of strict semantic considerations with respect to the wording of the incorporation clause, it seems that carriers are not at pains to introduce the charterparty clauses that are germane to shipment, carriage and discharge of the cargo.[197] As is clear from the observations, they will succeed in incorporating these clauses without having to concern themselves with the technicalities of forming the ideal wording.

However, regarding the ancillary charterparty provisions, the carriers under English law run the risk of not being able to achieve incorporation of these terms into the bill of lading if the incorporating language does specifically refer to such provisions. Having to make an express reference may put a strain on the carriers' intentions to incorporate, and their failure to do so usually turns out to be costly. Due to the practical significance of forum selection clauses, this rule has

[195] *Habas Sinai ve Tıbbi Gazlar Isthisal Endustri AS v Sometal SAL* [2010] EWHC 29 (Comm).

[196] It must be noted that in exceptional cases parties to the charterparty may be the same as those of the bill of lading, see Chapter 1, n 57.

[197] See for instance *The Garbis* [1982] 2 Lloyd's Rep 283, where the Court took the view that even unusual charterparty provisions can be incorporated through general words of incorporation.

a profound effect on the parties to the bill of lading when they wish to bring the dispute before a court or tribunal different from that provided in the identified charterparty. From the perspective of the holders, the rule of making a specific reference to a particular charterparty clause has considerable benefits. These include the fact that the express reference to a particular charterparty clause alerts these parties to the carriers' intentions to incorporate this specific term. Moreover, this rule reduces the risk of holding a bill of lading with an incorporated forum selection clause, if they require in their sale contracts submission of bills of lading with an incorporation clause that contains no reference to such provisions.

These striking differences between the US and English approaches have significance to both carriers and the holders because the rules have a direct impact on their considerations as to where the dispute should be brought. In particular, the rules further reveal what practical strategies can be employed by the holders who are seeking to thwart incorporation of a forum selection clause: challenging incorporation of a charterparty forum selection clause before an English court could be fruitful for these parties where (1) the bill of lading contains unqualified incorporation language, which makes no express reference to the forum selection clause, and where (2) the law governing the incorporation issue is English law.[198] Whereas unwelcome results may arise if they refer the dispute to a US court: provided that the court applies US law to the incorporation issue, the forum selection clause will be carried into the bill of lading merely through the general incorporation wording.

From a practical perspective, the parties may thus try to take advantage of these differences by pursuing litigation in a more favourable jurisdiction. These tactical manoeuvres do not usually prove successful, since US and English courts have the right to grant anti-suit injunctions to ensure that proceedings are not brought other than in the forum designated in the incorporated charterparty forum selection clause.[199] However, following the ECJ decision in *Turner v Grovit*,[200] it is clear

[198] For the conflict of laws rules, see Chapter 1.

[199] For English law, see s 37 of the Senior Courts Act 1981 and s 44 of the 1996 Act. See also *Société Aerospatiale v Lee Kui Jak* [1987] AC 871 (HL); *The Angelic Grace* [1995] 1 Lloyd's Rep 87, 96 (CA); *South Carolina Insurance Co v Assurance Maatchappij 'De Zeven Provincien' NV* [1987] AC 24; *The Kallang* [2009] 1 Lloyd's Rep 124; *The Duden* [2009] 1 Lloyd's Rep 145. Under English law, the courts grant anti-suit injunctions in cases where the ends of justice require it and where a party can establish that the other party has breached his/her either legal or equitable right not to be sued in a foreign court. If a party can establish that the other party has brought foreign proceedings in breach of a forum selection clause, the courts tend to take the view that these conditions have been satisfied. Thus, they enforce forum selection clauses, unless there are strong reasons for not doing so, see *Donohue v Armco* [2002] 1 Lloyd's Rep 425 (HL). In the absence of a forum selection clause, the courts may also grant an anti-suit injunction where the ends of justice require it and where the English court is the natural forum and the foreign proceedings are vexatious or oppressive. See *Société Aerospatiale v Lee Kui Jak* above. See also the recent Supreme Court judgment in *AES Ust-Kamenogorsk Plant LLP v Ust-Kamenogorsk Hydropower Plant JSC*, where the Supreme Court held that an English court can grant an anti-suit injunction to restrain a party from continuing or commencing foreign proceedings in breach of an arbitration agreement, even in cases where no arbitration is commenced or contemplated, see [2013] UKSC 35 (SC). For US law, see *Ibeto Petrochemical Industries Limited v M/T Beffen et al* 2007 AMC 213 (2d Cir 2007).

[200] Case C-159/02 *Turner v Grovit* [2004] ECR I-3565; [2005] 1 AC 101.

that English courts cannot grant an anti-suit injunction to restrain a defendant to the English court proceedings from commencing or continuing proceedings in another Member State.[201] There, the ECJ refused to permit English courts to issue an anti-suit injunction against a party who chose, in bad faith, to bring court proceedings in another Member State. In support of this, the ECJ took the view that the grant of an anti-suit injunction in order to restrain a party from starting or continuing an action before the courts of another Member State undermined the 'mutual trust' between courts of Member States.[202] In the wake of the much-cited ECJ decision in *The Front Comor*, there is no question that English courts cannot also grant an anti-suit injunction against the defendant who brought proceedings in the courts of another Member State in breach of an arbitration agreement.[203] This is despite the fact that the Regulation excludes matters on arbitration from its scope.[204]

This restriction on the grant of anti-suit injunction undoubtedly makes one question critical: which court is entitled to decide whether there is a valid forum selection clause in the bill of lading? As has been discussed elsewhere in this book, the incorporation and validity of an exclusive jurisdiction clause is decided pursuant to the 'first-seised rule'[205] under the Regulation. With the Recast Regulation, an exception to the first-seised rule is created: where a court of a Member State chosen in an exclusive jurisdiction agreement is seised of proceedings, the courts of other Member States shall stay proceedings for the chosen court to rule on its jurisdiction.

On the incorporation and validity of arbitration agreements, the position under the Regulation is largely shaped by two decisions: *The Front Comor*[206] and *The Wadi Sudr*.[207] The ECJ's decision in *The Front Comor* suggests that the questions of validity and incorporation of arbitration agreements do not fall outside the scope of the Regulation where the subject matter of the dispute, which is tied up with the preliminary ruling on arbitration, falls within the scope of the Regulation.[208] This raises a further question as to whether the preliminary ruling of the court of a Member State pertaining to incorporation and/or enforcement of an arbitration agreement must be recognised by the courts of other Member States, if the actual dispute falls within the scope of the Regulation.[209] The Court of Appeal in *The Wadi Sudr* followed the opinion of the Advocate General in *The*

[201] See Art 1(1) of the Regulation, which states: 'the regulation shall apply in civil and commercial matters whatever the nature of the court or tribunal'.

[202] Case C-159/02 [2004] ECR I-3565; [2005] 1 AC 101, 113.

[203] Case C-185/07 *The Front Comor* [2009] AC 1138.

[204] See Art 1(2)(d) of the Regulation.

[205] See Chapter 2, Section III.B.i.

[206] Case C-185/07 [2009] AC 1138.

[207] [2009] 1 Lloyd's Rep 666, overturned in [2010] 1 Lloyd's Rep 193 (CA).

[208] Leaving aside such circumstances, matters on arbitration do fall outside the scope of the Regulation, see Case C-190/89 *The Atlantic Emperor* [1991] ECR I-3855; [1991] ILPr 524; [1992] 1 Lloyd's Rep 342, 350–51.

[209] See Case C-185/07 [2009] AC 1138 at paras 53, 54.

Front Comor,[210] holding that English courts were estopped by the Spanish court's preliminary ruling that the charterparty arbitration clause was not incorporated into the bill of lading. Furthermore, the Court of Appeal held that 'a Regulation judgment could give rise to an issue of estoppel in the same way in arbitration proceedings excluded from the Regulation as in any other proceedings'.[211]

The Recast Regulation gives teeth to the arbitration exception, with its preamble effectively reversing the decision in *The Wadi Sudr:* the decision of the courts of any Member State as to whether an arbitration agreement is null, void, inoperative or incapable of being performed shall not be subject to the rules of recognition and enforcement laid down in the Recast Regulation.[212] With this provision, it is now clear that no court shall have priority to determine the validity of arbitration agreements. Although this rule will create the risk of irreconcilable decisions on the validity of arbitration agreements within the EU, a further provision is introduced to resolve the conflict. Where a court of a Member State decides against the validity of an arbitration agreement and assumes jurisdiction, the judgment of that court will be recognised and enforced pursuant to the Recast Regulation. However, an arbitral award rendered in respect of the same dispute shall triumph over that judgment, and it will be enforced pursuant to the New York Convention, which takes precedence over the Recast Regulation.[213]

Under the Regulation, it is thus much easier for a bill of lading holder to avoid a London arbitration clause incorporated into the bill of lading by initiating the proceedings in the courts of a Member State that is likely to hold against incorporation. Against such abusive litigation tactics, for carriers who wish to rely on the arbitration clause, the counter strategy to employ is to initiate arbitration proceedings in London, to obtain the award and to have the award entered as a judgment under section 66 of the 1996 Act before a judgment on the merits is given in another Member State.[214]

Following the ECJ decision in *The Front Comor*,[215] both sets of London arbitration and Italian litigation proceedings were running concurrently, with the risk of conflicting decisions on the merits. The arbitral tribunal sitting in London rendered an award declaring that the shipowners were not liable to the charterers and their subrogated insurers in respect of the collision. The

[210] ibid.

[211] See Waller LJ in [2010] 1 Lloyd's Rep 193 (CA) at 205. On the issue of estoppel by *res judicata*, see *The Sennar (No 2)* [1985] 1 WLR 490. However, see the decision of Flaux J in *The Front Comor*, where he held that the arbitral tribunal had jurisdiction to award equitable damages for breach of the obligation to arbitrate.

[212] See para 12 of the Preamble to the Recast Regulation.

[213] ibid.

[214] However, this is only of value to the carrier if the assets of the cargo interest are in England. Where a cargo interest pursues litigation proceedings before the court of another EU Member State in breach of an arbitration agreement, the judgment of that court can be refused recognition in the English courts. However, it may have to be recognised in the courts of other EU Member States.

[215] [2012] 1 Lloyd's Rep 398 (CA).

shipowners in turn applied to the English Commercial Court to have the declaratory award entered as a judgment under section 66 of the 1996 Act. At the time the Court was dealing with this application, the unsuccessful party did not have an inconsistent judgment obtained in a Member State.[216] With the Recast Regulation, it is now clear that English courts can enforce an arbitral award pursuant to the New York Convention, irrespective of an adverse judgment obtained in a different Member State.

Given the 'first-seised' rule under the Regulation, it is even easier for the holders to avoid an English jurisdiction clause which, through the eyes of English courts, was incorporated into the bill of lading. By initiating the proceedings in the courts of a Member State that will hold against incorporation, the holders can effectively avoid English jurisdiction clauses in bills of lading. Against these tactics, the counter strategy for the carrier would be to initiate litigation proceedings before English courts to obtain a declaration of non-liability against the bill of lading holder who will potentially bring a cargo claim.[217] With the Recast Regulation, there is now no need to employ such strategies to keep jurisdiction clauses effective. With Article 31(2) of the Recast Regulation, the court chosen in the exclusive jurisdiction agreement has, in principle,[218] priority to determine the validity of the agreement, as well as its applicability to the dispute before it.[219] To put it another way, where the court of a Member State chosen in an exclusive jurisdiction agreement is seised, the courts of other Member States shall stay proceedings for the chosen court to rule on its jurisdiction.

As is clear from these observations, the Recast Regulation will reinforce the use of forum selection clauses in bills of lading. On the other side of the Atlantic, US courts already look favourably on the enforcement of forum selection clauses, although the courts are divided as to the standards of issuing anti-suit injunctions in support of forum selection clauses.[220] Consequently, the judicial uncertainty surrounding this matter also poses challenges to carriers when they seek to compel a recalcitrant bill of lading holder to litigate or arbitrate pursuant to the forum selection clause in the bill of lading.

[216] See Art 34(3) of the Regulation.

[217] For a similar view, see H Seriki, 'Anti-suit Injunctions, Arbitration and the ECJ: An Approach Too Far' (2010) 7 *Journal of Business Law* 24, 31.

[218] See Art 31(4) of the Recast Regulation.

[219] See, in particular, subsections (2) and (3) of Art 31 of the Recast Regulation. For the position under the Regulation, see Arts 23 and 27 of the Regulation.

[220] For the 'liberal view', whereby the grant of an anti-suit injunction is considered to be appropriate in the case of parallel proceedings in different jurisdictions, see *Seattle Totems Hockey Club Inc v National League* 652 F 3d 852, 855–56 (9th Cir 1981). For the 'conservative view', whereby an anti-suit injunction is granted by taking specific account of public policy considerations, see *Stonington Partners Inc v Lernout & Hauspie Speech Products* 310 F 3d 118, 126 (3d Cir 2002). For an overall analysis, see *Quaak v Klynved Peat Marwick Goerdeler Bedrijfsrevisoren* 361 F 3d 11 (1st Cir 2004) quoted in N Meeson, 'Comparative Issues in Anti-Suit Injunctions' in M Davies (ed), *Jurisdiction and Forum Selection in International Maritime Law: Essays in Honour of Robert Force* (The Hague, Kluwer Law International, 2005) 79–81. See Moses (n 141) 93.

The overall picture under US law and English law is that, whether or not the forum selection clause can be incorporated into the bill of lading, the holder should nevertheless be prepared to accept one key fact: incorporation clauses have the effect of carrying across to the bill of lading many provisions whose application may cause unexpected and onerous liabilities.[221] Even though such provision can be incorporated into the bill of lading, this does not lead to the mechanical application of all the incorporated clauses to the holder. The further rules of incorporation, which will be discussed in the following chapters, provide the effective grounds for these parties to challenge the application of the incorporated charterparty provisions.

II. Manipulation of the Incorporated Charterparty Provisions

In the charterparty drafting process, it can seem a wise approach to insert provisions that expressly refer to the respective parties to which the obligations or the rights therein relate. The rationale for this practice is to ensure the proper and clear allocation of the rights and responsibilities under the charterparty, without leaving any ambiguities. While the intention of clearly specifying the rights and obligations of parties can be achieved through such means, there is much to consider as to whether charterparty terms drafted in this fashion will survive after being incorporated. Unless such provisions are manipulated to adapt the wording in the bill of lading, they will be irrelevant in the bill of lading context and will therefore be inapplicable to the holder. Consequently, in order to bind the holders to these provisions, the question is: are we to read the incorporated words referring to charterer, owner and charterparty as though they are referring to bill of lading holders, carriers and the bill of lading, respectively?

To adapt the charterparty terms to the bill of lading context would appear justifiable given that not doing so might lead to the incorporation clause being ineffective. This is further supported by the well-established rule of construction that the intention of the parties that is apparent under the incorporation clause must be given effect to.[222] Even though it also seems understandable to have a charterparty wording that involves many references to the charterers, shipowners and charterparty, manipulation of some charterparty terms can be hard to justify. Serious doubts arise as to the manipulation of the charterparty wording in cases where an incorporated charterparty provision places the responsibility for the discharge operations on the charterer or the charterer's agent. When a charterparty term is couched in such restrictive language, will the courts stretch the words to

[221] See, for instance, the position of the holder in *The Jordan II* [2005] 1 Lloyd's Rep 57 (HL).
[222] See *Adamastos Shipping Co Ltd v Anglo-Saxon Petroleum Co* [1959] AC 133.

make them applicable to the holder, or will these clauses simply be jettisoned from the bill of lading?

A. English Law

The well-established English legal position suggests that incorporated charter-party provisions that are germane to the subject matter of the bill of lading can be modified so as to bind the parties to these provisions.[223] This rule has its roots in *The Merak* decision, where Russell LJ stated, *obiter*, that:[224]

> [C]lauses which are directly germane to shipment, carriage and delivery may be incorporated by general words though the fact that they are found in a charterparty may involve a degree of verbal manipulation to fit exactly a bill of lading.

In his *dictum*, Lord Denning in *The Annefield* further regarded this view as representing the law when holding against incorporation of a charterparty arbitration clause in the absence of an express reference to arbitration in the bills of lading.[225] Against this backdrop, Lord Diplock in *The Miramar* considered two main issues: whether the charterparty demurrage clause in an Exxonvoy 1969 form was incorporated into the bill of lading through general words of incorporation and whether it was binding upon the bill of lading holder.[226] While holding that the incorporation clause was apt to describe and carry the demurrage clause across to the bill of lading, Lord Diplock did not allow manipulation of the words 'charterer is to pay demurrage' in the incorporated demurrage clause.[227] Had the words been manipulated, this would have resulted in the imposition of demurrage charges personally upon the bill of lading holders. Hinging on the restrictive language in the demurrage clause as a justification for the ruling, he added:[228]

> My Lords, I venture to assert that no business man who had not taken leave of his senses would intentionally enter into a contract which exposed him to a potential liability of this kind; and this, in itself, I find to be an overwhelming reason for not indulging in verbal manipulation of the actual contractual words used in the charter-party so as to give to them this effect when they are treated as incorporated in the bill of lading.

One may expect *The Miramar* decision to provide a widespread solution to remove, or at least to lessen, unfair consequences of imposing demurrage onto the holders, which demurrage had accrued without any act or failure on their

[223] See *The Merak* [1965] P 223, 259–60.
[224] ibid.
[225] *The Annefield* [1971] P 168, 184.
[226] [1984] 2 Lloyd's Rep 129.
[227] See also *The Spiros C* [2000] 2 Lloyd's Rep 319 (CA), where the decision in *The Miramar* was followed and the holder was held to be not personally liable for the accrued demurrage under the incorporated charterparty demurrage clause.
[228] ibid, at 132. There, it was emphasised that the issue of whether or not the bill of lading covered the whole cargo or whether there was more than one loading and discharge port was not a factor that shaped the decision.

part. However, the decision only had the effect of relieving the holders of demurrage charges in cases where the incorporated demurrage clause places the liability squarely upon the charterer.

When drafting a charterparty to be incorporated, *The Miramar* case raises some questions which are of vital importance for all parties concerned: could the ruling in *The Miramar* be extended for all germane charterparty provisions that impose liability exclusively upon the charterers? More specifically, after *The Miramar* decision, will a freight provision containing the words 'charterer is to pay' or a FIOST clause which reads 'charterer is to be responsible for the loading, stowage, trimming and discharge of the cargo without the risk and expense of the vessel' also be open to manipulation? Or are we now to spell out charterparty obligations, either by also pointing to the receivers or by not making reference to any party?[229] Should manipulation of such a demurrage provision or another germane charterparty provision be allowed if there is a special reference to the provision in the incorporation clause?

So far, the courts have not extended the application of the decision in *The Miramar* to all other germane charterparty provisions that exclusively point to the charterers but not to the receivers. To put it another way, the courts have not applied the reasoning in the decision in *The Miramar* in the case of other charterparty clauses that are drafted in that fashion.[230] Hence, the Court in *The Constanza M* accepted the difficulty in manipulating the words 'charterer is to pay freight', while also emphasising that such manipulation was possible.[231]

Nevertheless, the decision in *The Miramar* highlights the possibility that a charterparty provision with restrictive language may not be manipulated in cases where its application would give rise to onerous liabilities to be borne by bill of lading holders. A decision against manipulation on such grounds is also consistent with other cases on incorporation. The Courts in *Siboti K/S v BP France SA* and *The Rena K* took the view that undue manipulation is not permissible.[232] Furthermore, in *The Nerano*, manipulation of an arbitration clause incorporated into the bill of lading was permitted inter alia because the arbitration clause did not impose an unusual burden on the bill of lading holders.[233] English courts have allowed for manipulation of provisions to the extent that doing so is in line with the intention of the parties and that this can be objectively ascertained by the incorporation wording.[234] Thus, in the absence of an express provision to the

[229] In practice this is usually done by using the passive voice. See for instance the demurrage clause in *Gray v Carr* [1871] LR 6 QB 522, which is drafted in that fashion.

[230] For a similar approach, see para 96 of the judgment in *The Eems Solar* [2013] 2 Lloyd's Rep 519.

[231] See *The Constanza M* [1981] 2 Lloyd's Rep 147, 154.

[232] See *Siboti K/S v BP France SA* [2003] 2 Lloyd's Rep 364 and *The Rena K* [1978] 1 Lloyd's Rep 377.

[233] *The Nerano* [1996] 1 Lloyd's Rep 1.

[234] ibid, at 3–4.

contrary, the courts presume that parties did not intend to agree to unreasonable or commercially nonsensical terms.[235]

In light of these observations, it is clear that the reasoning in *The Miramar* can be used to prevent the imposition of obligations, originally assumed by the charterers, on the bill of lading holders. At this point, a further question is: can the courts reject manipulating a charterparty FIOST clause or a similar clause given their onerous effects on the holders? With these clauses generally having the effect of imposing responsibilities on the holders for loading operations over which they have no control, one may take the view that to allow verbal manipulation would be unreasonable and commercially nonsensical.[236] In *The Eems Solar* an incorporated charterparty provision provided that the cargo would be stowed by the charterers 'free of any risk, liability and expense whatsoever to the Owners'.[237] Although the clause made some references to the charterers, the part of the clause spelling out the transfer of responsibility for stowage did not need manipulation. Consequently, the clause was held to be applicable to the holder. Time will tell whether the courts will extend the application of the reasoning in *The Miramar*, although the case law as it currently stands suggests that such an extension is unlikely.

As these explanations suggest, the courts are inclined to avoid manipulation of a charterparty provision if it clearly manifests the intention to limit the application of the clause to the original parties. However, a charterparty clause in restrictive language should perhaps be adapted to the bill of lading, where all the charterparty terms are drafted in the same restrictive manner.[238] Furthermore, when an express reference to a charterparty provision is made in the incorporation clause, this should also trigger manipulation, irrespective of the language used in that provision. In such cases, the intention of the original parties to the bills of lading should be taken as 'paramount'.[239]

With respect to the charterparty arbitration clauses and other ancillary provisions, different considerations arise under English law: these provisions can only be incorporated into bills of lading through special incorporation wording. Since this is the main hurdle, no difficulties in manipulating these provisions arise on the grounds that the express reference to such charterparty terms in the

[235] See *Schuler v Wickman Machine Tool Sales Ltd* [1974] AC 235. For this reason, unless there are clear words in the contract to that effect, English courts have been reluctant to allow manipulation of exclusion clauses, which would, if permitted, impose onerous liabilities upon the holders. See *The Starsin* [2004] 1 AC 715, paras 144, 171 (HL).

[236] See also *The Coral* [1993] 1 Lloyd's Rep 1, where the Court of Appeal preferred not to raise the question of manipulation despite the fact that the FIOST clause imposed the relevant risks and duties exclusively on the charterers.

[237] [2013] 2 Lloyd's Rep 487.

[238] See *The Happy Ranger* [2002] 2 Lloyd's Rep 357, 366; *The Amstelmolen* [1961] 2 Lloyd's Rep 1. For a similar view see Cooke et al (n 7) para 18.55.

[239] See *The Rena K* [1978] 1 Lloyd's Rep 377; *The Nerano* [1996] 1 Lloyd's Rep 1; *Adamastos Shipping Co Ltd v Anglo-Saxon Petroleum Co* [1958] 2 WLR 688 (HL). For a contrary view see Cooke et al (n 7) para 18.55.

incorporation clause will trigger both incorporation and manipulation.[240] The Court of Appeal judgment in *The Nerano* is perhaps the main authority for the rule that ancillary charterparty provisions can be manipulated when they are expressly referred to in the incorporation clause.[241] There, the scope of the charterparty arbitration clause was limited to the disputes between original parties to the charterparty. Nonetheless, Saville LJ took the view that this provision must be extended to cover the disputes arising under the bill of lading. In support of this, he distinguished the case from the decision in *The Miramar* in two respects.[242] First, considering the wide use of arbitration clauses, Saville LJ emphasised that these provisions do not impose onerous obligations on the holders. Secondly, he highlighted the fact that, unlike the facts in *The Miramar*, the arbitration clause was expressly referred to in the incorporation clause, and this was held to demonstrate that the parties to the bill of lading intended to arbitrate, just as if they were parties to the charterparty.

Consequently, whether the arbitration clause refers to disputes between the shipowners and the charterers[243] or to disputes 'under the charter party',[244] the clause will be manipulated to adapt the bill of lading. Since an express reference to arbitration in the incorporation clause triggers both the incorporation and manipulation, an arbitration clause referring to disputes arising 'under this contract' must also be manipulated. Provided that an express reference is made in the bill of lading to that effect, the exclusive jurisdiction clauses and other ancillary charterparty provisions must equally be manipulated.

When deciding whether to manipulate or to read the charterparty clauses verbatim into the bill of lading, the explanations made so far show that there is no invariable recipe to be followed for all incorporated charterparty provisions. In terms of making the holders bound by germane charterparty terms, the real barriers emerge under the rules of manipulation, although little effort is sufficient to incorporate these provisions. It is therefore beneficial for carriers to use extra care, inter alia, in the wording of such charterparty clauses, which may impose onerous liabilities when applied to the bill of lading holders. Furthermore, the reasoning used in *The Miramar* and *The Nerano* also suggests that these parties can achieve application of such provisions to the holders by expressly referring to them in the incorporation clause.

B. US Law

Under US law, specific account must be given to the language of charterparty arbitration clauses. In respect of manipulation of these clauses, US courts resolve

[240] See *The Federal Bulker* [1989] 1 Lloyd's Rep 103, 109.

[241] [1996] 1 Lloyd's Rep 1.

[242] ibid, at 3–4.

[243] *The Oinoussin Pride* [1991] 1 Lloyd's Rep 126. But see *The Nai Matteini* [1988] 1 Lloyd's Rep 452, which is overruled by the decision in *The Nerano* [1996] 1 Lloyd's Rep 1.

[244] See *The Delos* [2001] 1 All ER (Comm) 763 and *The Rena K* [1978] 1 Lloyd's Rep 545.

this issue by relying on the words of these clauses,[245] categorising them as either narrow or broad.[246] To this end, US courts do not manipulate the arbitration clauses nor adapt them to the wording of the bill of lading where the arbitration clause refers to disputes arising between the shipowner and the charterer.[247] While such clauses are regarded as 'narrow', those clauses referring to disputes arising out of 'the charter party'[248] or 'this contract'[249] are treated as broad.[250] The provisions drafted in this manner are construed, in the context of bills of lading, as though they refer to the disputes under 'this bill of lading' or 'this bill of lading contract'. Where the arbitration clause does not neatly fall into either category, it is likely that the court will treat the clause as broad[251] and will therefore decide in favour of its application in the bill of lading context, due to the strong policy favouring arbitration.[252] US case law suggests that the wording that describes the disputes to be arbitrated is decisive in categorising the arbitration clauses. For this reason, a reference made to 'shipowners and charterers' when spelling out the process with respect to selection of the arbitrators is not taken as decisive for present purposes.[253]

If the language used in the incorporated charterparty arbitration clause is broad, the holders will be bound by this provision 'just as they would be if the dispute were between the parties to the charterparty'.[254] However, in the case of a narrow arbitration clause, the carriers are not entitled to arbitrate disputes with

245 See *Alucentro Div Dell'alusuisse Italia SPA et al v M/V Hafnia etc et al* 1992 AMC 267, 268 (MDFla 1991).

246 *FD Import & Export Corp v M/V Reefer Sun* 2003 AMC 60, 65 (SDNY 2002); *Midland Tar Distillers Inc v M/T Lotos* 362 F Supp 1311, 1314 (SDNY 1973); *Progressive Cas Ins Co v CA Reaseguradora Nacional De Venezuela* 1993 AMC 2916, 2923 (2d Cir 1993); *Trade Arbed v M/V Kandalaksha* 2003 AMC 1732, 1735 (SDNY 2003); *Limonium Maritime SA v Mizushima Marinera SA* F Supp 2d, 1999 WL 46721 (SDNY 1999); *Lucky Metals Corp v M/V Ave* 1996 AMC 265 (SDNY 1995).

247 *Continental UK Ltd v Anagel Confidence Compania Naviera SA* 1987 AMC 2012 (SDNY 1987); *Joo Seng Hong Kong Co v SS Unibulkfir* 493 F Supp 35 (SDNY 1980); *Production Steel Co of Illinois v SS Francios LD* 1968 AMC 2529 (SDNY 1968); *Nissho Iwai Corporation v The M/V Thalia* 1996 AMC 723 (EDLa 1996).

248 See *Alucentro Div Dell'alusuisse Italia SPA v M/V Hafnia* 1992 AMC 267, 268 (MDFla 1991); *Midland Tar Distillers Inc v M/T Lotos* 1973 AMC 1924 (SDNY 1973); *Son Shipping Co Inc v De Fosse & Tanghe* 1952 AMC 1931 (2d Cir 1952).

249 *Associated Metals & Minerals Corp v M/V Venture* 554 F Supp 281 (DCLa 1983); *Lowry & Co Inc v SS Le Moyne D'Iberville* 1966 AMC 2195 (SDNY 1966); *Lowry & Co v SS Nadir* 1965 AMC 1340 (SDNY 1963); *In Re Southwind Shipping Co* 709 F Supp 79, 82 (SDNY 1989).

250 *Alucentro Div Dell'alusuisse Italia SPA v M/V Hafnia* 1992 AMC 267, 268 (MDFla 1991).

251 *Continental Insurance Company v M/V Nikos N* 2002 AMC 1287 (SDNY 2002); *Salim Oleochemicals Inc v M/V Shropshire* 169 F Supp 2d 194 (SDNY 2001).

252 See *Asoma Corp v M/V Seadaniel* 971 F Supp 140 (SDNY 1997).

253 See *Alucentro Div Dell'alusuisse Italia SPA v M/V Hafnia* 1992 AMC 267 (MDFla 1992); *Midland Tar Distillers Inc v M/T Lotos* 1973 AMC 1924 (SDNY 1973); *In the matter of Arbitration between Benship Int v Bangladesh Agricultural Development Corp* F Supp 1991 WL 710 (SDNY 1991); *Lucky Metals Corp v M/V Ave* 1996 AMC 265 (SDNY 1995); *Continental Insurance Company v M/V Nikos N* 2002 AMC 1287 (SDNY 2002).

254 *Citrus Marketing Board of Israel v M/V Ecuadorian Reefer* 1991 AMC 1042 (DMass 1990); *Coastal States Trading Inc v Zenith Navigation SA* 446 F Supp 330 (SDNY 1977); *Son Shipping Co Inc v De Fosse & Tanghe* 1952 AMC 1931 (2d Cir 1952).

subsequent bill of lading holders, despite the specific reference to arbitration in the incorporation clause.[255] Where the language used in the arbitration clause is narrow, its application is restricted to the immediate parties named in the charterparty. Thus, the application of such arbitration clauses cannot be extended to non-parties to the charterparty,[256] irrespective of the words of incorporation in the bill of lading.[257]

However, a charterparty arbitration clause referring to the disputes arising between the 'owner' and 'charterer' is applicable to the parties to the bill of lading where both the carrier and the holder can be treated as the 'owner' and the 'charterer', respectively.[258] For these purposes, the courts look at whether each party (1) is also a party to the incorporated charterparty or (2) has assumed all obligations or privileges of either party to the charterparty or (3) is an agent or alter ego of the charterer or the owner who entered into the relevant charter.[259]

Manipulation is also not allowed for other incorporated charterparty clauses, such as exclusive jurisdiction clauses, which manifest an intention to limit the scope of application to the parties to the charterparty.[260] However, such restrictive language can be manipulated, if the bill of lading provides that 'charterparty terms will be applicable to the holder as if he were the party to the charterparty'. This or a similar provision can justify manipulation.[261] Moreover, manipulation can also be permissible for other charterparty provisions, in cases where the bill of lading contains an express provision making the holder liable in respect of the matters stipulated under these provisions.[262] Similarly, an incorporation clause which makes a specific reference to a charterparty provision can trigger the manipulation of the restrictive language of that provision to adapt the bill of lading.[263]

[255] *Alucentro Div Dell'alusuisse Italia SPA v M/V Hafnia* 1992 AMC 267 (MDFla 1991), where existence of an express reference to arbitration in the incorporation clause played no role in determining the application of a charterparty arbitration clause to the bill of lading holder.

[256] *Midland Tar Distillers Inc v M/T Lotos* 1973 AMC 1924 (SDNY 1924); *FD Import & Export Corp v M/V Reefer Sun* 2003 AMC 60, 63–64 (SDNY 2002).

[257] See *Salim Oleochemicals Inc v M/V Shropshire* 169 F Supp 2d 194, 198 (SDNY 2001).

[258] See *Continental UK Ltd v Anagel Confidence Compania Naviera SA* 1987 AMC 2012 (SDNY 1987).

[259] *Ventura Maritime Co Ltd v ADM Export Co* 1999 AMC 1676 (EDLa 1999). The legal position under English law is contrary to that under US law, see *The Phonizien* [1966] 1 Lloyd's Rep 150, where the carriers unsuccessfully sought to compel the holder to arbitrate on the grounds that the holder was also the 'charterer' as per the definition of the incorporated charterparty contract. This was not regarded as sufficient reason for binding the bill of lading holder to the charterparty arbitration clause, which was not expressly referred to in the incorporation clause. Given that the arbitration clause was not incorporated, the question of manipulation did not arise.

[260] PV Martin and SE Balick, 'A Trader's Concern: What is the Complete Contract?' [1996] *International Journal of Shipping Law* 220–21

[261] See *Limonium Maritime SA v Mizushima Marinera SA* F Supp 2d 1999 WL 46721 (SDNY 1999) quoted in MH Bagot and DA Henderson, 'Not Party, Not Bound? Not Necessarily: Binding Third Parties to Maritime Arbitration' (2002) 26 *Tulane Maritime Law Journal* 455.

[262] See *United States of America v Lamborn & Co and William A Jamison* 1932 AMC 1228 (2d Cir 1932).

[263] ibid.

C. Are the Rules of Manipulation Justifiable?

In both jurisdictions, the barriers to manipulation only arise in limited circumstances, and even these barriers can easily disappear with the adoption of some simple contract drafting techniques for the charterparty. Since the main purpose of incorporation clauses is to make the charterparty referred to applicable in the context of bills of lading, the tendency of the courts towards manipulation is understandable. In particular, when an express reference to a charterparty provision is made in the incorporation clause, the intention to make the relevant term a part of the bill of lading becomes more apparent, and manipulation becomes even more justifiable in those circumstances. It is for this reason that English law has a more sensible approach with respect to manipulation of arbitration clauses: specific reference to arbitration in the incorporation clauses is enough to trigger manipulation, irrespective of the charterparty wording. What remains to be seen under English law is whether the reasoning in *The Miramar* will be applied to other types of charterparty provisions the application of which would give rise to onerous liabilities to be borne by the holder. It will also be interesting to see the effect of special words of incorporation on the manipulation of such onerous provisions.

The US approach regards the words of the charterparty forum selection clause as the only decisive factor in resolving the issue of manipulation. For this reason, the specific reference in the incorporation language is not sufficient to trigger manipulation. Giving priority to the charterparty wording in the case of special words of incorporation in the bill of lading overrides the intention that can clearly be ascertained from the bill of lading. It makes little sense to interpret the incorporated charterparty wording against the intention manifested in the bill of lading, particularly since the bill of lading is the incorporating contract. Despite its shortcomings, the rule is strictly followed by the courts and arbitral tribunals.[264]

III. Conclusion

The justifiability of the rules of incorporation comes down to one critical question: are they a set of rules that are based merely upon technical considerations, or do they balance the interests of parties to the bill of lading and help the efficient flow of international trade?

[264] For judicial decisions see n 254 and for arbitration awards see *In Re Arbitration between Alimentos Precocidos Guayana CA and Her An Shipping SA* SMA No 3468 (14 August 1998); *In Re Arbitration Between Cementos Andinos Dominicanos SA and East Bulk Shipping SA* SMA No 3993 (11 February 2008).

An evaluation of the rules of incorporation discussed so far suggests that the description test is particularly vital for the holders, who are only guided by the incorporation clause when seeking to anticipate what charterparty provisions might be incorporated. For this reason, certainty in the interpretation of the words of incorporation is essential for the good flow of international trade and for the reliability of bills of lading as transferable instruments. The US and English rules of incorporation on this issue are well developed, and they indeed make it possible for the holders to anticipate what type of charterparty clauses can be incorporated. The practice also appears to have adapted itself to these rules, with many standard bill of lading forms drafted in an appropriate fashion to import a wide range of charterparty clauses.

An incorporation clause in a bill of lading manifests an intention to incorporate. To give effect to this intention, the wording of the incorporated charterparty provisions needs to be adapted to the bill of lading. This commercially sensible approach nevertheless has its own limits, and it is clear in both jurisdictions that the courts are not engaged in a mechanical adaptation of the incorporated charterparty provisions of whatever nature. Undue manipulation is not permitted in either jurisdiction, although what makes manipulation 'undue' is not answered in the same way.

When determining which charterparty provisions can be brought into the bill of lading, one further question arises: does the extent of incorporation contemplated by the relevant charterparty have any role to play? It is not uncommon to see that some charterparty provisions are not incorporated into the bill of lading, even though the relevant charterparty expressly contemplates their incorporation into the bill of lading. Such mismatches between the bill of lading and the charterparty especially arise in cases where a charterparty lists the clauses to be incorporated into the bills of lading, while the incorporation clause is, of itself, not apt to describe them. In the next chapter, the issue of whether the terms of the bill of lading, or those of the charterparty, are the decisive factors for incorporation will be analysed.

4

The Operative Words of Incorporation

Given the observations made in the previous chapters, it is natural for the holders to take the wording of incorporation clauses as one of the main tools for anticipating the type of charterparty clauses that will be incorporated into the bill of lading. They can therefore try to envisage the possible contractual picture under the bill of lading by taking into account the wording of the incorporation clause. To achieve this objective, the holders would need to examine the rules of incorporation, whereby the words of incorporation are interpreted. Behind this approach lies the assumption that charterparty clauses do not play any role in the formation of the terms of the bill of lading before they are incorporated pursuant to the incorporation clause.

However, when a charterparty comes into play with a stipulation that some particular charterparty clauses are to be incorporated into the bill of lading,[1] the question arises as to whether this provision must be ignored in the ongoing incorporation process. A similar question also becomes relevant where the bill of lading provides for incorporation of 'all terms of the charterparty' and the relevant charterparty lists the clauses that are regarded as the 'terms' for the purposes of their incorporation into the bill of lading.[2]

In the event that a charterparty stipulates a narrower or a wider scope of incorporation than the bill of lading, the practical consequences of giving more weight to the charterparty as opposed to the latter are numerous: to allow charterparty clauses to operate as incorporation clauses would protect shipowners from the adverse results arising from a bill of lading whose incorporation clause is not apt to bring in the charterparty provisions as requested under the charterparty. More precisely, this would eliminate the shipowners' concerns of wider responsibility towards the holders than they anticipated under the charterparty. Given that the shipowners will generally have the right to look to their respective charterers to recover losses arising from a bill of lading that provides wider responsibilities, to give more weight to the charterparty would also be to the charterers' benefit.

However, to accept that the charterparty provisions can determine which charterparty will be incorporated into the bill of lading would have a profound effect on the holders. When the bill of lading is no longer the decisive factor for

[1] See, for instance, clause 20 of the Asbatankvoy Charterparty.

[2] See *The Varenna* [1984] QB 592.

determining the extent of the incorporation, the holders will be deprived of their major guidance to foresee their contractual position under the bill of lading. From a wider perspective, one can also argue that it would be improper to give a contract the effect of dominating the formation of another contract where at least one party to the latter seldom has the chance to see the former. However, it is also true that there are accepted views under English law and US law that may cast doubt on this argument. There is a presumption recognised under English law that bill of lading holders are provided with copies of the charterparty.[3] Under US law, some of the bill of lading holders are treated differently on the basis that they are the respective charterers of the charterparties referred to, or because of their close contractual relationship with the charterers.[4]

In this chapter, the issue of whether the charterparty, or the bill of lading, controls incorporation of the respective charterparty clauses will be considered. Thereafter, how workable the rules are in practice will be analysed.

I. Is the Charterparty or the Bill of Lading the Driving Force for Incorporation?

Under English law, it was first suggested in *The Emmanuel Colocotronis*[5] that the charterparty provisions which contemplate the incorporation of certain charterparty clauses should be decisive. Despite the incorporation wording in the bill of lading, the Court in *The Emmanuel Colocotronis* favoured incorporation of the charterparty arbitration clause by reason of the charterparty provision, which sought to achieve incorporation to that effect. In order to justify his findings, Staughton J relied on the decisions in *The Merak*[6] and *The Rena K*:[7] in both of these cases the Courts took the view that an arbitration clause that refers to the disputes 'under bill of lading' can be incorporated, though the incorporation clause is devoid of any specific reference to arbitration. The reliance of Staughton J on these two cases was in fact misplaced: the specified wording of the arbitration clause in both cases was different from the charterparty clause in *The Emmanuel Colocotronis*, which purported to introduce some particular charterparty clauses into the bill of lading. Nevertheless, Staughton J sought to draw support from these two cases when concluding that it was legitimate to look at the charterparty to determine the extent of incorporation once the bill of lading directs the holder to the charterparty.

[3] See *OK Petroleum AB v Vitol Energy SA* [1995] 2 Lloyd's Rep 160, 163, quoting *The Merak* [1965] P 223, 250; *The Annefield* [1971] P 168, 177.

[4] See *Chilean Nitrate Sales Corp v Steamship Nortuna* 1955 AMC 1576 (SDNY 1955).

[5] *The Emmanuel Colocotronis* [1982] 1 Lloyd's Rep 286.

[6] [1965] P 223.

[7] *The Rena K* [1979] QB 377.

Undoubtedly, the suggestion that the charterparty wording might be relevant in deciding on incorporation of the charterparty clauses had been made many years ago in the *obiter dictum* of *Thomas v Portsea*.[8] This was then recognised in many cases such as *The Rena K* and *The Annefield*.[9] Furthermore, the Court in *The Merak* also adopted this view as its *ratio decidendi* when allowing the incorporation of an arbitration clause referring to disputes under bills of lading. Nevertheless, in these cases, the permission to turn to the charterparty wording was exclusively proposed for charterparty arbitration clauses. In particular, the suggestion was confined only to incorporation of such charterparty provisions where they expressly referred to disputes arising under bills of lading. The decision in *The Emmanuel Colocotronis* was, therefore, well beyond the scope of the previous decisions.

For this reason, the Court of Appeal in *The Varenna*[10] overruled *The Emmanuel Colocotronis*. In so doing, the Court took no specific account of the intention of the parties to the charterparty when deciding which of the charterparty provisions should be included in the bill of lading.[11] The Court in *The Varenna* also distinguished the decision in *The Merak*, since the latter decision was not concerned with the effect of a charterparty clause that listed the provisions to be included in the bill of lading. The decision in *The Merak* involved a charterparty arbitration clause that required arbitration of the disputes arising out of 'any bills of lading issued hereunder'. In arriving at this conclusion, Oliver LJ in *The Varenna* took the view that the charterparty clause that mandates incorporation of some particular charterparty provisions cannot be incorporated.[12] He drew support from the rule that general incorporation wording is only apt to describe those charterparty clauses that are directly germane to shipment, carriage and discharge of cargo.[13]

Hobhouse J in the Queen's Bench Division rested his judgment in *The Varenna* on different legal grounds.[14] The assumption in English law that bill of lading holders have access to the relevant charterparties led Hobhouse J to raise the following arguments: when the charterparty and bill of lading do not stipulate incorporation of the same particular charterparty provisions, and a discrepancy arises between these two distinct documents, it should be inferred that the bill of lading purports to import different clauses from those sought to be incorporated by the charterparty.[15] Thus, even though bill of lading holders are presumed to know what is contemplated under the charterparty, they are nevertheless expected

[8] *TW Thomas & Co Ltd v Portsea Steamship Company Ltd* [1912] AC 1 (HL).

[9] *The Annefield* [1971] P 168.

[10] [1984] QB 592.

[11] For a view in favour of *The Emmanuel Colocotronis*, see EA Marshall, 'Incorporation of Arbitration Clauses into Charterparty Bills of Lading' [1982] *Journal of Business Law* 478–84.

[12] [1984] QB 592, 619 (CA).

[13] ibid.

[14] See [1983] 1 Lloyd's Rep 416. See also *Siboti K/S v BP France SA* [2003] 2 Lloyd's Rep 364, 374, where the decision was premised on both the previous and the present view.

[15] See [1983] 1 Lloyd's Rep 416, 423.

to discern that the difference between the bill of lading and the charterparty is intentional.[16]

Regardless of the different paths taken, the common view was: whatever the parties to the charterparty intend to incorporate into the bill of lading should not have any effect on the incorporation of charterparty provisions.[17] This led to the conclusion that at the stage of introducing the respective charterparty clauses into the bill of lading, the primary document to ascertain the intention of the parties in respect of incorporation was to be the bill of lading, rather than the charterparty.[18] The incorporation process was correctly regarded as the incorporation of the charterparty provisions only, and not the intentions of the parties to the charterparty.[19] What flows from this approach is twofold. First, the incorporation clause in the bill of lading is saved from being merely a stock phrase, which only demonstrates the intention to incorporate, without any capacity to shape the contractual context of the bill of lading.[20] Secondly, it becomes clear that where the extent of incorporation contemplated by the charterparty does not coincide with that under the bill of lading, the latter contract shall be taken as the basis for determining the charterparty terms to be incorporated.[21] Moreover, the picture emerging from the English case law suggests that there is no departure from this approach, even in cases where the bill of lading holder has actual or constructive knowledge of the charterparty that the bill of lading seeks to incorporate.[22] Nor does the assumption under English law, which treats the bill of lading holders as though they have access to the terms of the charterparty, change this pattern.

However, the law is unclear with respect to the effects of charterparty provisions describing any of the incorporation wording used in the bill of lading for incorporation purposes. The decision in *The Varenna* leaves the door open to the construction of these charterparty clauses, together with the incorporation clauses in the bill of lading.[23] A number of cases, on the other hand, suggest that the charterparty provisions which are not incorporated into bills of lading are not to be taken into account when construing the terms of the bills of lading, including the incorporation clause.[24] It is submitted that charterparty clauses of this type should not be relied on when determining the charterparty terms to be

[16] ibid.

[17] See *The Varenna* [1984] QB 592, 597 (CA) and *Siboti K/S v BP France SA* [2003] 2 Lloyd's Rep 364.

[18] See *The Federal Bulker* [1989] 1 Lloyd's Rep 103, 105.

[19] See *The Varenna* [1984] QB 592, 597 (CA) at 597.

[20] *The Delos* [2001] 1 Lloyd's Rep 703; *The Federal Bulker* [1989] 1 Lloyd's Rep 103.

[21] See *Siboti K/S v BP France SA* [2003] 2 Lloyd's Rep 364.

[22] See *The Varenna* [1984] QB 592, 597 (CA) at 619. See also, M Özdel, 'Incorporation of Charterparty Clauses into Bills of Lading: Peculiar to Maritime Law?' in M Clarke (ed), *Maritime Law Evolving* (Oxford, Hart Publishing, 2013) 181–95.

[23] See ibid. Also see *The Spiros C* [2000] 2 Lloyd's Rep 319.

[24] See *The Federal Bulker* [1989] 1 Lloyd's Rep 103, 105; *Siboti K/S v BP France SA* [2003] 2 Lloyd's Rep 364, 369–74.

incorporated.[25] The possible effects of such clauses, which define the words of incorporation contained in the bill of lading, are no different from those provisions stipulating which particular charterparty clauses are to be included in the bill of lading. Both types of charterparty clause purport to achieve incorporation, as contemplated by the parties to the charterparty, and therefore they should both be disregarded during the process of incorporation. When these observations are accepted, it becomes clear that charterparty clauses which are not incorporated into the bill of lading should not be construed along with the terms of the bill of lading. The intention of the parties to the latter should always be taken as the sole basis for determining which charterparty provisions can be carried across to the bill of lading.[26]

While the English approach is centred on the terms of the bill of lading,[27] the solutions provided under US law with respect to this matter are bound up with the facts of each individual case.[28] To this end, US law entails examination of the actual position of the individual bill of lading holder in order to determine whether the charterparty or the bill of lading has control over the incorporation of charterparty terms.

In certain circumstances, US courts tend to give more weight to what is contemplated in the charterparty as to the extent of incorporation into the bill of lading. Such circumstances arise where the holder is not a stranger to the charterparty, namely where the subsequent bill of lading holder is the actual charterer of the incorporated charterparty,[29] or where he or she is not at arm's length from the charterer in question.[30] In those cases, if the charterparty does not contain an express provision that manifests the parties' intention to incorporate, it is even legitimate to examine whether an implied intention to that effect can be discerned from the charterparty.[31] Where the holder is not a 'stranger' to the charterparty, it is also permissible to turn to the charterparty with a view to clearing up any ambiguities concerning the bill of lading.[32]

[25] For a similar view, see S Girvin, *Carriage of Goods by Sea*, 2nd edn (Oxford, Oxford University Press, 2010) 149.

[26] See *The Federal Bulker* [1989] 1 Lloyd's Rep 103, 105; *The Rena K* [1979] QB 377, 381; *Siboti K/S v BP France SA* [2003] 2 Lloyd's Rep 364, 368; and *The Oinoussin Pride* [1991] 1 Lloyd's Rep 126.

[27] See *Siboti K/S v BP France SA* [2003] 2 Lloyd's Rep 364, 370, where it was stated that the inquiry should start and end with the terms of the bill of lading.

[28] See *Cargill BV v S/S Ocean Traveller* 1989 AMC 953, 959 (SDNY 1989).

[29] See *Energy of Transport Ltd v M/V San Sebastian* 348 F Supp 2d 186, 206 (SDNY 2004); *Continental Insurance Company v M/V Nikos N* 2002 AMC 1287, 1292 (SDNY 2002); *Cargill BV v S/S Ocean Traveller* 1989 AMC 953, 959 (SDNY 1989).

[30] This becomes relevant where either the charterer or the bill of lading holder is the alter ego of the other, or where there is an agency relationship between these parties with respect to the relevant shipping transactions carried out. See *Amoco Overseas Co v ST Avenger* 1975 AMC 782, 785 (SDNY 1975); *Keytrade USA Inc v Ain Temouchent M/V* 2005 AMC 948, 951–52 (5th Cir 2005); *Steel Coils Inc v Captain Nicholas I M/V* 197 F Supp 2d 560, 567 (EDLa 2002).

[31] See *Keytrade USA Inc v Ain Temouchent M/V* 2005 AMC 948 (5th Cir 2005); *Energy of Transport Ltd v M/V San Sebastian* 348 F Supp 2d 186 (SDNY 2004).

[32] In this context, even the documented contract negotiations that demonstrate the parties' intention to incorporate some specific charterparty provisions may be a determining factor. See *Amoco*

The reason for giving the charterparty the effect of dominating incorporation in those instances is straightforward: the bill of lading holder who falls into any of the specified categories is different from the others who usually have no knowledge about the charterparty provisions referred to in the bill of lading. However, the holders of the former type are expected to be aware of the charterparty provisions that mandate incorporation of some particular charterparty clauses into the bill of lading.[33] Holding these parties to be bound by the charterparty provisions can to some extent be justified[34] on the grounds that such holders either have the chance to negotiate the charterparty or have a close relationship with the charterer.[35]

For a bill of lading holder who is not a stranger to the relevant charterparty, US law would appear to have an entirely charterparty-oriented perspective. However, the US approach is, in fact, closer to being 'bill of lading-oriented', even though charterparty provisions may dominate incorporation in certain circumstances. In the process of resolving the question of incorporation, the starting point is always the incorporation clause under the bill of lading.[36] Consequently, without an incorporation clause, the bill of lading could be completely ineffective in importing the charterparty clauses.[37]

It is for this reason that US courts tend to find against incorporation in cases where the bill of lading is devoid of necessary contractual details.[38] This bill-centric approach also explains why the courts are reluctant to incorporate the provisions of the charterparty referred to when the bill of lading contains exhaustive provisions that regulate the contractual relation between the carrier and the holder. Since these matters have a significant impact on the decision-making

Overseas Co v ST Avenger 1975 AMC 782, 785 (SDNY 1975). Conversely, under English law, where the intention to incorporate under the bill of lading remains in doubt, the charterparty provisions cannot lead the court to find in favour of incorporation, see S Mankabady, 'References to Charter-parties in Bills of Lading' [1974] *Lloyd's Maritime and Commercial Law Quarterly* 56, 57, quoting *Thomas v Portsea* [1912] AC 1 (HL). See *The Annefield* [1971] P 168, 181. For a contrary view, see *The Merak* [1965] P 223.

33 For this reason, the requirement of making unmistakable reference to the charterparty disappears in the case of a bill of lading holder who is a signatory to the incorporated charterparty. See *Federal Insurance Co v M/V Audacia* 1987 AMC 566 (SDNY 1986); *State Trading Corp of India v Grunstad Shipping* 582 F Supp 1523 (SDNY 1989).

34 *Steel Coils Inc v Captain Nicholas I M/V* 197 F Supp 2d 560, 567 (EDLa 2002).

35 ibid.

36 See *Keytrade USA Inc v Ain Temouchent M/V* 2005 AMC 948 (5th Cir 2005).

37 *Lykes Lines Ltd v M/V BBC Sealand* 2005 AMC 865 (5th Cir 2005).

38 See *Midland Tar Distillers Inc v M/T Lotos* 1973 AMC 1924 (SDNY 1973); *Production Steel Co of Illinois v SS Francios LD* 1968 AMC 2529 (SDNY 1968). However, depending on the surrounding circumstances of the case, this matter could be insignificant to the question of incorporation, see *Amoco Oil Company v MT Mary Ellen* 1982 AMC 1758 (SDNY 1982) where it was stated that there cannot be any contractual lacuna for the cargo moving to the United States, even though the bill of lading has no detailed provision to regulate the contractual relations between the parties. This is merely because the bill of lading will incorporate, by law, the terms of the United States Carriage of Goods by Sea Act, 1936.

process, it must be concluded that what the original parties to the bill of lading have decided over incorporation has a large-scale impact on incorporation.

To sum up, the dominant US approach suggests that the inquiry always starts with the bill of lading, which is expected to manifest, in one way or another, the intention to incorporate a charterparty. Consequently, depending on the position of the bill of lading holder, the charterparty provisions may, at a later stage, determine incorporation of specific charterparty clauses. When the bill of lading holder can be included in one of the identified categories, the inquiry will then entail construction of both documents.[39] This underpins the statement that the charterparty that spells out the provisions to be incorporated into the bill of lading cannot be solely dominating: the provisions of the bill of lading have, in any case, the potential to be decisive on the matter of incorporation.[40]

These fine distinctions between US law and English law disappear when a bill of lading holder is neither the charterer of the charterparty referred to nor has one of the specified relationships with the charterer. In such circumstances, the analysis revolves around the bill of lading provisions, and the charterparty is no longer effective in the process of deciding on the charterparty terms to be incorporated.[41] This 'bill-centric'[42] approach also sets barriers to any charterparty intervention, even though the bill of lading holder, who can be subsumed into one of the aforementioned categories, has actual knowledge of the charterparty.[43]

Consequently, all the previously mentioned rules of incorporation adopted under US law and English law can be condensed as follows. Under English law, the 'operative words of incorporation'[44] should be spelled out in the bill of lading. Under US law, this approach is maintained only in cases where the bill of lading holder has no connection in the prescribed manner with the charterparty referred to.

II. Are These Rules Workable?

Even though the intervention of the charterparty is limited under US law, it is still difficult to justify allowing the charterparty to become the determining factor

[39] See *Midland Tar Distillers Inc v M/T Lotos* 1973 AMC 1924 (SDNY 1973); *Cia. Platamon v Empresa Colombiana* 1980 AMC 538, 539 (SDNY 1979).

[40] *Keytrade USA Inc v Ain Temouchent M/V* 2005 AMC 948 (5th Cir 2005).

[41] *Bernuth Lembcke Co Inc v Steamship Acasta* 1952 AMC 1789 (ENDC 1951).

[42] See *Keytrade USA Inc v Ain Temouchent M/V* 2005 AMC 948 (5th Cir 2005), which regards the US approach with respect to this issue as 'bill-centric'. However, it seems to be the case that the charterparty intervention, which becomes relevant in the identified circumstances, prevents the legal position from being wholly 'bill-centric'.

[43] For US law, see *Amoco Oil Company v MT Mary Ellen* 1982 AMC 1758 (SDNY 1982). For English law, see *Serraino v Campbell* [1891] 1 QB 283, 297.

[44] See *The Varenna* [1983] 2 Lloyd's Rep 592, 594 (CA).

for incorporation. Although limited, this intervention prevents formation of a bill of lading in full compliance with the intentions of the original parties to the bill of lading. To put it another way, it does not recognise the possibility that a bill of lading holder, despite being a party to the charterparty referred to, may prefer the bill of lading to incorporate, or not to incorporate, some specific charterparty clauses, irrespective of the contrary charterparty requirements that are already known by the holder.

Consequently, taking the position of sub-charterers as an example, the chances of having a contract of carriage with shipowners under bill of lading terms different from those under their respective charterparties disappear with an incorporation clause. The overall commercial impact is that these parties become bound by the charterparty provisions, even in a different contractual context, despite their relations with the shipowner being different from those with the charterer.

Whether or not the discrepancy is intentional, it is still disingenuous to allow a charterparty to trigger incorporation. Before its provisions are duly imported into the bill of lading, the charterparty should be deemed as a separate and distinct contract from the bill of lading. Resorting to the charterparty to decide incorporation causes a vicious circle which neglects the major difference between the following issues: what bills of lading seek to incorporate, and what they should incorporate when the intention of the parties to the charterparty is taken into account.[45]

The suggestion above is in accordance with the fact that, in practice, the possibility that the bill of lading may fail to effect incorporation as required under the charterparty has long been anticipated. For this very reason, the shipowners introduce charterparty provisions that place the responsibility on the charterer for any losses or damages that they may suffer in cases where the charterer issues bills of lading contrary to the charterparty requirements.[46] Shipowners who wish their contracts of carriage with the bill of lading holders to be no less advantageous than their charterparties therefore safeguard their contractual positions with these provisions.[47] Consequently, the shipowners already have the tools to protect themselves from the adverse effects of a bill of lading which falls short of meeting the charterparty requirements.

This practice undoubtedly reinforces one conclusion: with the charterparty provisions contemplating incorporation of some specific charterparty clauses into the bill of lading, parties to the charterparty aim to create a contractual effect solely within the charterparty framework.[48] Therefore, it becomes more persuasive to allow the intention of the original parties to the bill of lading

[45] See Justice Garza in his judgment concurring in part and dissenting in *Cargill Ferrous International v Sea Phoenix M/V* 2003 AMC 1027, 1045 (5th Cir 2003).

[46] See, for instance, clause 10 of Gencon Charterparty of 1994, clause 31 of the New York Produce Exchange form 1993 (NYPE 1993) and clause 13 of Shelltime 4 form charterparty.

[47] See *The Federal Bulker* [1989] 1 Lloyd's Rep 103, 109–11.

[48] ibid.

to have control over incorporation,[49] for this conclusion is already within the contemplation of the parties to the charterparty, and they have introduced their own protective tools for such circumstances. For this reason, even though the charterer may breach his or her duty to issue a bill of lading that incorporates the charterparty provisions as manifested under the charterparty, this matter should not have any role to play in the incorporation process.[50]

From a practical point of view, the result of having the 'operative words of incorporation' under the bill of lading is that a potential third-party holder will have the chance to influence formation of the contract of carriage: where these parties ask their respective sellers to tender for payment a bill of lading in the desired form and content, the sellers will then need to procure a bill of lading that conforms to these requirements in order to receive payment. On requiring the tender of a bill of lading that contains a particular form of incorporation clause, the bill of lading holder will be in a position to pay for a contract of carriage whose terms can be anticipated to some extent despite the incorporation clause. For this reason, adoption of a 'purely bill of lading-oriented approach'[51] without giving any weight to the charterparty wording provides better solutions. This also helps the bill of lading, a transferable instrument, to be a more freestanding contractual document.

However, English courts may also depart from this 'bill-centric' approach in certain circumstances. There are a number of English cases suggesting that incorporation of the charterparty arbitration clauses that refer to disputes arising 'under bills of lading' should be allowed, despite the general incorporation wording.[52] Moreover, under English law, there is a possibility that ambiguities in the bill of lading may be resolved pursuant to the intention of the parties to the charterparty.[53] These approaches constitute a slight deviation from the rule that the intention of the parties to the bill of lading should prevail over the intention of the parties to the charterparty.

As regards these approaches, reference must again be made to the decision in *The Merak*, which involved a bill of lading holder who was a party to the charterparty referred to in the bill of lading.[54] There, the relevant incorporation clause, which was intended to refer to the arbitration clause, pointed, by mistake, to another provision of the charterparty. Nevertheless, this ambiguity was clarified on the basis of the charterparty provision that expressly provided for

[49] When the bill of lading is endorsed to a third party, this intention no longer becomes the common intention between the parties. Due to this reason, third-party bill of lading holders are bound by the intention of the original parties to the bills of lading which is reasonably ascertainable, see *Adamastos Shipping Co Ltd v Anglo-Saxon Petroleum Co* [1959] AC 133 (HL).

[50] See *The Federal Bulker* [1989] 1 Lloyd's Rep 103, 109.

[51] This can be defined as giving the words of incorporation the exclusive effect of importing charterparty clauses. See *The Varenna* [1984] QB 592.

[52] See Chapter 3.

[53] See *The Merak* [1965] P 223.

[54] ibid.

incorporation of the charterparty arbitration clause.[55] In reaching the conclusion that the charterparty arbitration clause was incorporated into the bill of lading, the majority view in *The Merak* did not give weight to the fact that the holder was a party to the charterparty.[56] The reason for disregarding the actual position of the bill of lading holder was the established English approach to incorporation, which does not permit any consideration of the holder's actual or constructive knowledge of the charterparty referred to.[57]

Unlike in English law, the picture emerging under US law suggests that the rules of incorporation have their roots in notice, and this significant feature explains why, in certain circumstances, the words of incorporation are held to be under the charterparty.

III. Conclusion

The question of whether it is the charterparty or the bill of lading that determines incorporation was discussed in a great number of cases, most of which are related to incorporation of the charterparty arbitration clauses. The key question in those cases was, in fact, whether the requirement of making an explicit reference to arbitration in the incorporation clause could, by any means, be bypassed with a charterparty term that dictates incorporation of the arbitration clause.

After numerous judicial decisions with respect to this matter, the self-explanatory answer was finally given under English law: since these contracts are distinct and separate from each other, the controlling effect should remain with the incorporating contract. In this context, no matter what knowledge the bill of lading holders may have of the charterparty referred to, it was agreed that the terms of the charterparty should have no effect on the bill of lading before its terms were duly incorporated pursuant to the provisions of the latter.

It is evident that under US law arbitration clauses are viewed in just the same way as any other contract provision.[58] For this reason, the question of whether it is legitimate to look at charterparty provisions becomes relevant in order to clear up any ambiguities arising from the bill of lading, especially with respect to the issues of (1) which charterparty is sought to be incorporated and (2) whether the charterparty provisions could be incorporated in the absence of an unmistakable reference under the bill of lading.

The overall picture emerging from the rules of incorporation, as they presently stand under US law and English law, is this: saving the exceptional circumstances

[55] ibid. See also *The Varenna* [1983] 1 Lloyd's Rep 416, 419 (CA).

[56] See *The Merak* [1965] P 223 at 259. However, Davies LJ found this matter to be an important factor to consider, see 254–55.

[57] See *Siboti K/S v BP France SA* [2003] 2 Lloyd's Rep 364. See also n 22.

[58] See Chapter 3.

under US law,[59] the incorporated charterparty clauses are construed without having regard to the actual intention of the parties to the charterparty.[60] In this new contractual context, the applicability of the incorporated charterparty provisions depends on a number of considerations other than the intention of parties to the charterparty. No matter whether the charterparty or the bill of lading has ultimate control over incorporation, the construction of the incorporated charterparty provisions brings forward one further inquiry, which will be analysed in the next chapter.

[59] See *Continental Insurance Company v M/V Nikos N* 2002 AMC 1287, 1292 (SDNY 2002). These cases are where the bill of lading holder either is the charterer to the charterparty referred to or has a close relationship with the charterer, such as being his or her agent, subsidiary or alter ego.

[60] For English law, see *The Heidberg* [1994] 2 Lloyd's Rep 287, where it was stated that even where the terms of the charterparty are incorporated into the bill of lading, they should nevertheless be interpreted without having regard to the actual intention of the parties to the charterparty. See also *The Federal Bulker* [1989] 1 Lloyd's Rep 103, 105 and *The Oinoussin Pride* [1991] 1 Lloyd's Rep 126, 130. Similarly, where the incorporating contract is the charterparty then the intention of the charterparty should prevail over the intention of the incorporated document, see *Adamastos Shipping Co Ltd v Anglo-Saxon Petroleum Co* [1959] AC 133 (HL). For US law, see *Amoco Oil Company v MT Mary Ellen* 1982 AMC 1758 (SDNY 1981); *Cargill v Golden Chariot M/V* 1995 AMC 1077 (5th Cir 1994); and *Keytrade USA Inc v Ain Temouchent M/V* 2005 AMC 948, 954 (5th Cir 2005).

5

The Consistency Test

Does the inquiry end with the incorporation of charterparty terms into the bill of lading? Do the manipulated charterparty terms survive under the bill of lading, and do they unconditionally bind the holders? For those who view the incorporated charterparty provisions as directly applicable to the holders, these questions can seem of little importance. As is clear under US law and English law, incorporation does not lead to mechanical application of the charterparty terms under the bill of lading, despite the fact that such terms may have sufficient scope to bind the parties. Further consideration is essential, therefore, where the integrated charterparty provisions are inconsistent with the express bill of lading terms, or where they cannot be reconciled with the Hague,[1] the Hague-Visby[2] or the Hamburg Rules[3] ('the Conventions'), any of which may be operative under the bill of lading by force of law. Against this backdrop, it is vital to raise one question: are such inconsistencies a barrier to the application of the incorporated charterparty clauses in the bill of lading?

Given that carriage of goods by sea is a 'commercial' activity, non-shipping lawyers might be forgiven for assuming that allocation of the risks of sea carriage is based on freedom of contract. Astonishingly for non-shipping lawyers, this specialist area of commercial law is largely regulated by a patchwork of different sets of mandatory rules contained in the Conventions. One of the main purposes of the Conventions is to protect the holders against the carriers' exclusion of liability clauses.[4] When the incorporated exclusion clause goes beyond the limits allowed in one of the Conventions applicable to the bill of lading by force of law, it will be in the interests of the holders to know whether the clause could be ousted from the bill of lading context as a result of this inconsistency. Similar issues also arise where the incorporated charterparty provision contains a longer time bar than was envisaged in the applicable Convention. In such cases, carriers need to examine whether they can avoid the longer time bar by invoking the repugnancy between the relevant provisions.

[1] The International Convention for the Unification of the Rules Relating to Bills of Lading 1924.

[2] The Hague Rules as Amended by Brussels Protocol 1968.

[3] The United Nations Convention on the Carriage of Goods by Sea 1978.

[4] See F Reynolds, 'The Hague Rules, the Hague-Visby Rules, and the Hamburg Rules' (1990) 7 *Maritime Law Association of Australia and New Zealand Journal* 16–18. See also *Cargill BV v S/S Ocean Traveller* 1989 AMC 953, 958 (SDNY 1989).

Both parties also have a stake in knowing the consistency test, where an incorporated forum selection clause cannot be reconciled with the bill of lading terms, or with the applicable Convention. The importance of this issue becomes particularly apparent in cases where the parties view the forum suggested in the incorporated forum selection clause as less favourable than those available to them. To defeat the undesirable forum, it is common to see the parties invoke the consistency test. Against this background, this chapter will be devoted to the question of the extent to which inconsistent charterparty clauses will find room for application in the bill of lading. After examining the issue of consistency in general, the chapter will focus on the applicability of the incorporated charterparty clauses when they contradict the express provisions in the bill of lading or the applicable Convention. Meanwhile, it will discuss the matters of consistency also by reference to the Rotterdam Rules.[5]

I. The Incorporated Charterparty Clauses Repugnant to the Bill of Lading

When an incorporated charterparty term cannot be reconciled with an express bill of lading provision, the question of which one of them is applicable must be addressed. The practical significance of this question is twofold. First, application of one provision as opposed to another can be beneficial for one party, while being disadvantageous to the other. Secondly, the answer to this question radically affects the rights and liabilities of the parties to the bill of lading. Assuming that a general paramount clause in the bill of lading provides for the Hague-Visby Rules, while the incorporated charterparty term refers to the Hague Rules, leaning towards either the former or the latter provision has a great impact on the legal positions of the parties. With the Hague-Visby Rules providing a less favourable package or unit limitation for carriers, it is natural for carriers to avail themselves of the incorporated charterparty clause, while the holders would seek to strike out the same due to inconsistency.

Despite the significance of this issue, it may in some cases be hard to draw a line between consistency and inconsistency. One of the most striking difficulties is that two seemingly conflicting provisions can, in certain circumstances, be construed as a whole, and it is impossible to create a formula to solve this issue in each case. Another difficulty arises when determining the scope of the consistency test: should the rules have the effect of jettisoning the incorporated charterparty terms which are surplus or insensible, or should their application be extended to oust the incorporated charterparty clauses which do not characteristically

[5] The United Nations Convention on Contracts for the International Carriage of Goods Wholly or Partly by Sea 2009.

belong to the bill of lading? Alternatively, should inconsistency be deemed to have arisen only in cases where there is more than one provision which contains diametrically opposite stipulations with respect to the same issue? As an example, if the bill of lading provides for a lien on the cargo for the unpaid freight, and if an incorporated charterparty clause gives the carrier the right to a lien for the unpaid demurrage, could it be said that there is inconsistency between these provisions? In these circumstances, the question is should we marry these two terms and allow the carrier to assert a lien for both claims, or should the incorporated lien clause be struck down by the rule of consistency?

Initially, the question of which terms are inconsistent with each other will be analysed. After this examination, the issue of which one of the conflicting provisions prevails over the other will be analysed.

A. When is there Inconsistency between the Provisions and Which One Prevails?

i. General

It is clear under both English law and US law that the incorporated charterparty clauses are not permitted to alter the express provisions in the bill of lading.[6] Thus, the charterparty provisions that stipulate issues that are already covered in the bill of lading are deemed inapplicable to the holder.[7] Consequently, where, for instance, the discharge port is stated as Rotterdam in the bill of lading, the incorporated charterparty clause providing for Hamburg as the discharge port is given no effect.

Nonetheless, the answer to the question of which one yields to the other is not so straightforward when the incorporated charterparty clause introduces an issue which is not covered under the bill of lading, or when the clause qualifies a general term stipulated therein. To solve this problem, US and English courts raise three main questions: (1) can such a charterparty clause be applied together with the express bill of lading terms?[8] (2) does it make any sense in the bill of lading context? and (3) are they in accordance with the main purpose and char-

[6] For US law, see *Goodpasture Inc v M/V Pollux* 602 F 2d 84, 86 (5th Cir 1979); *O'Connel v One Thousand and Two Bales of Sisal Hemp* 75 F 408 (DCAla 1896); *Energy of Transport Ltd v M/V San Sebastian* 348 F Supp 2d 186, 203 (SDNY 2004). For English law, see *Gardner v Trechmann* [1884] 15 QBD 154.

[7] For US law, see *The Robin Gray* 1933 AMC 766, (2d Cir 1933) *cert denied* 290 US 653 (US 1933). See also JW McKearn, 'Shipowner Denied Lien Against Third Party's Cargo For Charterer's Unpaid Charter Hire' (1980) 26 *Loyola Law Review* 416, 418. For English law, see *Gardner v Trechmann* [1884] 15 QBD 154.

[8] For US law, see *Yone Suzuki, et al v Central Argentine Railway Limited, Gano Moore Coal Mining Company, Inc* 1928 AMC 1521 (2d Cir 1928). For English law, see *Gullischen v Stewart Brothers* (1883) LR, 13 QBD 317. For the possible application of the qualifying charterparty provisions, see G Treitel and FMB Reynolds, *Carver on Bills of Lading*, 3rd edn (London, Sweet & Maxwell, 2011) para 3-025.

acter of the bill of lading?[9] In order to address these issues, both US and English courts initially seek to construe all the integrated and express terms as a whole.[10] Where the incorporated charterparty provisions cannot be reconciled with the express bill of lading terms due to being surplus, inapplicable or insensible, they are treated as inconsistent and ineffective.[11] Even where the incorporation clause expressly permits incorporation of inconsistent charterparty provisions, incorporation should only be permitted to the extent that the application of inconsistent provisions does not defeat 'the main object and intent' of the bill of lading.[12]

To prevent incorporation of the repugnant charterparty terms would increase reliance on the bills of lading in international trade and would help provide a less risky environment for traders. With the consistency test, the holders are also considerably protected from the unforeseeable charterparty provisions whose character and nature is inconsistent with the bill of lading. Thus, from the perspective of the holders, the rule helps them predict legal consequences arising from the incorporation clause in their bills of lading.

These general observations are not always helpful in resolving the consistency issue, given that construction of the incorporated charterparty terms in most cases varies depending on the nature and the function of the particular clause. For this reason, specific charterparty clauses the consistency of which with the bill of lading terms has most often been challenged will now be examined. For present purposes, the consistency issue will be examined by reference to freight, demurrage, cesser and arbitration clauses.

ii. Freight Clauses

On the question of whether a bill of lading holder can be subject to an incorporated charterparty freight clause, the first question to raise is: could a freight-prepaid stamp make the freight clause repugnant? In strictly legal terms, no such inconsistency can arise from its use because a freight-prepaid stamp can

[9] For English law, see *Gullischen v Stewart Brothers* (1883) LR, 13 QBD 317. See also *The Varenna* [1984] QB 599 (CA); *Hogarth Shipping Company Limited v Greene, Jourdain & Co Limited* [1917] 2 KB 534; *The Mata K* [1998] Lloyd's Rep 614; *GH Renton & Co Ltd v Palmyra Trading Co of Panama* [1957] AC 149, 152 (HL). See also DA Davies, 'Incorporation of Charterparty Terms into a Bill of Lading' [1966] *Journal of Business Law*, 327, 330. For US law see, *Yone Suzuki, et al v Central Argentine Railway Limited, Gano Moore Coal Mining Company, Inc* 1928 AMC 1521 (2d Cir 1928); *O'Connel v One Thousand and Two Bales of Sisal Hemp* 75 F 408 (DCAla 1896). See also R Lord, *Williston on Contracts*, 4th edn (Rochester, NY, Lawyers Cooperative Publishing, 2010) vol 11, §30:25.

[10] For English law, see *The Leonidas* [2001] CLC 1800. For US law, see Restatement (Second) On Contracts §202(d), §203(a).

[11] For English law, see *The Leonidas* [2001] CLC 1800. See also *Andreas Vergottis v Robinson David & Co Ltd* (1928) 31 Ll L Rep 23; *Hamilton & Co Mackie Sons* (1889) 5 TLR 677; *Porteus v Watney* (1877–78) LR 3 QBD 534, 542. For US law, see Restatement (Second) On Contracts §202(d), §203(a) and see also *Americas Ins Co v Stolt Nielsen Inc* 2004 AMC 2542 (SDNY 2004).

[12] For a similar view, see *Glynn v Margetson & Co* [1892] 1 QB 337, 355, per Fry LJ. See also *Renton v Palmyra* [1956] 1 QB 462. For a similar view under US law, see Restatement (Second) On Contracts, §202 para (c), where reference is made to 'principal purpose of the contract'.

only give rise to a representation of fact, not to a contractual promise.[13] For this reason, it is accepted in both jurisdictions that these stamps do not themselves make the incorporated charterparty freight clauses inconsistent, inapplicable or insensible.[14]

Under English law, this proposition draws support from the House of Lords decision in *The Nanfri*.[15] There, a dispute arose under a time charterparty with respect to the charterer's payment of the charter hire by repeatedly deducting the sums that were alleged to be due under the charterparty. Upon the charterer's refusal to pay the full charter hire as requested, the shipowner instructed the master not to sign any bills of lading which contained a freight-prepaid stamp and which did not incorporate the charterparty lien clause for freight. This instruction was held to be a repudiatory breach, entitling the charterer to terminate the charterparty. In reaching this decision, the Court in *The Nanfri* took the view that 'freight-prepaid' bills of lading do not necessarily prevent the shipowners from collecting the bill of lading freight and from asserting a lien for freight. To the same effect was the decision of the US Court of Appeals for the Ninth Circuit in *Logistics Management Inc v One Pyramid Tent Arena*.[16] In that case the Court found no inconsistency between the lien provision and the freight-prepaid stamp in the bill of lading, to the effect that the shipowner was entitled to assert a lien for freight against the holder by virtue of the lien clause.

It is clear in both jurisdictions that a 'freight-prepaid' stamp may triumph over an incorporated charterparty freight clause: despite a freight clause in the bill of lading, the carrier will be estopped from claiming freight from the holder who relied on the truth of the freight-prepaid stamp in the bill of lading.[17] In such circumstances, the carrier has no right to assert a lien on the cargo for the unpaid freight against such holders, irrespective of the statement under the bill of lading that freight be payable as per the charterparty.[18] However, a carrier can claim freight from the holders, despite a freight-prepaid stamp on the bill of lading, if the holders are not misled by the freight-prepaid stamp and are on notice that the freight has not yet been paid.[19]

[13] Treitel and Reynolds (n 8) para 2-001.

[14] For English law, see *The Nanfri* [1979] 1 Lloyd's Rep 201, 210 (CA); *The Indian Reliance* [1997] 1 Lloyd's Rep 52, 55–58. For US law, see *The Robin Gray* 65 F 2d 376, 378 (2d Cir 1933). See also McKearn (n 7) 416, 420; M Lynch, 'Pay the Man … Again! The Fourth Circuit Requires Shippers to Pay Freight Twice When Cargo Consolidators Default in Hawkspere Shipping Co v Intamex SA' (2003–2004) 28 *Tulane Maritime Law Journal* 602, 608.

[15] *The Nanfri* [1979] 1 Lloyd's Rep 201.

[16] *Logistics Management Inc v One Pyramid Tent Arena* 1996 AMC 1826 (9th Cir 1996).

[17] For English law, see *The Nanfri* [1979] 1 Lloyd's Rep 201 and *The Indian Reliance* [1997] 1 Lloyd's Rep 52. For US law, see *The Robin Gray* 65 F 2d 376, 378 (2d Cir 1933). See also *The Albert F Paul* F 2d 16, 1924 AMC 967 (2d Cir 1924); *Berdex International v M/V Kapitan Grishin* 1992 AMC 1559, 1565–66 (NDCal 1992).

[18] For US law, see *Hawkspere Shipping Co Ltd v Intamex SA* 330 F 3d 225, 237 (4th Cir 2003). For English law, see *The Nanfri* [1979] 1 Lloyd's Rep 201 and *The Indian Reliance* [1997] 1 Lloyd's Rep 52.

[19] ibid.

The legal effects of freight-prepaid stamps must be considered from the perspective of a holder—who is normally also the buyer under a sale contract. Due to the way that these stamps operate, it becomes possible for the holder to avoid liability to the carrier for freight by requiring his/her seller to tender for payment a bill of lading which has a freight-prepaid stamp on it. This is subject to the general condition that the holder does not have actual knowledge of the unpaid freight.

On the effect of freight-prepaid stamps, Article 42 of the Rotterdam Rules proposes a different solution, based on the question of whether the holder—who is labelled as the 'consignee'[20] under the Rotterdam Rules—is also the shipper. When the holder is not also the shipper, the carrier is estopped from claiming freight by reason of the freight-prepaid stamp in the bill of lading. This leaves open one question: if a holder who is not also a shipper happens to know that freight has not been paid, would it be possible for this party to shield itself under the freight-prepaid stamp on the bill of lading? It would be unjust to allow such a cargo receiver to shield itself under this stamp, but the wording of the Rotterdam Rules can hardly be stretched to create the desired result.

The solution proposed by the Hamburg Rules is far more beneficial to the holders: under these rules, a bill of lading that does not record the incurred freight or demurrage, or that does not indicate that freight or demurrage is payable is prima facie evidence that no freight or demurrage is due.[21] Where such a bill of lading is not in the hands of a shipper, it operates as conclusive evidence that no freight or demurrage is payable.[22] The aim of this rule would appear to be to prevent imposition of liability on holders to pay unpredictable sums, such as loading port demurrage, which may already have been incurred beyond their control.

Saving the peculiar case of freight-prepaid stamps, if an incorporated charterparty clause is inconsistent with an express bill of lading clause stipulating the rate of freight, the latter term will prevail over the former.[23] The holders are thus bound by the amount of freight and the payment method, which is expressly stated in the bill of lading, irrespective of the contrary terms in the integrated charterparty provisions.[24] However, where the incorporated charterparty clause envisages the payment method, while the bill of lading terms only stipulate the amount of freight, the courts may not find any inconsistency between these two provisions and may, therefore, treat both of them as equally applicable.[25]

[20] See Art 1.11 of the Rules.
[21] See Art 16(4) of the Hamburg Rules.
[22] ibid.
[23] For English law, see *Gardner v Trechmann* (1884) 15 QBD 154; *Ocean v Harding* [1928] 2 KB 371, 384. For US law, see *The Albert Dumois* 54 F 529 (DCNY 1893); *O'Connel v One Thousand and Two Bales of Sisal Hemp* 75 F 408 (DCAla 1896); *The Albert F Paul* 1924 AMC 967 (2d Cir 1924).
[24] ibid.
[25] For English law, see *The Indian Reliance* [1997] 1 Lloyd's Rep 52; *The Spiros C* [2000] 2 Lloyd's Rep 319. The same result must also follow under US law, given that US courts tend to presume that all integrated and express contract provisions are consistent with each other, and they seek to construe all the terms as a whole. For US law, see Restatement (Second) On Contracts, §202(d), §203(a).

Since an incorporated charterparty term yields to the express bill of lading clauses in the case of inconsistency, English and US courts restrict the carriers' right to lien on the cargo to the amount stated under the bill of lading.[26] Under English law, the leading authority for this proposition is the Court of Appeal judgment in *Gardner v Trechmann*, where the shipowner was not allowed to assert a lien for the sum in excess of the bill of lading freight.[27] A same view was also taken by a US court in *The Albert Dumois*.[28]

Consequently, in the absence of an express freight clause in the bill of lading, the freight clause incorporated from the charterparty must regulate the issue of payment of freight. When this is the case, the carrier must be entitled to claim payment of the sum provided in that clause against the holder,[29] and the right to lien must also exist for the amount of the unpaid charterparty freight. On the holder's liability for the charterparty freight, the further question is: could shipowners claim the lump-sum freight provided in the charterparty clause against a holder whose bill of lading only covers part of the cargo shipped on board the vessel? If so, could they also exercise a lien on such holder's cargo for the lump-sum freight? The English and US judicial decisions do not suggest any barriers to the imposition of such a disproportionate liability on bill of lading holders:[30] the courts tend to take the view that a charterparty freight clause incorporated into the bill of lading can regulate the amount of freight, as well as effecting the extent of lien for freight, in the absence of an express bill of lading provision relating to freight. Conversely, where the charterparty clause contains a freight rate, as opposed to lump-sum freight, it is clear in both jurisdictions that the holders are liable only for the amount of freight that is in proportion to the goods covered under their respective bills of lading.[31]

From an overall perspective, imposing the payment of lump-sum freight on a holder whose bill of lading covers only part of this cargo is an excessive hardship, as is asserting a lien on the same holder's cargo on this basis. In order to remove this burden from the shoulders of these parties, could the consistency test be used

[26] For US law, see *American Steel Barge Co v Chesapeake & Ohio Coal Agency Co* 115 F 669, 672 (1st Cir 1902). For English law, see *Gardner v Trechmann* (1884) 15 QBD 154, 157. In order to assert lien, the incorporated charterparty term should give the shipowner the right to lien upon all cargoes and all freights for the sums due under the charter. See also *The Spiros C* [2000] 2 Lloyd's Rep 319. For US law, see *Chembulk Trading LLC v Chemex Ltd* 393 F 3d 550, 555 (5th Cir 2005); *Hornbeck Offshore Operators Inc v Ocean Line of Bermuda Inc* 849 F Supp 434, 439 (5th Cir 1993).

[27] See *Gardner v Trechmann* (1884) 15 QBD 154 at 157.

[28] 54 F 529 (DCNY 1893).

[29] For a similar view, see *Gardner v Trechmann* at 158, per Cotton LJ. See also J Cooke et al, *Voyage Charters*, 3rd edn (London, Informa Law from Routledge, 2007) para 17-21. For US law, see McKearn (n 7) 417–18.

[30] For a similar opinion, see Cooke et al (n 29). See also W Poor, *American Law of Charter Parties and Ocean Bills of Lading*, 5th edn (New York, NY, Matthew Bender, 1968) 72.

[31] For English law, see *Fry v Chartered Mercantile Bank of India* (1866) LR 1 CP 689. For US law, see *The Lake Galera* 1932 AMC 1228 (2d Cir 1932), which can be used by way of analogy. There, the bill of lading holder was held to be liable for demurrage in proportion to the goods covered under his bill of lading pursuant to the incorporated demurrage clause, which contained a rate for passage of time and weight of the goods shipped on vessel.

in order to strike out that lump-sum charterparty freight which is not proportionate to the amount of cargo covered under the bill of lading? There are compelling reasons for saying that the consistency test must find room for application here.[32] Where the bill of lading merely covers part of the cargo carried on board the vessel, to impose the lump-sum charterparty freight on the holder would be contrary to commercial sense: a charterparty clause providing for a lump sum would not sensibly be applied in the bill of lading context, unless the incorporation clause expressly provided otherwise.[33] Thus, unless there is an express provision in the bill of lading to the contrary, parties cannot be presumed to have intended to bind the holder with the incorporated freight clause providing for lump-sum freight where the bill of lading does not cover the entire cargo on board the vessel.

iii. Demurrage Clauses

What happens to the incurred demurrage at the loading port when the vessel starts off her voyage immediately after loading, without the shipowner having received the demurrage? To ensure the payment of loading port demurrage at a later stage, the shipowner who is also the carrier in the bill of lading would look favourably to the incorporation of the demurrage clause into the bill of lading.[34] Leaving aside the rationale behind the use of incorporation clauses, one may find it hard to justify imposition on the holder of the responsibility for loading port demurrage, over which he/she has no control. For the same reason, it may be equally hard to accept the holder's liability for discharge port demurrage in its entirety where he/she is not the receiver of the entire cargo, or where demurrage is incurred by the delay during the discharge of someone else's cargo. Nonetheless, as will be explained below, holders in any of these circumstances may be liable for demurrage, if their respective bills of lading incorporate the relevant charterparty demurrage provision, and if there is no express provision in their bill of lading providing the contrary. For present purposes, the holder's liability for the loading port demurrage will be examined first. Thereafter, the question will be the extent to which the holder could avoid demurrage incurred during the loading or discharge of the entire cargo.

a. Liabilities of the Cargo Interests for Demurrage Incurred at the Loading Port

As is clear from US and English judicial decisions, transferees of bills of lading can be liable for loading port demurrage pursuant to an incorporated charterparty demurrage clause, which does not place the liability exclusively upon the

[32] See McKearn (n 7) 143, 144, where a similar view was taken.

[33] A similar line of reasoning was also adopted in *The Miramar* [1984] AC 676 (HL); *Gullischen v Stewart Brothers* (1883) LR 13 QBD 317; and *Fidelitas Shipping v V/O Exportchleb* [1963] 2 Lloyd's Rep 113, 124 (CA).

[34] See, for instance, *The Nanfri*, where the shipowner took such a measure in order to compel the charterer to pay the full charter hire, [1979] AC 757, 776 (HL).

charterer.[35] This result can seem harsh for those transferees who have, in most cases, no control over the loading operations. In order to remove this burden, it has been suggested that the incorporated charterparty clauses, providing for loading port demurrage, be rendered ineffective on the grounds that they are repugnant to the nature of bills of lading.[36] Despite the force of this argument, demurrage provisions appear to be one of the most apposite terms in the context of bills of lading,[37] as they are related to loading and discharging operations of the cargo covered thereunder. Although demurrage may be accrued during the operations over which the holder has no control, this fact is, of itself, insufficient to render demurrage clauses inapposite.

However, it may be argued that an incorporated charterparty provision regarding the loading port demurrage can be treated as insensible and inapplicable in the bill of lading context, where the bill of lading is no longer in the hands of the shipper. This proposition can be justified on three main grounds. First, demurrage liability for loading port demurrage cannot reasonably be anticipated by the transferees of bills of lading, who pay for these transferable instruments at their face value.[38] Secondly, transferees cannot be taken to have intended to assume such an onerous and unforeseeable liability when the bill of lading does not contain an express reference to the charterparty demurrage clause.[39] Thirdly, when interpreting a contractual provision, the courts presume that the parties to the contract did not intend the terms to operate in an unreasonable and commercially nonsensical way. On interpreting the incorporation clause in light of these arguments, one may therefore conclude that charterparty provisions imposing loading port demurrage on the transferees must be treated as 'insensible'[40] and inapplicable in the bill of lading context.

There are two difficulties with this interpretation. The first comes with the operation of the English Carriage of Goods by Sea Act (COGSA) 1992: a bill of lading holder, to whom the bill of lading has been transferred, can perfectly well be subject to liabilities under the contract, as if he/she had been an original party to that contract.[41] To put it another way, for the transfer of liability from the shipper to the subsequent holders, COGSA does not require the holder to make any

[35] For English law, see *Gray v Carr* (1870–1871) LR 6 QB 522. For US law, see *The Lake Galera* 1932 AMC 1228 (2d Cir 1932); *The Hans Maersk* 266 F 806, 808 (2d Cir 1920). Some US judicial decisions further suggest that despite the incorporation of a demurrage clause which embraces both loading and discharge demurrage, liability of the consignee for the loading demurrage is nevertheless secondary, see *Yone Suzuki et al v Central Argentine Railway Limited* 1928 AMC 1521, 1543 (2d Cir 1928).

[36] See Davies (n 9) 327, 330.

[37] For a similar view, see *Fidelitas Shipping Co v V/O Exportchleb* [1963] 2 Lloyd's Rep 113, 124, per Pearson LJ.

[38] A similar line was also taken by Lord Diplock in *The Miramar* [1984] AC 676.

[39] For English law, see ibid. For US law, see Restatement (Second) On Contracts, §203(a), where it is dictated that contracts be given reasonable meaning.

[40] For English law, see *The Varenna* [1984] QB 599. For US law, see *Encyclopaedia Britannica Inc v SS Hong Kong Producer* 422 F 2d 7, 14 (2d Cir 1969).

[41] See COGSA s 3(1).

contribution to the occurrence of the liability.[42] Provided that the holder takes a step, as defined under COGSA section 3(1), to enforce the contract of carriage, he/she is deemed to have assumed all liabilities of the original shipper, including liability for loading port demurrage and dangerous cargo. Given that the transfer of liability under COGSA is not conditional upon personal liability, it is difficult to argue that application of a charterparty clause providing for loading port demurrage to the holder is 'unreasonable' and 'commercially nonsensical'. The second difficulty comes with the decision in *The Eems Solar*.[43] There, the incorporated charterparty clause provided that the cargo would be stowed by the charterers 'free of any risk, liability and expense whatsoever to the Owners'. The bill of lading holder brought a cargo claim against the carrier for cargo damage that occurred during stowage. Against the holder, the carrier was entitled to invoke the incorporated clause, which was held applicable in the bill of lading context, although the holder had no control over the stowage operations which took place at the port of loading.

Consequently, it would appear that an incorporated charterparty clause providing for loading port demurrage would be equally applicable to the holders on the satisfaction of two conditions: the bill of lading does not contain any provision to the contrary, and the wording of the clause has sufficient breadth for application to the holder. The same conclusion will also follow in US law.[44] The shipowner who is also the carrier under the bill of lading can alternatively turn to the charterer for recovery of these sums.[45] The shipowner's right to recovery from the charterer can, however, be subject to a charterparty cesser clause: provided that the shipowner has a right to lien on the cargo which is commensature with these liabilities, a properly worded cesser clause will have the effect of releasing the charterer from liability for these sums.[46]

[42] ibid.

[43] *The Eems Solar* [2013] 2 Lloyd's Rep 487. See also *Gray v Carr*, where the Court allowed application of the charterparty clause providing for loading port demurrage to the bill of lading holder. There, the bill of lading made a specific reference to the demurrage clause in the charterparty, and the charterparty demurrage clause only provided for loading port demurrage. In order to give effect to the incorporation clause that referred to demurrage specifically, the charterparty clause providing for demurrage had to be treated as applicable to the holder. This decision must be treated with caution, however, following the decision in *The Miramar* [1984] AC 676 (HL), at 686 per Lord Diplock.

[44] *Yone Suzuki v Central Argentine Railway Ltd* 1928 AMC 1521 (2d Cir 1928); *The Lake Galera* 60 F 2d 876, 879 (2d Cir 1932).

[45] Under US law, the courts do not interpret cesser clauses in such a way as to release the charterers from liabilities arising before the issue of the bill of lading, such as demurrage at the loading port and dead-freight. Even though a commensurate lien with those liabilities is provided to the shipowner, the charterer remains primarily liable for these charges. See *Yone Suzuki v Central Argentine Railway Ltd* 1928 AMC 1521 (2d Cir 1928); *The Marpesia* 292 F 957, 973 (2d Cir 1923). Under English law, the courts tend to give the cesser clause a retrospective effect save that the shipowner has the right to assert lien which is coextensive with these liabilities and the wording of the cesser clause allows such an interpretation. See *Fidelitas Shipping Co v V/O Exportchleb* [1963] 2 Lloyd's Rep 113.

[46] For US law, see *Crossman v Burrill* 179 US 100 (US 1900). For English law, see *Fidelitas Shipping Co v V/O Exportchleb* [1963] 2 Lloyd's Rep 113.

b. Liabilities of the Cargo Interests for the Total Amount of Demurrage

Could demurrage for loading or discharge of the entire cargo be imposed on a holder, where his or her bill of lading only covers part of the goods carried on board the vessel, or where the delay is not attributable to loading or discharging of his or her cargo? As a solution to these problems, it can be argued that every bill of lading holder should be liable for demurrage in proportion to (a) the amount of the cargo covered under his or her respective bill of lading and (b) their contribution to any delay in the loading or discharge operations.

When this line of thinking is followed, a demurrage clause providing for a fixed rate for the delay in loading and discharge operations of the entire cargo is evidently repugnant to the bill of lading that covers only part of the cargo. Nonetheless, in *Porteus v Watney*, the Court of Appeal took the view that the holder was liable for demurrage incurred throughout the discharge of the entire cargo. This imposition of liability was rather harsh in that the holder's bill of lading covered only part of the goods carried aboard the vessel and the delay was due to the failure of other holders.[47] The main reason for the Court to hold the bill of lading holder liable for the full amount of demurrage due under the charterparty was that the incorporated charterparty demurrage clause merely provided a daily rate. Given the rate of demurrage, the Court refused to divide the total amount of the incurred demurrage between the individual holders, either in proportion to the part of cargo covered under their respective bills of lading or on the basis of the rate of their contribution to the delay. Such apportionment of liability between the holders can now be achieved under the Civil Liability (Contribution) Act 1978.[48]

The decision in *Porteus v Watney* must be treated with caution following the decision in *The Miramar*. Lord Diplock in *The Miramar* took the view that the decision in *Porteus v Watney* would have been decided differently, had it been tried 'in the last two or three decades'.[49] Against this backdrop, as with the charterparty freight provisions providing for lump-sum freight, provisions imposing liability for demurrage for the entire cargo should be inapplicable to a bill of lading that covers only part of that cargo. A holder of this type of a bill of lading should not be taken to have intended to assume such a disproportionate and unforeseeable liability. For this reason, these provisions should be treated as 'insensible' and inapplicable in the case of such a bill of lading.

Where the incorporated charterparty provision contains a fixed rate based on the weight of the cargo, it is clear that no difficulties arise in applying such a provision to a bill of lading that covers only part of the cargo:[50] in such cases, the demurrage liability will be calculated in proportion to the amount of cargo

[47] See (1877–78) LR 3 QBD 534.

[48] See Treitel and Reynolds (n 8) para 30-038.

[49] *The Miramar* [1984] AC 676 (HL), at 686 per Lord Diplock.

[50] See *Fry v Chartered Mercantile Bank of India* (1866) LR 1 CP 689, where a similar approach was taken in the presence of an incorporated freight provision, which provided a freight rate per ton.

covered by the bill of lading. Under US law, this method was adopted in *United States of America v Lamborn & Co.*[51] There, the holder was held liable for the amount of demurrage, which was in proportion to the weight of the cargo covered under his or her bill of lading on the grounds that the incorporated demurrage clause provided a rate to that effect.[52]

Even though a demurrage clause that contains a fixed rate per ton could ease the hardship to some extent, it will not protect the transferees of bills of lading against the demurrage charges arising from a delay that is not attributable to them. Nevertheless, unlike the lump-sum demurrage, a demurrage provision does not seem to run counter to bills of lading that cover only some part of the whole cargo carried aboard the vessel.

c. Lien for Demurrage

With respect to the carriers' right to lien for the incurred demurrage at the loading and/or discharge ports, the legal position in both jurisdictions would appear to be similar.[53] In both jurisdictions, carriers are entitled to lien the cargo for the incurred demurrage, where a lien clause to that effect is incorporated into the holder's bill of lading.[54] However, carriers' right to lien cannot be exercised pursuant to the incorporated charterparty lien clause in the case of an inconsistent lien provision expressly provided in the bill of lading.[55] In evaluating consistency between the incorporated and express lien clauses in bills of lading, the courts in both jurisdictions usually take the view that repugnancy exists only where there is an apparent contradiction between these two clauses. Therefore, where the express lien clause in the bill of lading is restrictive, as compared to the incorporated charterparty lien clause, the courts tend to construe these provisions as a whole.[56] As an example, if a charterparty lien clause refers to lien for freight, demurrage and dead freight, and a bill of lading provision merely talks of the right to lien for freight, the carrier's right to lien will also cover claims for demurrage and dead freight.[57]

Unlike the imposition of an *in personam* demurrage liability on the holders either for the loading port demurrage or for the full amount of demurrage, it is justifiable to give carriers the right to exercise lien over the holder's cargo for such demurrage. Lien provisions merely function as a security, and they do not have

[51] See 1932 AMC 1228 (2d Cir 1932).

[52] For US law, see *United States of America v Lamborn & Co* 1932 AMC 1228 (2d Cir 1932).

[53] Regarding liens for demurrage, see *Fidelitas Shipping Co v V/O Exportchleb* [1963] 2 Lloyd's Rep 113 (CA) for English law. For US law, see *O'Connel v One Thousand and Two Bales of Sisal Hemp* 75 F 408, 410 (DCAla 1896).

[54] ibid.

[55] For the decisions that were discussed in examining the consistency of lien provisions for unpaid freight can also be applied to these cases by way of analogy, see n 26.

[56] For English law, see *Fidelitas Shipping Co v V/O Exportchleb* [1963] 2 Lloyd's Rep 113 (CA). For US law, see *The Robin Gray* 1933 AMC 766 (2d Cir 1933) where it was stated that the bill of lading would incorporate only charterparty clauses that were not expressly provided for in the bill of lading.

[57] ibid.

any effect on the substantive rights of the parties.[58] For this reason, incorporated lien provisions—the application of which may give carriers the right to lien the cargo even for such extensive sums—is not repugnant to bills of lading. To remove the harshness of the operation of lien clauses, the solution is in the hands of the potential bill of lading holder. It will be in his or her best interests to take precautionary measures in their respective sale contracts: to require tender for payment of a bill of lading which contains a freight-prepaid stamp and a notation that all loading charges have been paid.[59]

iv. Cesser Clauses

Cesser clauses are designed to release charterers from payment of sums due under the charterparty in return for providing shipowners the right to lien the cargo that is 'commensurate' with the charterers' liability for payment.[60] It would appear that cesser clauses are introduced into charterparties mainly because charterers do not wish the costs arising at the discharge port to diminish their profits.[61] Since these parties seldom retain the title to goods during their transit, they usually cannot control the charges incurred at the discharge port. To avoid payment of such charges and anticipate the costs of carriage, they typically seek to insert a cesser clause into their charterparties.

In the context of bills of lading, difficulties arise when this clause is sought to be made applicable *mutatis mutandis* to the holders of bills of lading by reason of the incorporation clause. If the cesser clause were to be read as such in this context, this would have the effect of relieving the holders of all charges due under the bill of lading. Included in these charges are those relating to freight, loading and discharge port demurrage. Undoubtedly, such an extensive reading of the cesser clause would defeat the main purpose of the incorporation clauses. Perhaps for this reason, the courts in both jurisdictions have repeatedly rendered these clauses ineffective in bills of lading.

Hence, in *Gullischen v Stewart Brothers*,[62] the English Court refused to allow the holder to rely on the cesser clause incorporated into the charterparty. There, the holder was also the charterer of the incorporated charterparty. While accepting that this clause releases the charterer from liabilities, the Court held this party responsible for the charges under the bill of lading, given that he was also the cargo recipient. Designed to release charterers, but not the holders, from liability, the cesser clause was held to be not 'sensible' in the bill of lading context. US courts have also adopted a similar approach. Following *Gullischen v Stewart*

[58] See *Miramar Maritime Corporation v Holborn Oil Trading Ltd* [1984] AC 676 (HL). See also *The Spiros C* [2000] 2 Lloyd's Rep 319, 333 (CA). The position is the same under US law; see *Crossman v Burrill* 179 US 100 (US 1900).

[59] For a similar view, see MA Miller, 'Cesser Clauses' (2001) 26 *Tulane Maritime Law Journal* 85.

[60] For English law, see *Fidelitas Shipping Co v V/O Exportchleb* [1963] 2 Lloyd's Rep 113. For US law, see *Crossman v Burrill* 179 US 100 (US 1900).

[61] See Miller (n 59) 72.

[62] (1883–84) LR 13 QBD 317.

Brothers, the US Court of Appeal for the Second Circuit in *Yone Suzuki v Central Argentine Railway Ltd*[63] also did not allow the consignees to avail themselves of the charterparty cesser clause. In so doing, they held the consignees liable for the incurred demurrage.

It is evident that the *Gullischen* approach is necessary in order to prevent reliance of the holders on cesser clauses. For this reason, the Courts in *Gullischen* and *Yone Suzuki* did not err in arriving at such a conclusion. Nevertheless, the pattern of reasoning adopted in *Gullischen* is no longer recognised under English and US law. If the facts, identical to those in *Gullischen*, were brought before US and English courts, the courts would decide on the issue differently.[64] This is simply because it is now accepted that the contract of carriage that governs the relations between the charterer and the shipowner is the charterparty.[65] For this reason, the bill of lading held by the cargo recipient in *Gullischen* would be treated as a mere receipt.[66] Therefore, the dispute between the litigants would be resolved on the basis of the charterparty terms.

In light of all these explanations, could it be said that charterers can be relieved of liability in the case of a cesser clause under the charterparty, even though they are also cargo recipients?[67] It is clear that the courts in both jurisdictions do not allow charterers to escape liability in those cases.[68] In so doing, they take the view that shipowners could not have intended to forego their rights without being provided with a sufficient and effective remedy in return.[69] For those cargo recipients who hold the bill of lading as their contract of carriage, the position is also clear: given that the rulings in *Yone Suzuki* and *Gullischen* remain unchallenged, these parties cannot rely on the cesser clause in the charterparty referred to in order to avoid payment of sums due under the bill of lading.[70] This is a justifiable outcome. To give effect to cesser clauses in bills of lading would release holders

[63] 1928 AMC 1521 (2d Cir 1928).

[64] For a similar view, see Treitel and Reynolds (n 8) para 3-037.

[65] See Chapter 1, n 57.

[66] ibid.

[67] The cases where the charterparty is superseded by bills of lading pursuant to the charterparty supersession clause must be treated differently. See Cooke et al (n 29) para 17-44 and *Oriental Maritime Pte Ltd v Ministry of Food Government of People's Republic of Bangladesh* [1982] 2 Lloyd's Rep 371.

[68] For US law, see *Yone Suzuki, et al v Central Argentine Railway Limited Gano Moore Coal Mining Company Inc* 1928 AMC 1521 (2d Cir 1928). For English law, see *The Aegis Britannic* [1987] 1 Lloyd's Rep 119.

[69] See *Clink v Radford & Co* [1891] 1 QB 625, 627, which was also referred to in *Crossman v Burrill* 179 US 100 (US 1900). Some scholars, however, argue that a cesser clause can work well with the express bill of lading terms. See G Gilmore and C Black, *Law of Admiralty*, 2nd edn (Mineola, NY, Foundation Press, 1975) 221 and Treitel and Reynolds (n 8) para 3-041.

[70] This proposition can also be supported when the wording of the traditional and modern cesser clauses is taken into account. The traditional cesser clauses usually read 'charterer's liability under this charterparty to cease on the cargo being loaded, the owners having a lien on the cargo for the freight and demurrage'. See *Clink v Radford & Co* [1891] 1 QB 625. For modern cesser provisions, see clause 8 of Gencon Charterparty of 1976.

from all payment obligations therein. This would defeat one key objective of shipowners in introducing incorporation clauses: to be able to turn to the holder for the recovery of sums due under the charterparty. Thus, to keep incorporation clauses meaningful and effective, cesser clauses are jettisoned from the bill of lading for inconsistency.

v. Arbitration Clauses

Where the incorporated arbitration clause refers to disputes arising under the 'charterparty' or under the 'contract', the issue of whether it is consistent with the 'bill of lading' must be addressed before taking the step to decide applicability of such provisions to the holders. The question of consistency also arises in the case of incorporated charterparty clauses providing for arbitration of disputes between 'shipowners' and 'charterers'. The main question is: does such an arbitration wording make any sense under bills of lading, to which the holders and the carriers are parties? To resolve this issue, US and English courts have introduced the rules of manipulation,[71] which decide the extent to which such wording can be adapted to bills of lading and applied, *mutatis mutandis*, to the holders. Consequently, where the rules do not permit verbal manipulation of particular arbitration wording, the arbitration clause in that form will be inconsistent and ineffective in the bill of lading context.[72]

English courts tend to give effect to arbitration clauses, unless there is a clear inconsistency between the incorporated arbitration clause and bill of lading provisions. Hence, in *The Nerano*,[73] the Court readily reconciled an incorporated charterparty clause providing for London arbitration and a bill of lading clause referring to English law and jurisdiction.[74] The main reason for not treating these provisions as inconsistent with each other was the supervisory nature of the English courts over London arbitration proceedings. Accordingly, the carrier was held to have the right to arbitrate the dispute by virtue of the arbitration clause, regardless of the express jurisdiction clause in the bill of lading.

If the facts, identical to those in *The Nerano*, were brought before US courts, the result would probably be the same. When the courts have to choose between jurisdiction and arbitration clauses, they give effect to the arbitration clause due to the federal policy favouring arbitration.[75] The rule of consistency, which

[71] See Chapter 3.

[72] Such circumstances only arise under US law. Under English law the rules of manipulation do not have such significance in the case of arbitration clauses. For the arbitration clauses to be incorporated, English law requires specific reference to arbitration in the incorporation clauses, and this specific reference to arbitration automatically triggers manipulation. See Chapter 3.

[73] The Nerano [1996] 1 Lloyd's Rep 1.

[74] ibid.

[75] See *Paramedics Electromedicina Comercial Ltd v GE Med Sys Info Tech Inc* 369 F 3d 645, 654 (2d Cir 2004); *Moses H Cone Memorial Hospital v Mercury Construction Corp* 460 US 1, 24 (US 1983); *FD Import & Export Corp v M/V Reefer Sun* 2003 AMC 60, 63 (SDNY 2002).

gives effect to the express bill of lading terms as opposed to the inconsistent charterparty provisions, does not, therefore, find any room for application in such cases. Nonetheless, when the bill of lading contains both express and incorporated arbitration clauses that conflict with each other, the consistency test will come into play, to the effect that the arbitration clause expressly provided in the bill of lading will prevail over an incorporated arbitration clause.

For the sake of completeness, it must be noted that consistency of the incorporated arbitration clauses should also be discussed by reference to the Conventions, either of which may be applicable to bills of lading by force of law. This will be discussed below.[76]

B. Where do These Rules Take Us?

The discussions have shown that the rule of consistency comes into play where the conflict derives from an incorporated charterparty, and where the bill of lading does not explicitly stipulate whether the incorporated or express terms will prevail. Although not inconsistent with an express bill of lading term, a previously incorporated charterparty clause can be jettisoned from the bill of lading where its application does not make any sense in the bill of lading context.

With a view to incorporating consistent provisions into the bill of lading, US and English courts interpret the incorporation clauses to decide which particular charterparty provisions can be carried across to the bill of lading.[77] For the same purpose, the courts have devised the rules of manipulation in order to decide whether the incorporated charterparty clause should be adapted to the bill of lading. As a last remaining hurdle, the courts have also to apply the consistency test to rule out the repugnant charterparty clauses, which have somehow been incorporated through the words of incorporation. Nonetheless, unlike the other rules of incorporation, the consistency test comprises less technical and semantic considerations, for it allows the courts to assess the overall workability of the incorporated charterparty clauses in the bill of lading. Also, it gives the courts the opportunity to once again consider the effects of applying a particular charterparty clause to a third-party bill of lading holder, and to decide whether to do this.

In construing the incorporated charterparty clauses in the bill of lading context, consideration must also be given to the Conventions. Given that almost all bills of lading are now governed by the Hague or the Hague-Visby Rules, our focus will be on the inconsistency of the incorporated charterparty clauses with these sets of rules. Where appropriate, reference will also be made to the Hamburg and the Rotterdam Rules.

[76] See Section II.

[77] See Chapter 3.

II. Consistency of the Provisions with the Hague and the Hague-Visby Rules

A. Historical Background to the Conventions

Before addressing the issue of consistency, it is first necessary to discuss briefly the historic reasons for adopting the Conventions. While it is common for charterparties to be concluded between parties who have equal or similar bargaining power, the terms of carriage under the bill of lading cannot be negotiated between the subsequent holder and the carrier.[78] Even though there is a chance for shippers to negotiate with carriers, it is not always possible to see a balance between the bargaining positions of these parties.[79] During the eighteenth and nineteenth centuries, it was due to this inequality that contractual positions of the holders were adversely affected by the carriers' exclusion clauses, which were designed to relieve carriers of all liabilities whatsoever.[80] Throughout this period, English shipowners were dominant in international transport, and English courts were upholding the carriers' exclusion clauses.[81] Across the Atlantic, the international trade activities of US merchants were mainly carried out with vessels furnished by English shipowners.[82] Evidently, exclusion clauses were detrimental to US cargo interests, who constituted the majority of the US shipping market,[83] and to the development of this particular sector.[84]

In the late nineteenth century, US courts thus started to invalidate exclusion clauses.[85] The exclusion clauses were valid under English law, and English courts upheld the carriers' exclusion clauses in cargo disputes.[86] To keep their exclusion clauses effective, shipowners introduced exclusive jurisdiction clauses into bills of lading in order to designate the courts that were considered to be more receptive

[78] ibid.

[79] For the imbalance in bargaining power between the shipper and the carrier in the formation of the bill of lading terms, see *The Ardennes* [1951] KB 55, 59–60. At present, sophisticated shippers with equal bargaining power make arrangements with carriers other than in the form of charterparties.

[80] See R Force et al, *Admiralty and Maritime Law*, vol 1 (Washington, DC, Beard Books, 2005) 1, and Reynolds (n 4) 16.

[81] See CW O'Hare, 'Cargo Dispute Resolution and the Hamburg Rules' (1980) 29(2–3) *LQR* 219–20.

[82] ibid. See also Reynolds (n 4) 18.

[83] Force et al (n 80) 1.

[84] ibid.

[85] See SM Denning, 'Choice of Forum Clauses in Bills of Lading' (1970–1971) 2 *Journal of Maritime Law and Commerce* 17, 26. See also *CA Seguros Orinoco v Naviera Transpapel* CA 1988 AMC 1757, 1765 (D Puerto Rico 1988).

[86] See O'Hare (n 81) 219–20. Under the English common law of carriage of goods by sea, the 'default regime' is strict liability, and carriers' liability is subject to few exceptions. See Treitel and Reynolds (n 8) 593–95. In almost all cases, this default regime is displaced either by contract provisions or by the mandatory application of the Carriage of Goods by Sea Act ('the 1971 Act'), to which the Hague-Visby Rules are scheduled.

to the exclusion clauses.[87] These tactical manoeuvres by shipowners led US courts not only to take a hostile approach towards forum selection clauses,[88] but also to regard the forum selection clauses as a means to evade American public policy.[89] This hostility remained predominant until the twentieth century.[90]

With a view to protecting American cargo interests and balancing the competing interests of carriers and cargo holders, the United States enacted the Harter Act in 1893,[91] whereby carriers were prohibited from contracting out their liabilities where the loss or damage was caused by their failure to exercise due diligence in making the vessel seaworthy or in taking care of the cargo.[92] Following the Harter Act, similar legislation for the protection of cargo interests was also enacted in many countries such as Australia, Canada and New Zealand, where the international trade activities were mainly dependent upon vessels furnished by English shipowners.[93] In countries where cargo interests prevailed, carriers' forum selection clauses were struck down due to public policy considerations.[94] There were thus differing national policies around the world. This was obviously not in the interests of carriers: they were faced with different sea carriage rules in every country where they did business.[95]

i. The Hague Rules

Since this fragmented cargo liability was to the detriment of both carriers and cargo interests, there was a pressing need to have an international sea carriage Convention for the smooth running of international trade.[96] In search of a global solution for the reconciliation of conflicting interests of carriers and cargo interests, lengthy negotiations took place under the auspices of the International Law Association and the Comité Maritime International. Eventually, the International Convention for the Unification of the Rules Relating to Bills of Lading, commonly

[87] O'Hare (n 81) 220.

[88] See Denning (n 85) 17.

[89] See JC Sweeney, 'UNCITRAL Draft Convention on Carriage of Goods by Sea' (1975–1976) 7 *Journal of Maritime Law and Commerce* 69, 71 and O'Hare (n 81) 220.

[90] See *M/S Bremen v Zapata Off-Shore Co* 407 US 1 (US 1972).

[91] See 46 USC §§190–91. The Harter Act 1893 remains in force and is still applicable where the US Carriage of Goods by Sea Act 1936 ('the 1936 Act') does not operate in bills of lading. The 1936 Act also applies to contracts for the carriage of goods between US ports and to the period when the goods are in the custody of a carrier before loading and after discharge of the cargo, see 46 USC §1312 and §1307. See also Force et al (n 80) 20–22 and *Wemhoener Pressen v Ceres Marine Terminals Inc* 5 F 3d 734, 739 (4th Cir 1993). In fact, the first legislation in the United States relating to this topic was the Fire Statute 1851, which was designed to give the common carrier a restricted right to exclude its liability for losses arising from fire, JC Moore, 'The Hamburg Rules' (1978–1979) 10 *Journal of Maritime Law and Commerce* 2.

[92] See Force et al (n 80) 1. See also Reynolds (n 4) 18.

[93] Reynolds (n 4) 22; O'Hare (n 81) 220–21; Sweeney (n 89) 69, 70.

[94] A good illustration of this is the legal position under US law prior to the US Supreme Court decision in *Vimar Seguros y Reaseguros v M/V Sky Reefer* 1995 AMC 1817 (US 1995).

[95] P Myburgh, 'Uniformity or Unilateralism in the Law of Carriage of Goods by Sea?' (2000) 31(2) *Victoria University of Wellington Law Review* 355, 359.

[96] O'Hare (n 81) 220–21.

referred to as the Hague Rules, was promulgated in 1924. The Hague Rules were the first international Convention relating to the standardisation of the laws governing international carriage of goods by sea, and they were widely accepted.[97] The rules can be considered a great success.[98] They provided a minimum and non-derogatory protection for cargo interests[99] and struck a balance between the conflicting interests of carriers and cargo interests. The United Kingdom implemented the Hague Rules through the enactment of the Carriage of Goods by Sea Act 1924.[100]

ii. The Hague-Visby Rules

A number of shortcomings in the rules were observed over the years. The particular problems encountered were in respect of the package and unit limitation, the legal position of carriers' servants and agents towards cargo interests, the evidentiary functions of bills of lading and the scope of the application of the rules.[101] The rules were revised by the Visby Protocol in 1968, and following this revision, became the Hague-Visby Rules.[102] While the United Kingdom implemented these rules within its Carriage of Goods by Sea Act 1971 ('the 1971 Act'),[103] the United States enacted its own Carriage of Goods by Sea Act in 1936 ('the 1936 Act'), which embodies the Hague Rules with some alterations.[104] Although important, the changes brought about by the Visby Protocol were limited: a number of crucial issues, including the liabilities of actual carriers and independent contractors,[105] non-contractual claims of cargo interests and through carriage, were again not covered.[106] Some countries were dissatisfied with this simplistic approach, and the

[97] At the time of their promulgation, the rules were highly criticised, most notably in the UK and the USA. See M Sturley, 'Changing Liability Rules and Marine Insurance: Conflicting Empirical Arguments about Hague, Visby and Hamburg in a Vacuum of Empirical Evidence' (1993) 24(1) *Journal of Maritime Law and Commerce* 120.

[98] A Diamond, 'The Hague-Visby Rules' (1978) 2 *Lloyd's Maritime and Commercial Law Quarterly* 225, 226.

[99] By virtue of Art I(b) of the Hague Rules, the mandatory application of the rules is confined to 'bills of lading or any similar document of title'.

[100] Although the Hague Rules officially entered into force in 1931, the rules came into effect in the United Kingdom through the enactment of the Carriage of Goods by Sea Act 1924. See Treitel and Reynolds (n 8) 625–26.

[101] Diamond (n 98) 228–31.

[102] The limitation amount provided under the package and unit limitation provision of the Hague-Visby Rules was later replaced by the Protocol signed in Brussels in 1979 ('the SDR Protocol'). Under this protocol, the limitation was to be calculated on the basis of Special Drawing Rights, determined by the International Monetary Fund.

[103] Reynolds (n 4) 18.

[104] Force et al (n 80) 2–3.

[105] See Art IV*bis* (2), which enables the carrier's servants and agents (not being an independent contractor) to avail themselves of the defences and limits of liability which the carrier is entitled to invoke under the rules.

[106] Diamond (n 98) 264.

Hague-Visby Rules attracted criticism for being unsatisfactory in accommodating the needs of modern trade.[107]

iii. The Hamburg Rules

The negative responses to the Hague-Visby Rules largely came from developing countries, where the rules were believed to tip the balance in favour of carriers.[108] This prompted a search for a Convention affording more protection to cargo interests.[109] Shortly afterwards, steps were taken under the auspices of the United Nations Commission on International Trade Law (UNCITRAL) for a new carriage Convention. After the drafting process, which, some authors thought, lacked the necessary discussions over the empirical analysis of shipping and trade practice,[110] the Hamburg Rules were adopted in 1978.

The Hamburg Rules provide for a more comprehensive set of rules allocating the risk of loss of or damage to cargo between cargo interests and carriers, as well as setting out a liability regime based on presumed carrier fault or negligence.[111] The Hamburg Rules appear to be favourable to cargo interests,[112] although some provisions in the rules are to the carriers' advantage.[113] A brief look at the Hamburg Rules suggests an improvement over the Hague and the Hague-Visby Rules in some respects. This can perhaps be best illustrated by reference to one of the main shortcomings of the Hague and the Hague-Visby Rules: the well-known actual carrier problem. Unlike the Hague and Hague-Visby Rules, the Hamburg Rules provide that all the provisions governing the responsibility of contractual carriers would also apply to actual carriers for the parts of the voyage that they actually performed.[114] One of the other important advances of the

[107] See Sweeney (n 89) 69, 74.

[108] Reynolds (n 4) 27–29.

[109] DA Werth, 'The Hamburg Rules Revisited—A Look at US Options' (1991) 22(1) *Journal of Maritime Law and Commerce* 63, 64.

[110] W Tetley, 'The Hamburg Rules—A Commentary' [1979] *Lloyd's Maritime and Commercial Law Quarterly* 1, 4.

[111] The Hamburg Rules, Annex ('principle of presumed fault or neglect'). In contrast, the Hague and the Hague-Visby Rules provide rules on burden of proof which are applicable in limited circumstances.

[112] The most striking provisions favourable to cargo interests are, inter alia, those relating to the abolition of error in navigation (Art 5.1), damages for delay (Arts 5.2 and 6.1.b), extended time bar (Art 20.1), limitation of the carriers' rights to enforce their forum selection clauses against cargo interests (Arts 21 and 22), extension of carriers' scope of liability to cover live animals (Art 1.5) and all types of transport documents excluding charterparties (Arts 1.6, 2.1 and 18), and making the carrier's obligation as to seaworthiness a continuous duty (Art 5.1).

[113] Some of the provisions favourable to carriers are, inter alia, those relating to the extension of the scope of the rules to cover non-contractual claims against carriers and their servants and agents (Art 7.1 and 7.2), the almost unbreakable limitation of liability in favour of carriers and their servants (Art 8.1 and 8.2) and the imposition of the burden of proof on cargo claimants in the case of fire claims (Art 5.4).

[114] Articles 1.2 and 10 of the Hamburg Rules. As with the Hague and Hague-Visby Rules, the Hamburg Rules are silent on the issue of independent contractors. Nonetheless, a brief reading of Art 7(2) of the rules suggests that independent contractors are left outside the protective sphere of the

Hamburg Rules was the express provision on through transport. The Hague and Hague-Visby Rules had no provisions on the effect of transhipment clauses seeking to relieve carriers of liability after transhipment. Such transhipment clauses would be invalid under the Hamburg Rules if the name of the on-carrier were not recorded in the transport document.[115]

As with the Hague and Hague-Visby Rules, the Hamburg Rules were not free from controversy: the latter rules received even more criticism, especially from the major shipping and trading nations, thereby failing to provide a widely accepted replacement for the Hague and the Hague-Visby Rules. A variety of reasons lurked behind the objections: the rules were believed to tip the balance too much in favour of cargo interests, leaving carriers with more risks[116] and higher carriers' insurance[117] premiums.[118] Also, the changes were significant, and they thus required not just an overhaul of carriers' liability by the national courts, but also the painstaking process of adapting trade, shipping and insurance practices to the new circumstances.[119] Another point of criticism was that the Hamburg Rules envisaged a severe limitation to carriers' rights to enforce their forum selection clauses under transport documents on cargo interests. In many jurisdictions where parties were traditionally allowed to designate the forum for resolution of their disputes,[120] this limitation was also highly objectionable. Finally, the Hamburg Rules were intensely criticised for not reflecting true commercial interests and for being driven by political motives.[121]

The Hamburg Rules aim at minimising the inequalities between the parties' bargaining powers. Given that the Hamburg Rules depart from the Hague and Hague-Visby Rules in many key aspects, they have not been attractive to those jurisdictions the case law of which has largely been developed under the Hague

Hamburg Rules. The provision enables the servants and agents of carriers to rely on limitations and defences in the rules, provided that they prove that they acted within the scope of their 'employment'.

[115] Article 11 of the Hamburg Rules.

[116] As an example, see the wording under Art 5.1 of the Hamburg Rules, which would appear to provide a regime close to strict liability despite the express mention of the rule of presumed carrier fault or negligence. Reynolds (n 4) 31. In contrast, some commentators took the view that adoption of the Hamburg Rules would have the effect of decreasing the carriers' liability. Tetley (n 110) 17.

[117] If carriers are also shipowners, they normally obtain indemnity cover from a Protection and Indemnity (P&I) Club in order to protect themselves against cargo liabilities arising from carriage of goods on their vessels.

[118] This so-called 'insurance argument' does not actually provide a solid base for choosing the preferable set of rules from the carriers' and cargo interests' perspectives. This is particularly because freight rates are likely to increase as the carriers pay higher insurance premiums. For a thorough analysis of the impact of changing liability rules on insurance, see Sturley (n 97) 119 *et seq*.

[119] Reynolds (n 4) 32.

[120] This is the case under English law; see *The El Amria* [1981] 2 Lloyd's Rep 119 (CA), where it was held that English courts would enforce the foreign jurisdiction clauses unless there were strong reasons for not doing so. See also *The Eleftheria* [1969] 1 Lloyd's Rep 237 and *Donohue v Armco* [2002] 1 Lloyd's Rep 425 (HL).

[121] DC Frederick, 'Political Participation and Legal Reform in the International Maritime Rulemaking Process: From the Hague Rules to the Hamburg Rules' (1991) 22 *Journal of Maritime Law and Commerce* 82.

and Hague-Visby Rules.[122] Furthermore, the Hamburg Rules' perspective, with regard to forum selection clauses, also runs counter to the rooted traditions of some countries, including the United Kingdom, on freedom of contract.[123] It would be difficult to argue that the entry into force of the Hamburg Rules was a step towards the promotion of harmonisation and certainty. The Rules failed to replace the pre-existing Conventions, namely the Hague and Hague-Visby Rules, and therefore brought about even more fragmentation to the international carriage of goods by sea.

iv. The Rotterdam Rules

Given that the Hamburg Rules did not completely replace the Hague and Hague-Visby Rules, preparations for another Convention on the carriage of goods by sea were initiated within the Comité Maritime International (CMI) after just a short period of time.[124] At a later stage, from the beginning of the twenty-first century, the preparations continued within UNCITRAL.[125] The draft Convention, which became known as the Rotterdam Rules, was approved on 8 July 2008 and signed by a number of countries including the United States. For the rules to enter into force, they need to be ratified by at least 20 states. At the time of writing, the Rotterdam Rules have been signed by 24 states, only two of which have so far ratified them.[126]

The Rotterdam Rules cover a wide range of topics: they go beyond regulating carriers' liability, addressing notably the obligations of the shipper,[127] delivery of goods,[128] the rights of the controlling party[129] and the transfer of rights.[130] Furthermore, the rules stretch the scope of carriers' responsibility beyond tackle-to-tackle and port limits for the purposes of accommodating door-to-door carriage. Although their main ambit is sea carriage, the rules introduce the modified network solution in respect of carriage of goods prior and/or subsequent to sea carriage.[131] The rules also expand freedom of contract in international sea carriage by introducing the volume contract exception. Parties to volume contracts

[122] Reynolds (n 4) 32–33.

[123] See MF Sturley, 'Overruling Sky Reefer in the International Arena: A Preliminary Assessment of Forum Selection and Arbitration Clauses in the New UNCITRAL Transport Law Convention' (2006) 37 *Journal of Maritime Law and Commerce* 19. English law has a liberal policy towards the enforcement of forum selection clauses, and this is in conflict with Arts 21 and 22 of the Hamburg Rules, which are related to jurisdiction and arbitration.

[124] See W Tetley, 'Reform of Carriage of Goods—The UNCITRAL Draft and Senate COGSA '99, "Let's Have a Two-Track Approach"' (2003) 28 *Tulane Maritime Law Journal* 4.

[125] ibid.

[126] See Art 94 of the Rotterdam Rules.

[127] See Chapter 7 of the Rotterdam Rules. It must be noted that the existing liability regimes do contain express provisions on the liability of shippers but only in respect of dangerous goods. See Art IV/6 of the Hague and Hague-Visby Rules and Art 13 of the Hamburg Rules.

[128] Chapter 9 of the Rotterdam Rules.

[129] Chapter 10 of the Rotterdam Rules.

[130] Chapter 11 of the Rotterdam Rules.

[131] See Arts 26 and 82 of the Rotterdam Rules.

are allowed to derogate from the rules to a certain extent,[132] and these contracts are made subject to the rules as a default position.[133] This expansion of freedom of contract marked a drastic change in the attitude to harmonisation of the law governing contracts of carriage: the central concern of protecting the weak, which was the rationale behind the Hague and Hague-Visby Rules, shifted to the objective of striking a 'fair' or 'right' balance of risk between carriers and cargo interests.[134] Finally, the rules contain provisions to facilitate the use of electronic transport records,[135] adhering to the objectives originally raised in the draft instrument.[136] With a set of 96 articles, the rules are comprehensive, although the issues of freight[137] and right to suit[138] are not covered in the rules.

The Rotterdam Rules are vulnerable to the same criticisms as those that can be levelled at the Hamburg Rules. Given that various jurisdictions developed their case law under the Hague and Hague-Visby Rules, ratification of the Rotterdam Rules, which envisage drastic changes, especially in terms of the carriers' liability regime, may not seem attractive to many. Perhaps the most controversial provisions of the Rotterdam Rules are those relating to jurisdiction and arbitration, simply because they considerably hinder enforcement of forum selection clauses against cargo interests. Since this particular aspect of the Rotterdam Rules falls into conflict with the rooted liberal approaches of various jurisdictions towards choice-of-forum clauses, adoption of these provisions is rendered optional.[139]

v. *The Conventions and the Consistency Test*

The Conventions are of great significance to both carriers and holders, given that in almost all cases one of the Conventions becomes operative under bills of lading. When they apply, whether by force of law or not, and run counter to the express or integrated bill of lading provisions, the question of consistency inevitably arises. When addressing this issue, it is naïve to think that the Conventions only serve the purposes of the holder and therefore they have the effect of invalidating all provisions that are to the carrier's interest. Some provisions, such as the time bars spelled out in all Conventions, will be more favourable to the carriers when the bill of lading expressly provides a time-bar clause with a longer period. While the parties may thus have varying preferences between the Conventions and the provisions in the bill of lading, it is in their best interests to know the prevailing provision in the case of inconsistency.

[132] Parties are not allowed to derogate from 'super mandatory' rules in the Rotterdam Rules, and their right to derogate is subject to a number of formal requirements, see Art 80 of the Rotterdam Rules.

[133] Article 80 of the Rotterdam Rules.

[134] T Fujita, 'Report on UNCITRAL Convention on Contracts for the International Carriage of Goods Wholly or Partly by Sea', *CMI Yearbook 2007–2008* 277.

[135] Chapters 3 and 8 of the Rotterdam Rules.

[136] Chapter 2 of the draft instrument.

[137] Chapter 9 of the draft instrument.

[138] Chapter 13 of the draft instrument.

[139] See Art 91 of the Rotterdam Rules.

In the next section, how the identified inconsistencies are resolved under US law and English law will be explained under three main headings. First, the US and English approaches towards the resolution of the inconsistencies between the bill of lading terms and the Conventions will be discussed. In this context, the legal position under US law will be examined by reference to the US Carriage of Goods by Sea Act 1936 ('the 1936 Act'), while that under English law will be discussed by reference to the Carriage of Goods by Sea Act 1971 ('the 1971 Act'). Secondly, the issue of whether forum selection clauses are in conflict with these Conventions will be addressed. A final question will be whether the Conventions can override the express or incorporated bill of lading provisions which relieve the shipowner of the responsibilities for loading and discharge of the cargo.

B. Which Prevails?

When discussing the consistency issue, our discussions will not be confined to those charterparty provisions incorporated into the bill of lading. A closer look will also be taken at the express bill of lading terms to discuss the extent to which they can survive together with the 1971 Act and the 1936 Act. For the purposes of this analysis, it is important to start off by establishing when and the extent to which the 1936 Act and the 1971 Act could govern a bill of lading.

i. Scope of Application

In terms of its geographical scope, the 1971 Act applies by force of law,[140] where (a) the carriage is from a port in a contracting state,[141] (b) the contract contained in or evidenced by the 'bill of lading'[142] provides that the rules or the legislation of any state giving effect to them are to govern the contract,[143] or (c) the 'bill of lading'[144] is issued in a contracting state.[145] Moreover, under section 1(3) of the

140 See s 1(1)–(2) of the 1971 Act and Art X of the Hague-Visby Rules.

141 See Art X(b) of the Rules. No state other than those having formally ratified the Hague-Visby Rules should be treated as a 'Contracting State' for the purposes of the Article, see *The MSC Amsterdam* [2007] 2 Lloyd's Rep 622. The carriage need not take place between the ports of two different contracting states. It is enough for the carriage to be from a contracting state. The rules apply to such sea carriage, even if it is preceded by the carriage of goods from an inland point, see M Özdel, 'Multimodal Transport Documents in International Sale of Goods' (2012) 23(7) *International Company and Commercial Law Review* 238 *et seq*.

142 This provision must be read together with Art 1(b) of the Hague Rules, and it must be taken to mean 'bills of lading or any similar document of title'.

143 See Art X(c) of the Rules. Since the Article talks of 'any state', incorporation of the legislation of a state which is not a contracting state would suffice provided that the legislation gives effect to the whole or a substantial part of the rules, Diamond (n 98) 259. Under English law, a mere reference to 'British Law' in the bill of lading is insufficient to satisfy Art X(c), as it does not refer to the national legislation giving effect to the rules. *The Komninos S* [1991] 1 Lloyd's Rep 370. For this purpose, a reference to the 1971 Act will suffice.

144 See n 142.

145 See Art X(a) of the Hague-Visby Rules. In order for the rules to apply under this trigger, the place of issue of the bill of lading must be in a contracting state, and carriage must be between two different states. The place of shipment need not be in a contracting state.

1971 Act, the rules are applicable by force of law, where the carriage is from any port in the United Kingdom, whether or not it is between ports in two different states. If a contract of carriage contained in or evidenced by a bill of lading expressly provides that the rules shall govern the contract, this will also trigger mandatory application of the rules by virtue of section 1(6)(a) of the 1971 Act. Under section 1(6)(b) of the Act, the same is also true of a contract of carriage contained in or evidenced by a receipt which is a non-negotiable document marked as such and which expressly provides that the rules are to govern the contract as if the receipt were a bill of lading.[146] In terms of its contractual and documentary scope, the rules apply to contracts of carriage that either expressly or by implication provide for the issue of a bill of lading or any similar document of title.[147]

By virtue of Article I(c) of the Hague-Visby Rules, which are scheduled to the 1971 Act, the rules do not apply to carriage of live animals and deck cargo. The exception as to deck cargo finds room for application where the cargo is actually on deck where the contract also states that the cargo is so carried.[148] Where a contract of carriage is contained in or governed by a bill of lading or a non-negotiable receipt marked as such expressly incorporates the rules pursuant to section 1(6), the rules will have force of law even in the case of carriage of live animals or of deck cargo.[149] Finally, in terms of the carrier's scope of responsibility, the Hague-Visby Rules cover mandatorily the period from the time when the goods are loaded to the time they are discharged from the ship—a period described as 'tackle-to-tackle'.[150] Outside tackle-to-tackle, the terms of contract of carriage that have been freely negotiated find room for application. Therefore, the application of the rules can be extended by contract, although the rules will only have contractual force outside tackle-to-tackle.

The US 1936 Act contains the amended version of the Hague Rules, and it applies to every bill of lading covering goods shipped from or to the ports of the United States.[151] As with the 1971 Act, this Act is not compulsorily applicable

[146] *The European Enterprise* [1989] 2 Lloyd's Rep 185.

[147] See s 1(4) of the 1971 Act and Art I(b) of the Hague-Visby Rules. See also *Pyrene v Scindia* [1954] 2 QB 402; *The Rafaela S* [2005] 2 AC 423 (HL); *The Happy Ranger* [2002] 2 All ER (Comm) 24 (CA).

[148] *Svenska Traktor v Maritime Agencies* [1953] 2 QB 295.

[149] See s 1(7) of the 1971 Act.

[150] See Art I(e) of the Hague and Hague-Visby Rules; *Pyrene v Scindia* [1954] 2 QB 402. See also Treitel and Reynolds (n 8) para 9-131, where it is suggested that 'rules may apply as implied terms after receipt of the goods but before loading, and after discharge but before delivery or up to the time of the operation of any separate warehousing arrangements, except in so far as this result has been excluded or modified'. This view was followed by Longmore LJ in *The MSC Amsterdam* [2007] 2 Lloyd's Rep 622.

[151] See USC §30701(13) and *Steel Coils Inc v M/V Lake Marion* 2001 AMC 115 (EDLa 2001). Therefore, the parties cannot by agreement change US COGSA, where it is applicable by force of law under the bill of lading.

for the period before loading and after discharge,[152] nor is it effective by force of law in the case of deck carriage[153] or live animals.[154] Other excluded types of carriage are domestic carriage[155] and carriage between foreign ports.[156] The parties are free to make the rules applicable before loading and after discharge of the goods, as well as to those excluded types of carriage by way of incorporation.[157] In such cases, the rules incorporated have a contractual effect in the bill of lading context. For the purposes of deciding whether or not the rules have a prevailing effect over bill of lading terms, the wording of the clause paramount will be the decisive factor.[158] Saving cases where the rules are incorporated into the bill of lading that is issued for domestic carriage, whether the rules will prevail over the bill of lading terms is a matter of contract construction.[159] Leaving aside the cases of domestic carriage, it is clear on authority that the rules are merely treated as contract provisions when they are incorporated into the bill of lading, in order to cover the extended period[160] or those excluded types of carriage.[161]

With respect to incorporation of the rules into bills of lading covering the carriage of goods between domestic ports, US law is unclear as to whether the

[152] See 46 USC §30701(1)(e). See also *Royal Insurance Company of America v Orient Overseas Container Line Ltd* 2008 AMC 337 (6th Cir 2008) and S Sorkin, *Goods in Transit*, vol 1 (New York, NY, Matthew Bender, 1990) s 5.13[1][c], p 5-142.

[153] See 46 USC §30701(1)(c), where it is provided that the rules will not be applicable to the goods actually carried on deck, provided that the cargo is stated to be carried on deck. *See Royal Insurance Co v Sea-Land Service* 50 F 3d 723, 727 (9th Cir 1995) at 727. Under the Hamburg and Rotterdam Rules, deck carriage is not excluded from application. See Art 9 of the Hamburg Rules and Art 25 of the Rotterdam Rules.

[154] See ibid.

[155] See *Commonwealth Petrochemicals Inc v S/S Puerto Rico* 1979 AMC 2772, 2779 (4th Cir 1979). See also MF Sturley, *Benedict on Admiralty*, vol 2A (New York, NY, Matthew Bender, 2007) s 41, pp 5–4 and s 44, pp 5–15.

[156] See *Royal Insurance Company of America v Orient Overseas Container Line Ltd* 2008 AMC 337 340 (6th Cir 2008). See also Sorkin (n 152) s 5.13[1][c], p 5-142, quoting *FD Import & Export Corp v M/V/ Reefer Sun* 248 F Supp 2d 240 (SDNY 2002).

[157] Where the rules are not applicable by force of law, the parties are also free to incorporate only some or part of the rules. See Sorkin (n 152) s 4.02, pp 4-21 and 4-20.2. See also *The Firestone Tire & Rubber Co v Almaneces Miramar Inc* 1980 AMC 1590, 1593 (D Puerto Rico 1978).

[158] See *St Paul Fire & Marine Insurance Company v Sea-Land Service Inc* 1991 AMC 523, 526 (SDNY 1990) where the rules prevailed over the express bill of lading terms with respect to the definition of 'package', as the clause paramount provided that any bill of lading term conflicting with the 1936 Act would be null and void.

[159] See also *Foster Wheeler Energy Corp v An Ning Jiang MV* 2004 AMC 2409 (5th Cir 2004).

[160] See *The Firestone Tire & Rubber Co v Almaneces Miramar* 1980 AMC 1590, 1593 (D Puerto Rico 1978); *Hartford Fire Insurance Company v Orient Overseas Containers Lines (UK) Ltd* 2001 AMC 25, 33–34 (2d Cir 2000). Therefore, if the Harter Act governs that period and if it conflicts with the 1936 Act, the latter rules yield to the Harter Act, see *Ralston Purina Co v Barge Juneau* 1981 AMC 2829 (5th Cir 1980) and Sorkin (n 152) s 4.02, p 4-21.

[161] For deck carriage, see *Institute of London Underwriters v Sea-Land Service Inc* 881 F 2d 761 (9th Cir 1989) where it was held that the 1936 Act will not apply compulsorily, despite the fact that the clause also contemplated application of these rules to deck cargo. For carriage between foreign ports, see also Sturley (n 155) s 41, p 5-4 and s 44, p 5-15 quoting, inter alia, *Foster Wheeler Energy Corp v An Ning Jiang MV* 2004 AMC 2409 (5th Cir 2004).

incorporated rules should be given statutory or contractual force.[162] The literal meaning of the provision under section 13 of the 1936 Act suggests that statutory force be given to the rules that have been incorporated into the bill of lading.[163] It would appear that this uncertainty could hardly be removed without any alterations to the Act.

ii. The Issues of Consistency

Despite the differences between US law and English law as to when the rules have force of law, it is common ground that this issue must be addressed before taking any step to resolve inconsistencies. When the rules do have the force of law, the parties may not agree to terms that run counter to the applicable non-derogation provision under the rules. However, the parties may do so where the rules do not have a statutory force in the bill of lading. For the purposes of this assessment, Article III(8) of the Hague-Visby Rules—which are scheduled to the 1971 Act—and section 3(8) of the 1936 Act play a vital role: as non-derogation provisions, they prohibit carriers from removing or lessening their liabilities any more than is allowed under the rules. Consequently, where any of these sets of rules are operative in a bill of lading by force of law, the applicable non-derogation provision can strike out the incorporated or express bill of lading terms that purport to exclude or lessen the carrier's liability beyond the limits.[164] On the contrary, where the rules do not compulsorily apply to a bill of lading, it is clear on authority that the consistency issue will be treated within the realms of contract construction, and the question of which one prevails will not necessarily hinge on the non-derogation provisions.[165]

It must be recalled that carriers are allowed to assume further obligations and liabilities in addition to those outlined in the rules.[166] For this reason, provisions to that effect will not be struck down due to inconsistency, nor does the applicable non-derogation provision debar their application. Therefore, not every conflicting bill of lading clause will be considered as null and void. Those provisions which do not lessen or remove carriers' liability, as defined under the non-derogation provisions, will survive, even when the rules are operative under the bill of lading by force of law.

[162] Sorkin (n 152) s 5.13[1][c], p 5-142 and see also Sturley (n 155) s 42, p 5-6.

[163] See Sturley (n 155) s 42, p 5-6.

[164] For US law, see *Uniwire Trading LLC v M/V Wladyslaw Orkan* 2008 AMC 2152 (SDNY 2008) where generally the applicability of the rule enunciated under 46 USC §30701(3)(8) is discussed. For English law, see *Dairy Containers Ltd v Tasman Orient Line CV* [2004] 2 CLC 794, 800; *The Hollandia* [1983] 1 AC 565 (HL).

[165] For US law, see Sturley (n 155) s 42, p 5-7. For English law, see Cooke et al (n 29) para 85.237 At English common law, clearly drafted exclusion clauses are in principle given effect to and these clauses are not ruled out just because they are unreasonable, see *The Irbenskiy Proliv* [2005] 1 Lloyd's Rep 387. The courts may, however, limit the effects of an exclusion clause so as to avoid absurd results, considering the main objectives of the contract of carriage, see *Glynn v Margetson & Co* [1983] AC 351.

[166] See Art V of the Hague-Visby Rules and 46 USC §30701(5).

In order to see the further effects of the non-derogation provisions on bills of lading, the issues pertaining to package or unit limitation of carriers' liability must be analysed. Evidently, under both the 1971 Act and the 1936 Act, the carriers' liability for, and in relation to, goods lost or damaged during sea carriage is limited.[167] When the 1971 Act comes into operation by force of law, the carriers' exclusion clauses, which contain a lower amount of limitation than that provided under the Act, are invalidated pursuant to the non-derogation provision, Article III(8) of the Hague-Visby Rules. By section 3(8) of the 1936 Act, such clauses are also overridden.[168] However, where the incorporated or express bill of lading terms contain a higher amount of limitation, the non-derogation provisions will not bite against such terms.[169]

Under English law, Article III(8) of the Hague-Visby Rules may also have the effect of striking out time-bar clauses which contain a period within which the cargo claimant is required to commence litigation or arbitration against the carrier. Thus, where an arbitration or a jurisdiction clause contains a time bar shorter than one year, which is the minimum mandatory period envisaged under Article III(6),[170] the offending time bar is treated as invalid while the remaining part of the clause on jurisdiction or arbitration remains in effect.[171] A jurisdiction or an arbitration clause is not therefore invalidated in its entirety, regardless of the fact that the bill of lading does not expressly contemplate partial invalidation.[172] Most importantly, English courts have repeatedly taken the view that the reference to 'suit' under Article III(6) must be taken to comprise both litigation and arbitration proceedings: this is to the effect that the time bars contained in arbitration clauses are also considered to be subject to the one-year threshold spelled out under Article III(6) of the Hague-Visby Rules.[173] The leading authority for this interpretation is *The Merak*. There, the Court held that the cargo interests' claim was time barred by reason of Article III(6) of the Hague-Visby Rules, given the

[167] See USC §30701(4)(5) and the Hague-Visby Rules Art IV(5). In order for the carrier to rely on this limitation, US law established a 'fair opportunity rule' whereby carriers need to give shippers an opportunity to declare a higher value for the goods shipped. Sturley (n 155) s 166, p 16-34.

[168] For US law, see *Hanover Insurance Co v Shulman Transport Enterprises Inc* 1979 AMC 520 (1st Cir 1978). See also Sorkin (n 152) s 4.02, p 4-20.1, and see also Sturley (n 155) s 166, p 16-31. For English law, see *Svenska Traktor Aktiebolaget v Maritime Agencies (Southampton) Ltd* [1953] 2 QB 295. Also a provision that redefines 'package' for the purposes of the package unit limitation will be struck down by Art III(8) if the provision has the effect of lessening the carrier's liability more than is allowed by the Rules. See *The River Gurara* [1988] QB 610.

[169] Therefore, if the carriers introduce into the bill of lading a clause paramount incorporating the Hamburg Rules, the higher package or unit limitation under the Hamburg Rules will be valid and enforceable. For US law, see *Daval Steel Products v M/V Acadia Forest* 1988 AMC 1669 (SDNY 1988), and Sturley (n 155) s 166, p 16-31. See also 46 USC §30701(4)(5). For English law, see Art IV(5) of the 1971 Act. See also Cooke et al (n 29) para 85.412.

[170] See Art III(6) of the Hague-Visby Rules for English law. See also *The Ion* [1971] 1 Lloyd's Rep 541.

[171] For English law, see *The Ion* [1971] 1 Lloyd's Rep 541.

[172] For English law see ibid.

[173] *The Merak* [1965] P 223, 253.

cargo interests' failure to commence arbitration within 12 months of the date of discharge.[174]

Under US law, time-bar provisions providing for less than a one-year time bar are struck down by section 3(8) of the 1936 Act, given the minimum mandatory period of a one-year time bar under section 3(6) of the Act. Where the offending time bar is contained in a jurisdiction clause, parts of the clause relating to forum selection remain intact.[175] However, US courts have established an exception to this rule in favour of arbitration clauses that impose a shorter period for the commencement of arbitration proceedings. The underpinning of this exception is the well-accepted view that the reference to 'suit' in section 3(6) of the 1936 Act is not taken to cover arbitration proceedings.[176] Hence, in *Son Shipping Co v De Fosse & Tanghe*, the US Court of Appeal for the Second Circuit adopted this view when holding that the cargo interest was entitled to institute arbitration proceedings, even more than one year after the delivery of cargo.[177] Following the *Son Shipping* decision, the New York State courts have repeatedly upheld the arbitration clauses that give less than a one-year period for commencing arbitration proceedings.[178] In so doing, they have consistently taken the view that the question of whether the claim is time barred is for the arbitrators to decide when the parties agree to resolve their disputes by arbitration.[179]

As a result of these judicial opinions, it is necessary to examine the extent to which arbitral tribunals sitting in New York give effect to the arbitration clauses that provide less than a one-year time bar. In light of the leading decision in *The Eastern Saga*, it is true to say that the arbitrators are inclined to consider such clauses as inconsistent with section 3(8) of the 1936 Act, especially in the context of bills of lading.[180] Hence, the arbitrators in *The Eastern Saga* overrode the three-month time bar in the Centrocon arbitration clause, which was held to be incorporated into the bill of lading. In so doing, they clarified that application of the *Son Shipping* decision, wherein a narrow meaning ascribed to the word 'suit' in section 3(6) could not be extended to prevent cargo interests from seeking remedy against carriers within the statutory period.

A long line of arbitration awards further reveal that *Son Shipping* is also not applicable to those cases where the cargo interests have failed to institute

[174] ibid.

[175] See 46 USC §30701(3)(6). See also *Vimar Seguros y Reaseguros SA v M/V Sky Reefer* 1995 AMC 1817, 1822 (US 1995) and *Ansell Healthcare Inc v Maersk Line* 545 F Supp 2d 339, 345 (SDNY 2008), quoted in Sturley (n 155) s 163, p 16-9.

[176] See *Son Shipping Co v De Fosse & Tanghe* 1952 AMC 1931 (2d Cir 1952).

[177] ibid.

[178] See *Kurt Orban Co v S/S Clymenia* 1971 AMC 778 (SDNY 1970); *Empreza Publica v SS Yukon Mart* 1976 AMC 2235 (SDNY 1976); *Lowry & Co Inc v SS Le Moyne D'Iberville* 1966 AMC 2195 (SDNY 1966). Conversely, see *Steel Warehouse Company v Abalone Shipping* 1998 AMC 2054, 2059 (5th Cir 1998). See also Sturley (n 155) s 163, p 16-9.

[179] See the cases cited in n 178.

[180] See *The Eastern Saga* SMA no 1742 (16 September 1982) quoting *The Osrock* SMA no 654 and *The Silverhawk* SMA no 1041.

arbitration proceedings within one year of the discharge of cargo. Thus, in *The John Weyerhaeuser*, the arbitrators held that the holder's cargo claim under the bill of lading was time barred by virtue of section 3(6) of the 1936 Act, since the arbitration proceedings were brought after the statutory period.[181] Following the award, the holder in *The John Weyerhaeuser* moved for *vacatur* before the US Court, alleging that the arbitrators were not entitled to decide whether the claim was time barred. On appeal, the Second Circuit affirmed the denial of the motion by the District Court.[182] In so doing, the Court established how the *Son Shipping* decision operates: restrictive reading of the word 'suit' in section 3(6) of the 1936 Act, which was suggested in *Son Shipping*, must only be adopted in order to give parties access to arbitration, even though they have not commenced proceedings within the statutory period.[183] Consequently, while the Second Circuit took the view that parties must not be debarred from utilising arbitration proceedings, they also accepted that it is for the arbitrators to decide whether the claim is time barred.[184]

The overriding effect of the non-derogation provisions under the 1971 Act and the 1936 Act is not confined to time bars and package or unit limitations: the non-derogation provisions also strike down the incorporated or express bill of lading provisions the application of which has the effect of removing or lessening carriers' liability more than is allowed by these sets of rules. For this reason, the non-derogation provisions must have the effect of overriding not only the provisions relating to the obligations of carriers, but also those provisions that define such obligations.[185] Furthermore, the non-derogation provisions are not taken to invalidate a provision merely because it appears to be offensive: when deciding whether to invalidate a provision, the courts assess whether application of that provision has the effect of lessening or removing the carrier's liability contrary to the rules applicable by force of law.[186] It naturally follows from these arguments that the non-derogation provisions in both sets of rules can invalidate various types of contract provision in the bill of lading provided that their application has such an effect on the carrier's liability.

For these reasons, the non-derogation provisions are one of the most effective tools in the hands of those holders who seek to avoid both express and incorporated bill of lading terms. From a practical standpoint, if application of an incorporated charterparty term has the effect of lessening liability of the carrier contrary to the applicable non-derogation provision, the term will be treated as invalid. Consequently, this overriding effect of the non-derogation provisions helps

[181] See SMA no 654 (August 1971).

[182] *Office of Supply, Government of the Republic of Korea v New York Navigation Co* 1973 AMC 1238 (2d Cir 1972).

[183] 1973 AMC 1238, 1242 (2d Cir 1972).

[184] ibid.

[185] For a similar view, see Treitel and Reynolds (n 8) para 9-237.

[186] See *The Hollandia* [1982] 1 AC 565, 575 (HL) where the Court took the view that, for the choice of forum clauses to be invalidated, the carriers' reliance on the relevant provision should be proved.

promote certainty under bills of lading, and it enables the holders to anticipate, to some extent, their contractual position towards their respective carriers.

It should be noted that neither the Rotterdam Rules nor the Hamburg Rules provide the traditional wording of the non-derogation provision found in the Hague and Hague-Visby Rules. They explicitly prohibit both direct and indirect derogation from the mandatory provisions therein.[187] The non-derogation provision in Article 79 of the Rotterdam Rules invalidates any term *to the extent that* (a) it directly or indirectly excludes, limits and increases the obligations and liabilities of the shipper, consignee, controlling party, holder or documentary shipper or (b) it directly or indirectly excludes or limits the obligations and liabilities of the carrier and maritime performing party. There is another reason why the non-derogation provision in the Rotterdam Rules would appear to bite against a wider range of provisions in contracts of carriage than the Hague and Hague-Visby Rules: Article III(8) of the Hague and Hague-Visby Rules invalidates only those provisions which have the effect of lessening or removing the carrier's liability *for loss or damage to, or in connection with goods arising from negligence, fault, or failure in the duties and obligations provided.* On the other hand, the non-derogation clause in the Rotterdam Rules invalidates any provision which has either the direct or indirect effect of lessening and removing *any obligations and liabilities of the carrier* under the Rules.[188]

Turning back to the discussions on the non-derogation provisions under the Hague and Hague-Visby Rules, it is important to highlight their effects on the validity of other carriage terms. It is clear in both jurisdictions that the non-derogation provisions also invalidate clauses purporting to exclude liability of carriers for failing to exercise due diligence in making the vessel seaworthy before and at the beginning of the voyage[189] and/or for damages arising from their reckless acts or omissions or from their wilful misconduct.[190] It is possible that the application of seemingly non-offending clauses could also have the effect of removing or lessening carriers' liability. This raises the question of whether those clauses which indirectly lessen the carriers' liability can be invalidated by the non-derogation provisions. In this respect, the question of whether the non-derogation provisions invalidate forum selection clauses has been hotly disputed in courts and

[187] See Art 23 of the Hamburg Rules and Art 79 of the Rotterdam Rules. It can be argued that by introducing the word 'indirect', the Rotterdam Rules leave the door open for the courts to invalidate a foreign forum selection clause whose application may indirectly lessen carriers' liability.

[188] It must be noted that the non-derogation provision has this wide application in cases where the conditions for the volume contract exception do not find room for application. The derogations which satisfy the formal requirements set out in Art 80 and which are contained in a volume contract as described in the same Article are not subject to Art 79. What the parties cannot derogate from, even in the context of volume contracts, is the so-called 'super-mandatory provisions' listed in Art 80(4). With the super-mandatory provisions talking of the obligations of both carriers and shippers, the duality approach also appears here.

[189] Regarding the obligations of carriers as to seaworthiness, see Art IV(1) for English law, and see 46 USC §30701(4)1 for US law.

[190] See Art IV(5)(e) of the Hague-Visby Rules and 46 USC §30701(4)/2(q).

tribunals. It has become common practice for holders to object to the validity of these clauses by arguing that their application results in lessening carriers' liability. A similar argument has also been raised with respect to the clauses purporting to delegate carriers' duties to load, stow, trim and discharge the cargo to the shippers/charterers/consignees. In the following subsections, the question of whether these particular types of clause run counter to the non-derogation provisions, namely Article III(8) of the Hague-Visby Rules and section 3(8) of the 1936 Act, will be analysed.

C. Validity of Incorporated Forum Selection Clauses under the Rules

It has always been the intention of parties to be able to refer their disputes to the court or tribunal that they consider to be the most beneficial and convenient. Since the eighteenth century, carriers have been introducing forum selection clauses into bills of lading either expressly or by way of incorporation. Inasmuch as third-party bill of lading holders play no role in the formation of carriage terms in bills of lading, the forum selection clauses therein are usually treated as exclusively beneficial to carriers. Unsurprisingly, application of these provisions against the holders has provoked criticism, especially in countries where the cargo interests prevail. Such countries have treated these clauses as a tool to circumvent their mandatory rules and policies.[191] On the other hand, in countries where the shipowners' interests prevail, the forum selection clauses are regarded as merely the exigencies of freedom of contract.[192]

Leaving aside these conflicting views, it is true to say that the forum designated in the forum selection clause generally comes as a surprise to the holder, when this clause becomes part of the bill of lading by way of incorporation. In particular, it becomes a rather unwelcome surprise for the holder where the chosen forum seems to give him or her less protection than other available jurisdictions. With a view to avoiding the charterparty forum selection clause that the bill of lading seeks to incorporate, the holder may attack the clause by relying on the rules of incorporation. However, where the forum selection clause overcomes all the hurdles of incorporation, or where they are expressly stipulated in the bill of lading, could the non-derogation provisions invalidate the clause?

In a great number of cases, the holders have sought to invalidate forum selection clauses in bills of lading by raising the argument that these clauses lessen carriers' liability contrary to the applicable non-derogatory provision.[193] Alternatively, they have attempted to render such clauses ineffective by invoking the rules of *forum non conveniens*, applicable in the jurisdiction where the proceedings have

[191] *See Indussa Corporation v SS Ranborg* 377 F 2d 200 (2d Cir 1967).
[192] O'Hare (n 81) 219–20.
[193] See *Organes Enterprises Inc v M/V Khalij Frost* F Supp 1989 AMC 1460 (SDNY 1989).

been brought. To address these issues, we will initially examine the extent to which these or similar grounds are sufficient to defeat forum selection clauses in bills of lading. We will then discuss enforceability of forum selection clauses under the Hamburg Rules, the Rotterdam Rules and the US COGSA Draft Instrument. Following the observations on these issues, we will discuss the future of forum selection clauses in the context of bills of lading.

i. Could Article III(8) Invalidate Forum Selection Clauses?

Due to the previously outlined historical reasons, the early US judicial decisions demonstrated a persistent hostility towards forum selection clauses,[194] which remained dominant under US law for a long time.[195] On the other hand, the English approach to forum selection clauses has always been more liberal and receptive. Given that the Hague Rules and the Hague-Visby Rules do not address the validity of forum selection clauses, it is left to contracting states to decide whether to enforce or invalidate foreign arbitration and jurisdiction clauses in bills of lading. Although both sets of rules are silent on this matter, whether forum selection clauses lessen the liability of carriers contrary to the non-derogation provisions has frequently come into question in cargo claims under bills of lading.

With the leading decision in *William H Muller & Co v Swedish American Line Ltd*,[196] US courts took a firm stand in favour of enforcing forum selection clauses in bills of lading. There, the Court refused to hold that enforcement of foreign forum selection clauses would directly result in exonerating carriers from liability.[197] Hence, considering that the dispute was closely connected to Sweden, and the Swedish courts would afford the same protection to cargo interests as US courts, the Court gave effect to the jurisdiction clause designating the courts of Sweden.[198] However, this liberal view was later abandoned and was taken over by an intensified territorial approach with the decision in *Indussa Corporation*

[194] See Denning (n 85) 17; Delaume, 'Shorter Articles and Comment: Choice of Forum Clauses and the American Forum Patriae: Something Happened on the Way to the Forum: Zapata and Silver' (1972–1973) 4 *Journal of Maritime Law and Commerce* 295.

[195] See *Bremen v Zapata Off-Shore Co* 1972 AMC 1407 (US 1972).

[196] *William H Muller & Co v Swedish American Line Ltd* 1955 AMC 1687 (2d Cir 1955). In this context, *Bremen v Zapata Off-Shore Co* 1972 AMC 1407 (US 1972) is illustrative, since the Court upheld the foreign jurisdiction clause designating the courts of England under a towing contract made between an American drilling rig owner and a German towing company. The Court found no reason to obstruct the parties' intention to refer the dispute before the courts of England pursuant to a 'freely negotiated' contract.

[197] See *William H Muller & Co v Swedish American Line Ltd* 1955 AMC 1687 (2d Cir 1955).

[198] Relying on the principles of *forum non conveniens*, the Court founded its decision on two headings. First, all evidence was available in Sweden, given that the cargo was shipped in Sweden, the vessel and its owner were Swedish, and the crew was residing in Sweden. Secondly, by anticipating the possible outcome of the dispute brought before the Swedish courts, the Court found that the substantial rights of the cargo interests would not be adversely affected. On this basis, the Court held that the jurisdiction agreement was 'reasonable' and should be given effect. See ibid, at 1690. See Denning (n 85) 28.

v SS Ranborg.[199] Overruling the *Muller* decision, the Court therein accepted the holder's argument that foreign jurisdiction clauses must be struck down by section 3(8) of the 1936 Act.[200] There were two main reasons for the decision. First, the Court held that the dispute was to be litigated in the United States because the 1936 Act applied to the bill of lading by force of law.[201] Secondly, the Court viewed the forum selection clause as lessening the carrier's liability, regardless of the fact that the chosen country was a Hague state. In support of this second ground, the Court took the view that the courts of the chosen country might not apply the Rules in the same way as a US court would.[202]

In light of the ruling in the *Indussa* case and its progeny,[203] US courts thus restored the old traditional policy towards forum selection clauses. Given that there is a federal policy favouring arbitration under the Federal Arbitration Act 1925 ('the 1925 Act'),[204] which also governs arbitration agreements in bills of lading, the decision was, nevertheless, restricted to foreign jurisdiction clauses.[205] Despite this restriction, the *Indussa* approach was also adopted in those cases concerned with the enforcement of foreign arbitration clauses. Thus, in a great number of US judicial decisions, foreign arbitration clauses were also held to run counter to section 3(8) of the 1936 Act.[206]

However, the courts in some US judicial decisions exhibited a receptive approach to foreign arbitration clauses with a view to following federal policy favouring arbitration,[207] and these polarised decisions left the issue shrouded in uncertainty. Nevertheless, the battle against the territorial and non-territorial

[199] 377 F 2d 200 (2d Cir 1967). Before the ruling in *Indussa*, there were other bill of lading cases which ousted the application of foreign forum selection clauses, despite the decision in *Muller*. See, for instance, *Carbon Black Export Inc v The SS Monrosa* 1958 AMC 1335 (5th Cir 1958).

[200] See 377 F 2d 200, 203–4.

[201] ibid, at 203. In this context, giving effect to a foreign forum selection clause was stated to enable carriers to enforce provisions contrary to the 1936 Act.

[202] ibid, at 203–04. See also A Nakazawa and BA Moghaddam, 'COGSA and Choice of Foreign Law Clauses in Bills of Lading' (1992–1993) 17 *Tulane Maritime Law Journal* 1.

[203] See *Hughes Drilling Fluids v M/V Luo Fu Shan* 1988 AMC 2848 (5th Cir 1988); *Northern Assurance v M/V Caspian Career* 1977 AMC 421 (ND Cal 1977); *Conklin & Garrett Ltd v M/V Finnrose* 1988 AMC 318 (5th Cir 1987); *State Establishment for Agricultural Product Training v M/V Wesermunde* 1988 AMC 2328 (11th Cir 1988); *Siderius Inc v M/V Ida Prima* 613 F Supp 916 (SDNY 1985); *Organes Enterprises Inc v M/V Khalij Frost* 1989 AMC 1460 (SDNY 1989).

[204] See 9 USC §1. For federal policy favouring arbitration, see *Japan Sun Oil v M/V Maasdijk* 1995 AMC 726, 727 (EDLa 1994).

[205] See 1967 AMC 589 (2d Cir 1967).

[206] See *Conklin & Garret v M/V Finnrose* 1988 AMC 318 (5th Cir 1987); *Organes Enterprises Inc v M/V Khalij Frost* 1989 AMC 1460 (SDNY 1989); *Pacific Lumber & Shipping Company Inc v Star Shipping* 1980 AMC 2101 (9th Cir 1979) *cert denied in* 444 US 1017 (US 1980); *Siderius Inc v M/V Ida Prima* 613 F Supp 916 (SDNY 1985). See also *State Establishment for Agricultural Product Trading v M/V Wesermunde* 1988 AMC 2328 (11th Cir 1988), *cert denied in* 488 US 916 (US 1989), where the court disfavoured a foreign arbitration clause on the basis of s 3(8) of the 1936 Act. Despite the reference to the Act, the court's reasoning appears to be mainly founded on the principles of *forum non conveniens*.

[207] See *Japan Sun Oil Co Ltd v M/V Maasdijk* 1995 AMC 726 (EDLa 1994); *Citrus Marketing Board of Israel and Agrexco v M/V Ecuadorian Reefer* 1991 AMC 1042 (DMass 1990); *Kurt Orban Co v S/S Clymenia* 1971 AMC 778 (SDNY 1970); *Midland Tar Distillers, Inc v M/T Lotos* 1973 AMC 1924

approach finally ended with the decision in *Vimar Seguros y Reaseguros v M/V Sky Reefer*,[208] wherein a foreign arbitration clause incorporated into the bill of lading was upheld. In particular, the Court took the view that section 3(8) of the 1936 Act did not itself invalidate the foreign arbitration clause,[209] and the costs of litigation in the chosen foreign forum did not lessen the carriers' liability within the meaning of this section.[210] In so doing, they accepted that section 3(8) of the 1936 Act only invalidates carriage terms if they lessen any of those carriers' liabilities enumerated under section 3.[211] The upshot of this view was that section 3(8) was not a barrier to the enforcement of forum selection clauses, for they are not even regulated under the 1936 Act.[212] Therefore, the possible effects of a prospective decision given by the chosen forum were found to be not sufficient to trigger the non-derogation provision, which would, if applied, nullify the foreign arbitration clause.[213] In the wake of *The Sky Reefer*, it has become clear, on authority, that section 3(8) does not mechanically invalidate forum selection clauses. Moreover, even though *The Sky Reefer* was concerned with enforcement of a foreign arbitration clause, the ruling has been treated as equally applicable in the case of foreign jurisdiction clauses.[214]

However, it would be wrong to say that section 3(8) no longer affects the validity of foreign forum selection clauses after *The Sky Reefer*: the courts in New York are still relying on the non-derogation provision to oust these clauses, albeit in a different context. It is clear that the ruling in *The Sky Reefer* does not support the use of section 3(8) to invalidate foreign forum clauses by reason of a speculation that the law applicable under the chosen forum might lessen carriers' liability.[215] Nevertheless, the courts in New York have repeatedly taken the view that, if the substantive law to be applied by the chosen forum might lessen any of those carriers' liabilities under section 3 of the 1936 Act, the foreign selection clause must be null and void as per section 3(8).[216] Consequently, while these judicial decisions

(SDNY 1973); *Travelers Indemnity Co v M/V Mediterranean Star* F 1988 AMC 2483 (SDNY 1988); *Kaystone Chemical v Bow-Sun* 1989 AMC 2976 (SDNY 1989).

208 1995 AMC 1817 (US 1995).

209 See ibid, at 1826–27.

210 See ibid, at 1822.

211 See ibid, at 1826–27.

212 See ibid, at 1822. This view was then recognised in numerous cases. See, for instance, *Steel Warehouse Co v Abalone Shipping Ltd* 1998 AMC 2054 (5th Cir 1998); *Lucky Metals Corp v M/V Ave* F Supp 1996 AMC 265 (SDNY 1996); *Kanematsu Corp v M/V Gretchen W* 1995 AMC 2957 (D Oregon 1995); *Thyssen Inc v Calypso Shipping Corp SA* 2002 AMC 2332 (2d Cir 2002).

213 See 1995 AMC 1817, 1827 (US 1995).

214 See ibid, at 1821. See also *Mitsui & Co v M/V Mira* 1997 AMC 2126 (5th Cir 1997); *Hyundai Corp USA Inc v M/V An Long Jiang* 1998 AMC 854 (SDNY 1998), where the courts upheld the foreign jurisdiction clauses by reason of the ruling in *The Sky Reefer*. See also M Davies, 'Forum Selection Clauses in Maritime Cases' (2003) 27(2) *Tulane Maritime Law Journal* 367, 377.

215 See 1995 AMC 1817, 1827 (US 1995).

216 See *American Home Assurance Co v M/V Jaami* 2007 AMC 1461, 1466 (SDNY 2007); *Asoma Corp v M/V Southgate* 2000 AMC 399, 401 (SDNY 2000); *Chiyoda Fire & Marine Insurance Co of America v M/V Hundai Freedom* 1999 AMC 1603, 1605 (SDNY 1999); *New York Marine & General Ins Co v M/V Admiralengrancht* 1999 AMC 1647 (SDNY 1999); *Silgan Plastics Corp v M/V Nedlloyd*

demonstrate an intention to narrow the scope of application of *The Sky Reefer*, they fall into conflict with the reasoning adopted in the *Sky Reefer* decision.

Unlike US courts, English courts do not invalidate forum selection clauses as a direct result of having Article III(8) of the Hague-Visby Rules effective by force of law under bills of lading.[217] The reason for this is clear: forum selection clauses are believed to make only procedural differences in resolving the dispute, and they are thought to have no effect on the substantive rights of the parties to the contract of carriage.[218] These well-accepted views, however, could be misleading for those who are unaware of the decision in *The Hollandia*.[219] In that particular case, Article III(8) was applied to invalidate a clause which required that disputes be resolved under Dutch law, and exclusively before the courts of Amsterdam. The reasoning of the Court was that upholding the forum selection clause would result in carriers being subject to a lower amount of limitation than that provided under the Hague-Visby Rules. Thus, the Court refused to stay the action on the grounds that the courts of the Netherlands, which would apply the Hague Rules, would give the cargo interests a significantly lower amount for damages than the English courts.[220]

In the wake of *The Hollandia*, could it be said that Article III(8) necessarily overrides all foreign forum selection clauses, merely because they designate foreign courts or tribunals? As has been made clear in the decision itself, *The Hollandia* decision does not support mechanical invalidation of foreign forum selection clauses.[221] It suggests that the courts should forecast the possible outcome of the dispute when resolved in the selected forum.[222] Hence, the effect of *The Hollandia* is limited to those cases where the possible outcome of the dispute in the chosen forum has the effect of relieving the carrier of more liability than is allowed by the Hague-Visby Rules.[223] Another restriction to the application of *The Hollandia* decision was made in *The Benarty*.[224] There, the carriers were allowed to bring the dispute pursuant to the jurisdiction clause before the courts of Djakarta, where the Hague-Visby Rules would not be applied. The decision was based on two grounds. First, the Court was convinced that the carriers relinquished all of their rights under the laws of Indonesia, which might offend against Article III(8). Secondly, instead of resorting to the package or unit limitation, the carriers sought to limit their liability on the basis of the registered tonnage of the vessel under the

Holland 1998 AMC 2163 (SDNY 1998); *Glyphics Media Inc v MV Conti Singapore* 2003 AMC 667, 675 (SDNY 2003); *Central National-Gottesman Inc v MV Gertrude Oldendorff* 204 F Supp 2d 675, 682 (SDNY 2002). See also *Fireman's Fund v Cho Yang* 1998 AMC 583, 586 (9th Cir 1997).

[217] See O'Hare (n 81) 219, 226. See also, *The Merak* [1965] P 223, 259.

[218] See O'Hare (n 81) 219, 226.

[219] See [1982] 1 AC 565.

[220] See ibid, at 571. In this context, while under the Hague-Visby Rules the cargo interests would be entitled to about £250, the amount under the Hague Rules was around £11,000.

[221] ibid, at 574.

[222] ibid, at 575.

[223] ibid.

[224] *The Benarty* [1984] 2 Lloyd's Rep 244.

Commercial Code of Indonesia, which was permissible pursuant to Article VIII of the Hague-Visby Rules. The decision in *The Benarty* further suggested that the decision in *The Hollandia* was not a barrier towards enforcement of foreign forum selection clauses, where carriers relinquished their rights available in the chosen fora, which rights would offend against Article III(8).[225]

ii. The Effects of the Decisions in The Sky Reefer *and* The Hollandia

What are the effects of these decisions in the jurisdiction battle between carriers and cargo interests? As is clear from both decisions, express and incorporated forum selection clauses in bills of lading do not themselves offend against the non-derogation provisions. However, US and English courts are divided as to whether there are any exceptions to this proposition: the decision in *The Hollandia* suggests that Article III(8) could, in certain circumstances, invalidate a forum selection clause: although the clause that was invalidated by Article III(8) was an exclusive jurisdiction clause, Lord Diplock's reasoning for the decision was also targeted at arbitration clauses in bills of lading. The situation is quite the reverse under US law. Although the decision in *The Sky Reefer* was concerned with enforcement of a foreign arbitration clause, the ruling has been treated as equally applicable in the case of foreign jurisdiction clauses.

The decision in *The Hollandia*, which creates an exception to the cardinal rule that forum selection clauses are only procedural and must therefore be given effect, gives rise to a series of questions: with respect to invalidation of the law and forum selection clause, is this decision in line with Article 3(1) of Rome I,[226] the Regulation and the Recast Regulation? If the ruling in *The Hollandia* were to be applied to invalidate a foreign arbitration clause, would this be consistent with the Convention on the Recognition and Enforcement of Foreign Arbitral Awards?[227] Since the Hague and Hague-Visby Rules do not regulate the issues of arbitration and jurisdiction, is it proper to use Article III(8) to invalidate foreign forum selection clauses, or should this matter be decided under the rules of *forum non conveniens*?

The decision in *The Hollandia* is consistent with Rome I, given that the reasoning of the decision is based on the statutory force of the 1971 Act. When this is accepted, it must be recognised that the decision neatly falls into the exception of 'mandatory rules of the forum' under Article 9(2) of Rome I.[228] To put it another way, it is perfectly legitimate for an English court not to enforce the applicable law of the contract, determined by reference to Articles 3 and 4 of Rome I, where the Hague-Visby Rules apply mandatorily.

[225] See also Cooke et al (n 29) para 85.238.

[226] Regulation (EC) No 593/2008 of the European Parliament and of the Council of 17 June 2008 on the law applicable to contractual obligations ('Rome I').

[227] Hereinafter referred to as the New York Convention.

[228] To the same effect is Art 7(2) of the Rome Convention 1980.

On the question of whether the decision in *The Hollandia* is in accordance with the New York Convention, reference should first be made to Article II(3) of the Convention, which provides that:

> The court of a Contracting State, when seised of an action in a matter in respect of which the parties have made an agreement within the meaning of this article, shall, at the request of one of the parties, refer the parties to arbitration, unless it finds that the said agreement is null and void, inoperative or incapable of being performed.

Similarly, under section 9(4) of the Arbitration Act 1996 ('the 1996 Act'), an English court shall stay proceedings brought in breach of an arbitration agreement, unless the agreement is 'null and void, inoperative or incapable of being performed'. An arbitration agreement can be considered as null and void by reason of public policy. When this is considered together with the statutory force of the Hague-Visby Rules, the question is: should a court refuse to stay proceedings because the arbitration agreement is null and void, where the resolution of the dispute at the seat of the arbitration might offend Article III(8) of the Hague-Visby Rules due to the mandatory rules at the seat of the arbitration? Given the United Kingdom's obligation under the New York Convention to give effect to arbitration agreements, it would appear that the grounds for refusal to stay proceedings must be applied restrictively. This lends support to the argument that application of the decision in *The Hollandia* should not be extended to arbitration clauses in bills of lading.

However, it is not clear whether *The Hollandia* could prevail over Article 23 of the Regulation, which renders choice-of-court agreements exclusive where at least one of the parties is domiciled in a Member State and the jurisdiction of a Member State is chosen. The reason for this uncertainty is that there has not been any English or ECJ decision on whether the Judgments Regulation gives way to the Hague-Visby Rules by reason of Article 71 of the Judgments Regulation. The Article provides that the Regulation does not detract from application of the Conventions 'which in relation to particular matters, govern jurisdiction or the recognition or enforcement of judgments'. On its restrictive interpretation, Article 71 comes into play only in case of a Convention containing jurisdictional provisions. However, when the extensive reading of the Article is adopted, those Conventions having jurisdictional effects are also covered. Such an extensive reading surely brings the Hague-Visby Rules within the scope of the Article, particularly since the ruling in *The Hollandia* recognises the application of Article III(8) to choice-of-court agreements. On the question of whether a restrictive or extensive meaning must be given to Article 71 of the Judgments Regulation, for present purposes, suffice it to say that English scholars are divided.[229] On entry into force of the Recast Regulation, this position will be clarified. Given the operation

[229] See Cooke et al (n 29) para 85.15, where the author supports the extensive reading of Art 71. For a contrary view, see R Aikens et al, *Bills of Lading* (London, Informa Law by Routledge, 2006) para 10.50.

of Article 31(2) of the Recast Regulation, the decision in *The Hollandia* will not find any room for application: where an English court is faced with a jurisdiction clause designating the courts of another Member State, the chosen courts will in principle[230] have priority to determine the validity of the agreement.

Leaving aside its compatibility with the New York Convention and the European Legislation, the decision in *The Hollandia* unjustifiably extends the application of Article III(8) to cases pertaining to enforcement of forum selection clauses. It is common ground that the Hague and Hague-Visby Rules do not contain any provisions on jurisdiction because the contracting states sought to keep their own national rules applicable to the jurisdictional issues.[231] Thus, Article III(8) was introduced merely for the purposes of invalidating provisions that exonerate carriers from those liabilities that are defined under Article III of the Hague and Hague-Visby Rules.[232] Even if we assume that the scope of 'carriers' liability' is more extensive than that envisaged under Article III,[233] the wording of Article III(8) does not justify ruling out those clauses that are solely concerned with procedural rights of the parties to bills of lading.[234]

Furthermore, it is also hard to suggest that interpretation of Article III(8) should go so far as to invalidate bill of lading terms on the basis of the speculation that their application may in the future indirectly lessen carriers' liability.[235] Forum selection clauses do not have a direct impact on the substantial rights and obligations of the parties. Instead, these clauses envisage before which forum the parties wish to resolve their disputes arising thereunder. Therefore, no forum designated in forum selection clauses can be treated as exclusively beneficial to carriers or to cargo interests,[236] even though application of some of those rules applicable in that forum may have the effect of lessening or removing carriers' liability vis-à-vis the cargo interests. For this reason, the Court in *The Hollandia* was at pains to restrict the striking out of forum selection clauses by reason of Article III(8).

Under US law, the effect of section 3(8) on the question of enforcement of forum selection clauses has been considerably diminished after the courts' departure from the approach in *The Indussa*. However, the courts of New York still follow a similar approach to that adopted in *The Hollandia*. They therefore retain the power to invalidate foreign forum selection clauses where the substantive law to be applied by the foreign forum might relieve carriers of liability. On the whole,

230 See Art 31(1) of the Recast Regulation.

231 Cooke et al (n 29) para 85.9.

232 See *Vimar Seguros y Reaseguros SA v M/V Sky Reefer* 1995 AMC 1817, 1822 (US 1995). But see *The Jordan II* [2005] 1 Lloyd's Rep 57 (HL), where the Court refused to rely on the *travaux préparatoires* of the Hague-Visby Rules in resolving the dispute.

233 See *The Hollandia* [1983] 1 AC 565, 573 (HL) where it was stated that construction of the rules should be purposive rather than literal.

234 MF Sturley, 'Bill of Lading Choice of Forum Clauses: Comparisons between United States and English Law' [1992] *Lloyd's Maritime and Commercial Law Quarterly* 248, 258.

235 See *Vimar Seguros y Reaseguros SA v M/V Sky Reefer* 1995 AMC 1817, 1827 (US 1995).

236 See *The Makefjell* [1976] 2 Lloyd's Rep 29, 32.

the scope of application of section 3(8), as adopted by the New York courts, is somewhat narrower than that under English law: as will be recalled, a time-bar clause providing for less than a one-year period is generally taken not to offend section 3(8) of the 1936 Act.

As an alternative to non-derogation clauses, the holders may consider relying on the rule of *forum non conveniens* in order to avoid the forum designated in the forum selection clause.[237] Undoubtedly, this raises the question of whether the cargo interest in *The Hollandia* could have relied on the rule of *forum non conveniens* while seeking to circumvent the exclusive jurisdiction clause. Under US law, it is unlikely that cargo interests will be able to avail themselves of the rule of *forum non conveniens* in such cases, since the change in the substantive law is not of itself sufficient to trigger the rule.[238]

Given the absence of uniformity between the legal systems with respect to the rules governing bills of lading, this position may seem detrimental to the bill of lading holders. However, this view is misconceived in many respects. Since a great number of countries are now either Hague, Hague-Visby or Hamburg states, it is clear that the holders are afforded a certain degree of protection in various jurisdictions. Another important point to be made is that the rights of cargo interests are protected at any rate, even where English and US courts stay the proceedings in favour of the forum selection clause: those holders who believe that the dispute has been unfairly resolved, in the foreign forum designated in the forum selection clause, have the chance to seek relief from these courts.[239] Thus, the US Court in *The Sky Reefer* followed this approach when it stayed proceedings and retained the supervisory power for the benefit of the holder, while upholding the foreign arbitration clause.[240]

Under English law, those cargo interests who are in a similar position to that in *The Hollandia* could rely on the rule of *forum non conveniens* with a view to avoiding the forum selection clauses in bills of lading. Thus, an English court may refuse to enforce a forum selection clause on the grounds that the chosen forum is not appropriate for the trial of the action.[241] Pursuant to the rule of *forum non conveniens* under English law, English courts may not uphold a foreign forum selection clause where the legal system in the chosen forum is different *in material respects*.[242] Therefore, it is possible for cargo interests to oust the forum selection clause on the basis of this rule, since the dissimilarities between the limitations of carriers' liability in *The Hollandia* can be regarded as a difference in *material*

[237] Sturley (n 234) 248, 258.

[238] See *Piper Aircraft Co v Reyno* 454 US 235 (US 1981). See also *Travelers Indemnity Co v S/S Alca* 1989 AMC 1843, 1846–47 (SDNY 1989); *Maria Arlete az Borralho v Keydril Co* 1984 AMC 728 (5th Cir 1983).

[239] For English law, see also *The Sibi* [1998] 2 Lloyd's Rep 229.

[240] See 1995 AMC 1817, 1826 (US 1995).

[241] *Donohue v Armco* [2002] CLC 440 (HL).

[242] See *The Eleftheria* [1970] P 94, 99.

respects.[243] This also supports the argument that, had *The Hollandia* not been decided, English courts would have provided the same protections to the cargo interests with this rule.

However, the considerations of *forum non conveniens* cannot find room for application where the question of jurisdiction falls within the scope of the Regulation.[244] In principle, the same is also true in the context of the Recast Regulation. Where an English court has jurisdiction under the Recast Regulation pursuant to some particular jurisdictional grounds, other than Article 25,[245] and where the court of a non-EU Member State is the court first seised, different considerations will arise: the English court may exercise its discretion to stay proceedings in favour of the non-EU Member State court, where, inter alia, it is satisfied that a stay is necessary for the proper administration of justice.[246] An exclusive jurisdiction clause designating the courts of that non-EU Member State may constitute a good reason for the court to stay proceedings.[247] On the whole, it would appear that what is necessary for the proper administration of justice would entail similar considerations to those of *forum non conveniens.*[248]

iii. Enforcement of Forum Selection Clauses and the Doctrine of Forum Non Conveniens

Given that the non-derogation provisions under the 1971 Act and the 1936 Act do not automatically render the forum selection clauses invalid, the holders need to know when the rule of *forum non conveniens* can be used in order to bypass these clauses. In practice, the bill of lading holders usually become aware of the contractually designated forum only after the dispute, given that many forum selection clauses become part of the bill of lading by way of incorporation. Could it be said that this fact is, of itself, sufficient to trigger the rule of *forum non conveniens*?

Both English and US courts tend to give effect to what the original parties to the bill of lading have promised in their choice of forum clauses.[249] As with the position under English law, the exception to this proposition under US law is the rule of *forum non conveniens*. Pursuant to this rule, US courts may refuse to enforce a foreign forum selection clause which is considered to be 'unreasonable'.[250] Under English law, the court may refuse to enforce a forum selection clause where

[243] See Sturley (n 234) 259–60.
[244] Case C-281/02 *Owusu v Jackson* [2005] ECR I-1383; [2005] 1 Lloyd's Rep 452.
[245] See Arts 33(1) and 34(1) of the Recast Regulation.
[246] See Arts 33 and 34 of the Recast Regulation.
[247] See Recital 24 of the Recast Regulation.
[248] See Recitals 23 and 24 of the Recast Regulation.
[249] For US law, see *Bremen v Zapata Off-Shore Co* 407 US 1, 20 (US 1972). For English law, see *The Angelic Grace* [1995] 1 Lloyd's Rep 87; *Akai Pty Ltd v People's Insurance Co Ltd* [1998] 1 Lloyd's Rep 90.
[250] For US law, see generally 28 USC §1404, which governs the rules of *forum non conveniens.*

there is a 'strong reason' for not doing so.[251] In both jurisdictions there are some common factors that the courts consider for the purposes of the rule of *forum non conveniens*.

While not limited, the recognised factors for consideration are (1) ease of accessing evidence,[252] (2) expense and expedition of the litigation in the chosen forum,[253] (3) strength of the connection between the dispute and the chosen country,[254] (4) parties' actual willingness to bring the dispute to the chosen forum,[255] (5) recognition and enforcement of the judgment of the selected forum,[256] (6) fair trial[257] and (7) availability of remedies.[258] Although these are contributing factors to the evaluation of the courts,[259] there is no invariable test for the assessment of the appropriateness of the selected forum. Both English and US courts use wide discretion in determining whether the chosen forum would be appropriate for the trial of the action.[260] Thus, the presence of one or more of those highlighted factors does not necessarily lead the courts to hold that the forum so chosen is not 'appropriate'.[261] While in *The Eleftheria*[262] the time bar in the chosen forum was treated as a 'strong reason' for disturbance of the choice, the Court in *The Adolf Warksi* regarded this as a 'neutral factor.[263]

[251] See *Donohue v Armco* [2002] CLC 440, 449, per Lord Bingham. See also *The Eleftheria* [1970] P 94, 99.

[252] For US law, see *Piper Aircraft Co v Reyno* 454 US 235 (US 1981). See also *Travelers Indemnity Co v S/S Alca* 1989 AMC 1843, 1848 (SDNY 1989). For English law, see *Amin Rasheed Shipping Corporation v Kuwait Insurance Co* [1984] AC 50, 68, 72 (HL). See also *The Eleftheria* [1970] P 94, at 104, where it was emphasised that despite the difficulties in bringing all evidence to the selected forum, it may nevertheless be the intention of the parties to have the disputes resolved in that forum.

[253] For US law, see *Piper Aircraft Co v Reyno* 1982 AMC 214, 241 (US 1981). For English law, see *Amin Rasheed Shipping Corporation v Kuwait Insurance Co* [1984] AC 50, 68, 72 (HL) and *The Eleftheria* [1970] P 94.

[254] For English law, see *The Abidin Daver* [1984] AC 398, 415 (HL); *The Fehmarn* [1958] 1 WLR 159, 162. For US law, see *Travelers Indemnity Co v S/S Alca* 1989 AMC 1843, 1848 (SDNY 1989).

[255] For English law, see *The Eleftheria* [1970] P 94, 99 and for US law, see *Bremen v Zapata Off-Shore Co* 407 US 1, 12 (US 1972).

[256] For US law, see Sturley (n 234) 256 and for English law, see *The Eleftheria* [1970] P 94.

[257] For US law, see *CA Seguros Orinoco v Naviera Transpapel* 1988 AMC 1757, 1771 (1988 D Puerto Rico). For English law, see *The Eleftheria* [1970] P 94.

[258] For US law, see *AP Moller-Maersk v Ocean Express Miami* 2008 AMC 1236, 1251 (SDNY 2008). For English law, see *The El Amria* [1981] 2 Lloyd's Rep 119, 127. However, it must be noted that mere existence of 'a legitimate personal or juridical advantage' is not given any weight when deciding over the appropriateness of the available fora, see *The Abidin Daver* [1984] AC 398, 410 (HL).

[259] Under US law, the evaluation factors are divided into two headings, namely, 'private interest factors' and 'public interest factors', see *Monsanto International Sales Co v Hanjin Container Lines Ltd* 1991 AMC 2741, 2744 (SDNY 1991); *Gulf Oil Corporation v Gilbert* 330 US 501, 507–08 (US 1947). Also, see generally, Sturley (n 234) 257–60.

[260] For US law, see Sturley (n 234) 256. See also *Travelers Indemnity Co v S/S Alca* 1989 AMC 1843, 1848 (SDNY 1989). For English law, see *The Fehmarn* [1958] 1 WLR 159, 163–64.

[261] For US law, see *Piper Aircraft Co v Reyno* 1982 AMC 214, 241, 256 (US 1981), which supports the argument that a chosen forum which is unnecessarily burdensome and which has 'administrative and legal problems' will not be regarded as 'appropriate' for that purpose.

[262] See [1970] P 94, 99.

[263] See [1976] 1 Lloyd's Rep 107, 112–13. It is clear under English law that time bars could lead English courts to refuse to stay proceedings where it is proved that reasonable steps have been taken by the relevant party to suspend the running of time, see *The Blue Wave* [1982] 1 Lloyd's Rep 151.

In light of these explanations, two important conclusions can be drawn for those holders willing to set aside an incorporated forum selection clause in the bill of lading pursuant to the rule of *forum non conveniens*. First, the argument that they have neither negotiated nor seen the charterparty choice of forum clause is not, of itself, sufficient to render the chosen forum 'inappropriate'.[264] Secondly, where the holders prove that the law applicable in the chosen forum materially differs from English law in that they will not obtain justice in the designated foreign jurisdiction, English courts may refuse to enforce the forum selection clause.[265]

For the purposes of the assessment of 'unreasonable forum', US courts have consistently refused to take into account whether or not the chosen forum is less advantageous to the cargo interests than US jurisdiction.[266] Although the courts do not generally give specific account of the differences between the legal systems, they have found the chosen fora 'unreasonable' in cases where such fora deprive the cargo interests of those remedies that are available in US jurisdiction.[267] These observations raise one question: could the chosen forum be deemed 'unreasonable' merely because it imposes on carriers a considerably smaller amount of package or unit limitation than that provided under US law? Undoubtedly, the holders in such circumstances may feel that they have not been provided with any remedy at all. It may be possible for US courts to refuse to enforce a foreign forum selection clause in such cases, given that US courts have considerable discretion to assess the factors before them.

Having considered carriers' chances of enforcing foreign forum selection clauses in bills of lading, it must be concluded that US law is surprisingly more favourable to them than English law for two reasons.[268] First, under US law, the holders cannot avoid a forum selection clause by invoking section 3(8) of the 1936 Act. Secondly, it is in principle impermissible to rely on the rule of *forum non conveniens* when seeking to avoid a forum selection clause, in the case of a mere difference between US law and the law applicable in the chosen forum.

These observations raise two questions. First, is the United States, which has a long history of adopting a conservative approach to forum selection clauses, now satisfied with the legal position as it currently stands, or is a change of direction

Under US law, a time bar is not necessarily a factor for consideration, see *Nippon Express USA Inc v M/V Chang Jiang Bridge* 2008 AMC 1735 (SDNY 2007); *Travelers Indemnity Co v M/V Mediterranean Star* 1988 AMC 2483 (SDNY 1988).

264 For US law, see *Mitsui & Co v M/V Mira* 1997 AMC 2126 (5th Cir 1997); *Carnival Cruise Lines v Shute* 111 S Ct 1522, 1523 (US 1990). For English law see, generally, *The KH Enterprise* [1994] 2 AC 324.

265 See *Donohue v Armco* [2002] CLC 440, 449, per Lord Bingham (HL). See also *The Eleftheria* [1970] P 94, 99.

266 Sturley (n 234) 260.

267 See *Indemnity Insurance Company of North America v M/V Eastline Tianjin* 2008 AMC 716 (SDNY 2008); *AP Moller-Maersk v Ocean Express Miami* 2008 AMC 1236, 1251 (SDNY 2008).

268 See Sturley (n 234) 260.

being prepared? Secondly, will the approach in *The Hollandia* survive under English law?

iv. The Future of Forum Selection Clauses

a. English and US Perspectives

From the perspective of the American shipping industry, the solution reached in *The Sky Reefer* is perhaps unsatisfactory.[269] It would appear that the US Supreme Court in *The Sky Reefer* went against the grain in adopting an even more liberal view than the one adopted under English law, which has a long tradition of giving effect to foreign forum selection clauses. Somewhat surprisingly, US law currently stands out as more liberal than English law: while the US decision in *The Sky Reefer* has been considered as equally applicable to jurisdiction clauses, there is room, albeit rather limited, for English courts to invalidate such provisions by reason of *The Hollandia*.

It is evident that the objective of the Court in *The Sky Reefer* was to facilitate efficient flow and improvement of American business in the international arena.[270] The Court took the view that the mistrust of foreign fora should give way.[271] Nonetheless, introducing such a non-territorial approach in the context of bills of lading contracts has aroused criticism. The criticism largely emanates from the intention to provide additional layers of protection to the holders who seldom have any means of negotiating the terms of a bill of lading.[272]

To remove the undesirable effects of *The Sky Reefer*, the Maritime Law Association of the United States prepared the 'Draft COGSA', whereby the holders are given a wide range of optional fora to bring their claims.[273] Moreover, the Draft COGSA provides that bill of lading holders can alternatively commence arbitration or litigation in the United States, where any of the specified places are in the United States, regardless of the foreign forum selection clause.[274] With similar concerns, the courts of New York brought an exception to the application of *The Sky Reefer* for those cases where the substantive laws to be applied by the chosen forum lessen the carrier's liability.[275]

Under English law, the decision in *The Hollandia* may also look promising to a holder seeking to avoid a forum selection clause in the bill of lading. When invalidating the exclusive jurisdiction in the bill of lading by reason of Article III(8) of the Hague-Visby Rules, Lord Diplock's reasoning was also targeting arbitration clauses in bills of lading. Traditionally, English courts have always been

[269] See Tetley (n 124) 5.
[270] See 1995 AMC 1817, 1824 (US 1995).
[271] ibid.
[272] See MF Sturley, 'Proposed Amendments to the Carriage of Goods by Sea Act' (1996) 18 *Houston Journal of International Law* 609, 657–58.
[273] See s 7(i) of the Draft US COGSA.
[274] ibid.
[275] See n 216.

in favour of enforcement of forum selection clauses. For this reason, arbitration clauses in bills of lading have never actually been invalidated by reason of Article III(8). In fact, the scope of application of the decision in *The Hollandia* has been even more restricted. While it is arguable that decision in *The Hollandia* survives the Regulation, the decision will have no teeth to bite an 'Article 25-compliant' exclusive jurisdiction clause under the Recast Regulation. With the decision in *The Hollandia* losing its impact, the traditional pro-enforcement policy towards forum selection clauses is even more dominant under English law.

b. The Hamburg and Rotterdam Rules

However, the recent international movements demonstrate a rather conservative approach to forum selection clauses. First the Hamburg Rules and now the Rotterdam Rules, both of which are prepared within UNCITRAL, set high hurdles to the enforcement of these clauses.[276] Pursuant to the Hamburg Rules, it is at the option of the cargo claimant to refer the cargo dispute before the forum which is designated in the choice of forum clause. In this respect, the cargo claimants are permitted to choose any of those fora listed under Articles 21 and 22 thereof. Perhaps with a view to recognising freedom of contract to some extent, the Rotterdam Rules favour the middle ground. Hence, the rules provide a number of available fora to which the parties may bring their claims, while giving carriers the right to enforce forum selection clauses in only limited circumstances.

Before examining the Rotterdam Rules on jurisdiction and arbitration, it is important to note that the chapters on arbitration and jurisdiction only bind those contracting states which have made a declaration to that effect.[277] When the chapters are operative, cargo interests are entitled to institute court proceedings against carriers in any of the jurisdictions listed in Article 66. These include the competent courts situated in the domicile of the carrier and those designated in the exclusive jurisdiction agreements made between the respective shippers and carriers. Under Article 75, these parties also have the right to commence arbitration proceedings in the places identical to those provided in Article 66.

The main exception to the cargo interest's right to choose the forum arises in the case of a volume contract made between the shipper and carrier.[278] Accordingly, the Rotterdam Rules stipulate that the forum selection agreement contained in a volume contract is binding upon its original parties provided, inter alia, that the agreement is individually negotiated or the contract concluded between the parties contains a 'prominent statement' as to the existence of the agreement by specifying the relevant sections of the volume contract.[279] Application of these forum selection agreements to third parties is also recognised in limited cases where (1) the designated court or tribunal is situated in one of those places listed under the

[276] See chapters 14 and 15 of the Rotterdam Rules, and Arts 21 and 22 of the Hamburg Rules.

[277] See Arts 74 and 78 of the Rotterdam Rules.

[278] See Art 75(3) for arbitration agreements and Art 67(1)(a) for choice-of-court agreements.

[279] See Art 67(1)(a)–(b) for choice-of-court agreements and Art 75(3) for arbitration agreements.

rules,[280] (2) the agreement is expressly provided in the transport document—such as a bill of lading—or electronic transport record, and (3) the cargo interest is 'timely' and 'adequately' informed regarding the exclusivity of the clause and the place of the designated forum. In the case of arbitration agreements, the rules further require that enforcement of such agreements against third parties be permitted under the applicable law.[281] Similarly, where the volume contract contains an exclusive choice-of-court agreement, the rules also dictate that the court seised recognise application of the agreement to the third party.[282]

In the case of non-liner transportation, the rules considerably relieve carriers of the burden of having to satisfy a chain of conditions when they seek to enforce an arbitration clause that is incorporated from a charterparty, or a similar contract, into a transport document such as a bill of lading. According to Article 76(2), carriers may thus avoid the requirements stated above and enforce the charterparty arbitration clauses against the holders if (1) the parties to the charterparty and the date of its making are stated under the transport document and (2) the charterparty arbitration clause is expressly specified in the transport document.[283] Where the transport document does not have the required content, the arbitration agreement in that document will be subject to the conditions under Article 75.

Adopting an exceptional solution for non-liner transportation is best understood by the fact that exclusive jurisdiction clauses are popular in the liner trade, while arbitration clauses are frequently used in the non-liner trade.[284] In non-liner transportation, the contractual relationships between the carriers and cargo interests are usually governed by charterparties or similar contracts.[285] In liner trade, on the other hand, the contract of carriage is usually contained in bills of lading or a similar transport document, and parties in such cases do not usually have equal negotiating power.[286] Perhaps due to these differences, the Rotterdam Rules envisage stricter requirements in the case of liner transportation and adopt a liberal approach where there is non-liner transportation.

Despite the underlying reason behind this, treating the holders in non-liner transportation differently from those in liner transportation is not immune to criticism. If the carrier's right to enforce arbitration clauses in bills of lading needs to be curbed vis-à-vis the holders, then it is difficult to justify a holder in liner trade being 'protected' from an arbitration clause more than a holder in non-liner trade. One may expect that the position of the holder of the latter should raise more concerns: as has been said many times in this book, holders do not generally

[280] See Art 75(2) for arbitration agreements and Arts 67(2)(a) and 66(1) for choice-of-court agreements.

[281] See Art 75(4)(d).

[282] See Art 67(2)(d).

[283] See Art 76. The same rules apply also in cases where an electronic transport document is issued.

[284] See Sturley (n 123).

[285] ibid. Note that these agreements are also outside the scope of the Rotterdam Rules, see Art 6.

[286] ibid.

have any means of negotiating, or even knowing, the terms of the charterparty referred to in the bill of lading.

Furthermore, since the exception under Article 76(2) provides an expedient method for the enforcement of arbitration agreements in non-liner transportation, this may also lead to a change in shipping practice: arbitration agreements may become more prevalent than choice-of-court agreements in non-liner transportation.[287] For those parties who expect the Rotterdam Rules to set high hurdles to the application of forum selection clauses in bills of lading, such a shift in practice would perhaps be undesirable.

The conditions for the exclusivity of the forum selection clauses in volume contracts are equally open to criticism. In particular, the requirement that original parties to the volume contract must either negotiate the exclusive forum selection agreement contained in a volume contract or make a 'prominent' reference to such an agreement raises one practical difficulty: the decision on this matter will be bound up with the factual circumstances of the case, and this will surely reduce the predictability as to the application of the forum selection clause.[288]

A similar difficulty derives from the conditions for binding the third parties with the forum selection clauses in volume contracts. In both Articles 67(1)(c) and 75(4)(c), an 'adequate' and 'timely' notice is required to be given to the third parties against which the forum selection clause is invoked. Hence, the issue of the circumstances in which these parties will be deemed to have given such notice is again not clear, and the courts in various jurisdictions may certainly have different views on this matter.[289] While stipulating a number of rigid formalities for the choice-of-court agreements in volume contracts, Article 67 further states that these clauses are binding upon third parties only if the court seised recognises the binding effect: having experienced abusive litigation tactics due to the 'first-seised rule' under the Regulation, this requirement would appear to give rise to even more problems than it solves.

Above all, from the perspective of the countries that have a long tradition of enforcing forum selection clauses, the Rotterdam Rules could be criticised principally for restricting the applicability of these clauses to certain cases. From the standpoint of the cargo interest, however, this particular feature may well constitute a compelling reason to support the rules.

The discussions during the preparations of the Rotterdam Rules[290] have demonstrated, yet again, that these jurisdictional issues will in the future remain to attract debates in the international arena. The solutions suggested under the rules attest that there is an enduring historical scepticism surrounding forum selection clauses and there remains also a belief that these clauses can be used to circumvent

[287] See generally Sturley (n 123).

[288] For a similar view, see Y Baatz, 'Choice of Court Agreements' in Y Baatz et al, *The Rotterdam Rules: A Practical Annotation* (London, Informa Law by Routledge, 2009) para 67-12.

[289] ibid.

[290] See generally Sturley (n 123).

the rules favouring cargo interests. In assessing whether forum selection clauses should be enforced, it must be borne in mind that these clauses are vital for carriers, who run the risk of being sued in various jurisdictions.

It also proves valuable to consider that giving the cargo interests the option of choosing from a number of fora, the Rotterdam Rules may lead to multiple proceedings brought against the same carrier by several claimants in different jurisdictions. This could, evidently, result in conflicting judicial decisions over the same incident.[291] Are the Rotterdam Rules on jurisdiction and arbitration conducive to the harmonisation of legal systems and certainty? As the explanations above have shown, the current legal position under English law and US law appears to provide better solutions for the attainment of the specified objectives. Hence, in order to avoid parallel proceedings and uncertainty, a strong presumption favouring choice-of-forum agreements is more desirable than the restrictions under the Rotterdam Rules.

Only time will tell the extent to which forum selection clauses remain enforceable in this new era. Recent developments within the European Union have enhanced significantly the enforceability of forum selection clauses, although the pendulum would swing back if the Rotterdam Rules were to enter into force. Having examined the enforcement of forum selections clauses in bills of lading, the validity of FIOST and similar clauses will now be discussed.

D. Validity of Carrier's Terms on Loading and Discharge of the Cargo

It is not uncommon to see charterparty clauses whereby shipowners transfer the responsibility for loading and discharge operations, including the expenses arising therefrom, to their respective charterers. Equally common is that these 'liability and expense sharing agreements' are introduced into charterparties with the use of acronyms such as FIO, FIOS, FIOST and FILO.[292] When shipowners shift their

[291] For a similar view, see *Carnival Cruise Lines Inc v Shute* 499 US 585, 594–95 (US 1991).

[292] FIO clauses, which are also referred to as 'FIFO', represent the shorthand form of 'free in and (free) out'. In introducing these clauses into the charterparty, shipowners purport to transfer the duty to load and discharge the cargo and the costs arising therefrom to the charterers, see *Atlas Assurance Ltd v Sterling International* 1975 AMC 2358 (9th Cir 1975). In the case of FIOS clauses, shipowners seek to relieve themselves of the duties and costs with respect to, inter alia, stowage of the cargo, whereas FIOST clauses purport to relieve shipowners, inter alia, of the operations and expenses of trimming the cargo. See *Jindal Iron and Steel Co Ltd v Islamic Solidarity Shipping Co* [2005] 1 WLR 1363 (HL); *The Jordan II* [2002] EWHC 1268 (Comm) para 16; *Sigri Carbon Corp v Lykes Brothers Steamship Co Inc* 1988 AMC 1787 (WDKy 1987). Pursuant to 'FILO' clauses, which stands for 'free in liner out', shipowners assume only the costs and responsibility for discharge of the cargo but not for loading the same. See *Sumitomo Corporation of America v M/V Sie Kim* 1987 AMC 160, 170 (SDNY 1985). It must be borne in mind that the terms of loading, stowage, trimming and discharge of the cargo depend exclusively on the wording of the provision. Thus, it can be concluded that fiost and similar clauses relieve shipowners at least of the costs of such operations, and it depends on the lan-

responsibilities for carrying out these operations to charterers, they also seek to relieve themselves of liabilities for these operations vis-à-vis the bill of lading holders. To achieve this purpose, carriers purport to make these charterparty clauses part of bills of lading by way of incorporation. It can seem justifiable to allow carriers to relieve themselves of responsibilities arising from the operations that they have not carried out. Nevertheless, one may naturally take the view that the shipowner who is also the carrier under the bill of lading must assume responsibility vis-à-vis the holder for these operations even in the case of a FIOST or a similar clause. Where the carrier is subject to a liability to the holder due to these operations, as the shipowner, he/she will be able to look to the charterer for indemnity. From the holder's perspective, looking to the charterer for remedy is eminently problematic in cases where they hold a shipowner's bill of lading.

This position raises the question of whether these parties have any chance of avoiding application of these provisions under the bill of lading. Undoubtedly, holders can rely on the rules of incorporation, where a FIOST or a similar charterparty provision is sought to be incorporated into the bill of lading through an incorporation clause. If the clause has restrictive language, which purports to shift the liability for discharge and loading operations of the cargo exclusively to the charterer, it is likely that it will not, in both jurisdictions, be applied *mutatis mutandis* to the bill of lading holders.[293] Nor will it be applicable where the bill of lading contains an express provision stipulating that shipowners assume responsibility for the performance of these operations.[294]

Where such a charterparty clause overcomes these hurdles of incorporation, could it be said that it is valid under a bill of lading governed by either the Hague or the Hague-Visby Rules? The answer to this question boils down to whether the clause is contrary to Article III(2),[295] which provides that 'the carrier shall properly and carefully load, handle, carry, keep, care for, and discharge the goods carried'. To conclude that there is a conflict would not, however, put the matter to rest. The further question would be: are these specified duties of carriers 'non-delegable'? An affirmative answer to this question would render the clause null and void by reason of Article III(8).[296]

Nevertheless, in order to arrive at such a conclusion, it is important to find the answers to some pivotal questions. Do the FIOST or similar clauses transfer only the costs and the duties with respect to these operations, or do they also transfer the responsibility for the operations? Can the shipowner who is also the carrier under the bill of lading narrow down the scope of his or her responsibility vis-à-vis

guage of the clause as to whether shipowners could also transfer the responsibility to the charterers. See *The Jordan II*, paras 15 and 16.

[293] See Chapter 3.

[294] ibid.

[295] Under US law, the Article is shown as 46 USC s 30701(3)/2.

[296] These or similar arguments have been raised in both jurisdictions in numerous cases. As an example, see *Associated Metals & Minerals Corp v M/V Arktis Sky* 1993 AMC 509 (2d Cir 1992).

the bill of lading holders? In other words, can the 'tackle-to-tackle rule', which is adopted in both jurisdictions, be tampered with to the detriment of the holder?

Under English law, the answer to these questions is centred on the House of Lords decision in *The Jordan II*.[297] The case was concerned with the responsibility of the shipowner vis-à-vis the shippers, cargo receivers and the voyage charterers for damage to the cargo. The damage occurred during loading and discharging operations, which were assumed by the charterer pursuant to the FIOST clause. It was not disputed that the charterparty FIOST clause was incorporated into the bill of lading. As the provision contained extensive language, which also embraced the cargo receiver,[298] the question of manipulation did not arise. For this reason, to avoid the application of the FIOST clause, the cargo interests contended that the clause was contrary to Article III(2) and was therefore invalid.

For the purposes of resolving the dispute, the decisive question was whether Article III(8) could override a FIOST clause that purported to transfer the liability of the shipowner under Article III(2). Holding against the cargo interests, the Court took the view that FIOST and similar clauses are not invalid under the Hague and the Hague-Visby Rules. In so doing, they took the view that Article III(2) did not oblige carriers to perform those duties.[299] Rather, the Article was said to make it compulsory for carriers to pursue these duties when they contractually assume the performance of these operations.

This judgment for the shipowners rested on two well-established decisions, one of which is *Pyrene Co v Scindia Navigation Co*.[300] On the interpretation of Article III(2), Devlin J in the latter case said *obiter*:

> Their [the Hague Rules] object … is to define not the scope of the contract service but the terms on which that service is to be performed … On this view the whole contract of carriage is subject to the rules, but the extent to which loading and discharging are brought within the carrier's obligation is left to the parties themselves to decide.[301]

This reasoning was later endorsed by the Court in *GH Renton & Co Ltd v Palmyra Trading Co*.[302] On the question of why these two decisions actually led the Court in *The Jordan II* to reach such a conclusion, it is important to look at the facts of these cases.

In the *Pyrene* case Devlin J was asked to decide whether or not the Hague Rules should be extended to cover the period commencing at the time when the ship's tackle is hooked onto the cargo.[303] On holding that the carrier's service could cover the tackle-to-tackle period, Devlin J used the reasoning that the carrier is free to define 'the terms on which that service is to be performed'. As is clear

[297] See *Jindal Iron & Steel Co Ltd v Islamic Solidarity Shipping Co* [2005] 1 WLR 1363 (HL).

[298] The clause provided that 'Shippers/Charterers/Receivers to put the cargo on board, trim and discharge cargo free of expense of the vessel'. See ibid, at 1336.

[299] See ibid, at 1370–71.

[300] *Pyrene Co v Scindia Navigation Co* [1954] 2 QB 402.

[301] See ibid, at 418.

[302] *GH Renton & Co Ltd v Palmyra Trading Co* [1957] AC 149, 170 (HL).

[303] [1954] 2 QB 402.

from these observations, Devlin J used this somewhat wide reasoning in order to impose on the carrier an extensive period of responsibility.[304] For this reason, the Court in *The Jordan II* could perhaps have refused the shipowners reliance on this reasoning to support the validity of the FIOST clause—which, in essence, narrows down the scope of responsibility of the carrier.

In *GH Renton & Co Ltd v Palmyra Trading Co*,[305] the question was whether changing the discharge port pursuant to a strike clause in a bill of lading was in accordance with the 'proper carriage of the goods' within the meaning of Article III(2). The strike clause giving the carrier the liberty to discharge the cargo at a port other than the contractual port of discharge was held not to offend Article III(8) for two reasons. The first reason was that Article III(2) had no geographical connotation. As the second reason, the Court took the view that Article III(2) required the carrier to perform properly and carefully only those obligations which he had agreed to perform, approving the *dictum* of Devlin J in the *Pyrene* case. As is clear from these facts, it was actually open to the Court in *The Jordan II* to distinguish this case: in essence, the *Renton* decision was concerned about the carrier's scope of responsibility in 'geographical terms' not in terms of his or her scope of responsibility for loading and discharge operations.

Nonetheless, the conclusion reached in *The Jordan II* was that FIOST and similar clauses did not offend Article III(8) and that the carrier was obliged to perform properly and carefully those obligations which he/she had agreed to perform. On the other side of the Atlantic, US courts take a diametrically opposed approach: the carrier's responsibilities under Article III(2) are 'non-delegable'.[306] This is irrespective of the fact that these operations are neither carried out by the carrier's employees nor handled by those stevedores engaged and/or controlled by carriers.[307]

Consequently, a provision seeking to transfer the responsibility for loading and discharge operations to charterers, shippers and/or cargo recipients is caught by Article III(8) and is treated as of no effect on the responsibility of carriers to bill

[304] Treitel and Reynolds (n 8) para 9-125.

[305] [1957] AC 149.

[306] See *Associated Metals & Minerals v M/V Arktis Sky* 1993 AMC 509, 513 (2d Cir 1992). See also *Continental Grain Company v Puerto Rico Maritime Shipping Authority* 972 F 2d 426, 430 (1st Cir 1993); *Great American Insurance v M/V Handy Laker* 2003 AMC 116, 137 (SDNY 2002); *Demsey & Associates Inc v S/S Sea Star* 1972 AMC 1440 (2d Cir 1972). However, it should be noted that there are also some district court decisions that declined to follow the decision in *The Arktis Sky*, see *Sigri Carbon Corp v Lykes Brothers SS Co* 1988 AMC 1787 (WDKy 1987); *Sumitomo Corporations of America v M/V Sie Kim* 1987 AMC 160 (SDNY 1985). Similar to the decision in *The Jordan II*, the Court in the latter case allowed carriers to limit the service they provide under the contract of carriage.

[307] See *Associated Metals & Minerals v M/V Arktis Sky* 1993 AMC 509, 513 (2d Cir 1992). Consequently, if the operations are handled by shippers, cargo interests, charterers or their agents, shipowners will still retain the overall responsibility for the operations under s 3(2) of the 1936 Act. *Nichimen Company Inc v M/V Farland and A/S Vigra* 1972 AMC 1573, 1587–88 (2d Cir 1972); *Tubacex Incorporation v M7V Risan* 1995 AMC 1305, 1309 (5th Cir 1995). Likewise, the position will be not different where the stevedores are arranged and controlled by any of these specified parties. See also *Stemcor USA Inc v M/V Archimedes* 2004 AMC 1651 (SNDY 2004).

of lading holders.[308] This raises the question of whether carriers can avoid liability for damage to cargo sustained during loading, stowing and discharge of the cargo, the duties under Article III(2) being non-delegable. Article III(2) is interpreted in such a way as to hold carriers prima facie liable for such damages.[309] As such, carriers are able to avoid liability, if they can bring themselves within one of the exceptions stated under Article IV(2).[310] Where, for instance, the cargo loss or damage was caused due to any act or omission on the part of the shipper, cargo owner or their agents or representatives or was caused without the actual fault or privity of the carrier, or without the actual fault or neglect of his or her agents or servants, the carrier will thus be able to avoid liability for such damage.[311]

It would appear justifiable to give effect to FIOST and similar clauses in cases where charterers seek to load a special cargo on the vessel.[312] The transfer of responsibility under a FIOST or a similar clause can further be justified on the grounds that it does not release carriers from liability arising from their own act or omissions. In essence, a FIOST or a similar clause only releases the carrier from responsibility for duties that they have not undertaken to perform, not for those services that they have assumed.

The difficulty with the FIOST and similar clauses can be understood when the effects of these clauses on bill of lading holders are considered. Against the carrier, the holder is generally left without any remedy for loss of or damage to cargo, if the carrier can prove that the cargo was lost or damaged during an operation for which he/she was not contractually responsible. Where, for instance, a cargo is damaged during stowage, over which a subsequent bill of lading holder has no control, a FIOST clause will make it much easier for the carrier to avoid liability, given the narrow confines of the catalogue of exceptions under Article IV(2).

If these clauses can be struck down by Article III(8), this will greatly improve the position of the holders, for they will be able to establish a prima facie case against carriers for loss or damage to the cargo caused during those operations. For these reasons, the rule established under *The Arktis Sky* is perhaps preferable: it provides a better solution for holders, whose reliance on bills of lading should be protected. Nonetheless, the recent international movements for unification of laws under bills of lading are in the direction of exempting carriers from liability for loading and discharge operations under FIOST and similar clauses. This is best illustrated by Article 13(2) of the Rotterdam Rules, which adopts a similar approach to that in the decision in *The Jordan II*.

[308] See *Associated Metals & Minerals v M/V Arktis Sky* 1993 AMC 509, 513 (2d Cir 1992).

[309] See ibid, at 514.

[310] ibid.

[311] In *The Arktis Sky* the carrier could not rely on the exemption clause under s 4(2)(q) and 4(2)(i) inter alia because the lashing statement signed by the vessel's chief mate contained a notation that the goods were stowed satisfactorily, and the operations were carried out under the control of the master. See s 4(2)(q) of the 1936 Act. For the assessments made under s 4(2)i and 4(2)q, see also *Yasuda Fire & Marine Insurance Co v M/V Tribels* 2000 AMC 2606 (EDLa 2000); *Thyssen Inc v Nobility M/V* 2005 AMC 2067 (5th Cir 2005).

[312] See CD Keedy, 'Maritime Law And Practice' (Tallahassee, Fla, Florida Bar, Continuing Legal Education, 2004) A [§6.17].

III. Final Remarks on the Consistency Test

On the whole, the rule of consistency puts a serious strain on the carrier's ability to invoke the incorporated charterparty provisions against the bill of lading holders. It protects the holder's rights arising from the express bill of lading terms, as well as from the Hague, the Hague-Visby and the Hamburg Rules, any of which could be operative under the bill of lading. Consequently, from the standpoint of the holders, this rule is an effective weapon to deploy when seeking to jettison the incorporated charterparty terms from bills of lading.

On the future of forum selection clauses in bills of lading, one may think that the promulgation of the Rotterdam Rules is a serious step towards weakening the effectiveness of forum selection clauses. In fact the potential effect of the Rotterdam Rules on enforcement of forum selection clauses is illusory: given that the chapters on arbitration and jurisdiction in the Rotterdam Rules can hardly be met with a universal approach, these chapters are made optional in order to permit states to ratify the Rotterdam Rules without them. The recent developments within the European Union further show that the pendulum has in fact swung back in favour of forum selection clauses: effectiveness of arbitration and jurisdiction clauses has now been enhanced with the Recast Regulation.

On the validity of FIOST and similar clauses in bills of lading, it would appear that the US and English approaches are diametrically opposed to each other. As is clear from the observations, what now appears to be the legal position under English law is the result of the reasoning of Devlin J in the *Pyrene* case that it is for the carrier to define the terms on which the carriage is to be performed. Initially this reasoning was used to extend the carrier's scope of responsibility. Following the *Pyrene* case, the use of this reasoning was stretched to strike clauses and recently to FIOST clauses. This raises the question of how far the courts can stretch the use of this reasoning. Can it be used in favour of a transhipment clause purporting to relieve the carrier of liability for loss of or damage to cargo during and/or after their transhipment? What are, if any, the limits to the carrier's freedom to define terms of the carriage?

From an overall perspective, could it be said that the rules of incorporation redress the balance between the competing interests of the bill of lading holders and the carriers? Or do they simply fail to do so by overburdening the issue with an excess of technical considerations? An examination of English and US judicial decisions with respect to this issue shows a number of grounds for defeating an undesirable charterparty provision that has been incorporated into the bill of lading through the words of incorporation. The arguments made so far support the view that the rule of consistency entails not mechanical but intelligent considerations.

Conclusion

The incorporation clauses in bills of lading have a long history in international carriage of goods by sea, and they remain prevalent without being strictly peculiar to a particular trade. The wide use of these clauses is best understood against the background of ongoing practice: when the vessel is under a charterparty, shipowners will wish to be well positioned both against their respective charterers and their third-party cargo interests, who hold the bill of lading as their contracts of carriage. This objective is of great importance to shipowners for two main reasons. Firstly, charterers naturally lose their interest in the cargo upon the submission of the bill of lading to third parties by virtue of their respective contracts of sale. Secondly, shipowners' most effective means of ensuring recovery of the charges under the charterparty will be the goods that they carry. In chartering the vessel to a seller or buyer who has undertaken to arrange carriage of the goods under the contract of sale, these parties understandably require that the bill of lading, issued under the charterparty, incorporates the provisions of the latter contract.

In light of the foregoing reasons, it is unsurprising to see that incorporation clauses are commonplace in bills of lading. However, through the eyes of bill of lading holders, this practice has been a cause for concern, inasmuch as they seldom have any means of knowing anything about the charterparty referred to. Perhaps with a view to mitigating the harsh consequences of incorporation, both US and English courts have been sensitive in their construction of these clauses and have determined the extent to which the charterparty referred to is applicable under bills of lading. As a result of this judicial sensitivity, the courts have developed a series of interlinked methods of construction, referred to in this book as the rules of incorporation.

This book has revealed that both English and US rules of incorporation are rooted in early judicial decisions, and there has been a persistent reluctance on the part of courts to depart from the rules in addressing the incorporation issue. The reason for this was crudely explained by the fact that definitive incorporation rules facilitate anticipation of carriage terms under bills of lading by commercial men, and this has the effect of increasing reliance on bills of lading, as well as promoting certainty in international trade. Despite this seemingly straightforward position, the book has underlined a number of complex areas that require clarification on account of their importance in shipping practice.

From the outset, the reader's attention was drawn to the fact that the English rules of incorporation are diametrically opposed to those recognised under US law in many respects. Due to the conflicting approaches taken on each side of the Atlantic, it was then emphasised that carriers and bill of lading holders first need to know what legal system is applied to the question of incorporation. Having set forth the general rule in both jurisdictions, that this issue is decided under the applicable law of the bill of lading, the book discussed the law governing the incorporation issue. Where the charterparty referred to contains an express or implied choice of law, the applicable law of the bill of lading cannot be determined with any degree of certainty before deciding whether the charterparty referred to in the bill of lading is incorporated. In order to ascertain under what law the incorporation issue must be addressed, US courts proceed upon the assumption that the charterparty is not incorporated, whereas English courts make a reverse assumption and ascertain the governing law as if the charterparty referred to were a part of the bill of lading. The logical shortcomings and the practical disadvantages of the two different modes of presumptive thinking were thoroughly analysed in the first chapter, and they will not be re-examined. For present purposes, suffice it to say that the question of conflict of laws adds an important practical dimension to the incorporation issue, which the parties must consider when choosing a forum for their claim.

Leaving aside the question of conflict of laws, the actual hurdles to incorporation emerge with the formalities that both the bill of lading and the charterparty to which it refers must satisfy for incorporation. In this respect, it is natural to think that the original parties to the bill of lading could only incorporate a pre-existing charterparty, which is specified in the incorporation clause, given that the holders are usually not in any way related to the charterparty referred to. It was seen in Chapter 2 that a similar line is taken under US law, and the incorporation clause which does not identify the charterparty in 'unmistakable' language is considered to have no force to incorporate where the holder is deemed to be a 'stranger' to the charterparty referred to. This line of thinking was criticised for creating variable carriage terms under bills of lading, which depend on the actual position of every holder. Given that the US rules of formality surrounding the charterparties referred to are also based on the status of the individual holders, these rules were also criticised on similar grounds. In light of these findings, Chapter 2 established one of the central premises of this book: to promote certainty in international trade, the holders' knowledge of the referred charterparty must not be taken into account in resolving the question of incorporation. On this basis, the well-rooted English rule, that the unqualified incorporation clause is not of itself fatal to incorporation, and those recognised presumptions for finding which charterparty is deemed to be incorporated, were applauded for providing straightforward and practical solutions to the problems involved in incorporation.

Even though both the bill of lading and the charterparty to which it refers may overcome the technicalities above, it is evident that the parties cannot be taken to have agreed any of the terms that are not clearly referred to in the bill of lading. Hence, in Chapter 3, the main focus was, essentially, on the construction of the incorporation wording in bills of lading. The examination of the English and US approaches demonstrated that these legal systems are divided on whether charterparty provisions that are ancillary to the subject matter of contracts of carriage, such as forum selection clauses, can be incorporated through general incorporation wording. There, it was stated that US courts do not require a specific reference to such charterparty provisions in bills of lading for the purposes of their incorporation, while the opposite is the case under English law. Considering the practical impacts of these differences, Chapter 3 suggested that the strict English requirement must be maintained on the grounds that the rule has been heavily relied on in practice. This proposition was also supported by the fact that making express reference to the ancillary contract terms gives the holders clear notice as to the intention of carriers to incorporate such provisions. Looking at recent decisions, it would appear that there is now a certain degree of flexibility in making specific reference to forum selection clauses for incorporation purposes: as long as the incorporation wording refers to one kind of dispute resolution, it can be read as extending to other types of dispute resolution clause in the charterparty.

Having identified the charterparty terms which can aptly be described through the words of incorporation, Chapter 3 went on to examine the extent to which the aptly described charterparty terms could be adapted to the bill of lading. In this respect, US and English rules of incorporation demonstrated how the courts, not 'mechanically' but rather 'ingeniously', decide in what circumstances the charterparty wording must be modified. Moreover, in this chapter it was highlighted that the incorporated charterparty clauses could, nevertheless, fall short of being applicable under bills of lading, given that the scope of every provision is limited to what it actually envisages.

In practice, parties to the charterparty frequently contemplate the form and content of the bill of lading to be issued thereunder, and, more often than not, they also stipulate what charterparty terms must be incorporated into such bills of lading. Regardless of the intention to incorporate, which can readily be discerned from the charterparty, these parties may simply not achieve this in the absence of appropriate incorporation wording in the bill of lading. In order to dispel doubts as to whether their intention could prevail over that of the original parties to the bill of lading, Chapter 4 explored the answer to one key question: are the charterparty terms or the respective incorporation clauses in bills of lading decisive in resolving the incorporation issue? The detailed examinations on this matter showed conflicting approaches between English and US courts: under English law, the incorporation clauses are conclusive in determining the scope of incorporation, while this 'bill-centric' approach is recognised under US law only in the case of a holder who is a 'stranger' to the charterparty referred to.

Through this analysis, Chapter 4 illustrated another key premise of this book: the incorporation clause must be the only driving force for incorporation, regardless of the actual position of the individual holder. From a practical perspective, this suggestion was justified on the basis of the fragile position of those holders who pay for bills of lading at their face value. At a conceptual level, it received support from the fact that the charterparty and bills of lading are distinct contracts made between different parties. On that basis, it was emphasised that bills of lading may not achieve incorporation simply as intended by the parties to the charterparty.

For those cargo interests who seek to thwart application of the incorporated charterparty terms, the final strategy to be employed is discussed in Chapter 5. There, the principal focus was on the question of consistency, which may arise between the express and incorporated bill of lading provisions. The judicial responses to such inconsistencies have repeatedly been to override any conflicting charterparty provision carried across to the bill of lading through the incorporation clause. Chapter 5 addressed this issue by analysing the consistency of various charterparty clauses, such as those relating to freight, lien, demurrage and forum selection, in the bill of lading context. In particular, a detailed examination was made of whether the incorporated charterparty terms could survive under bills of lading which are governed by the Hague, Hague-Visby or Hamburg Rules.

Since the early years, the incorporation issue has usually revealed itself as closely connected to disputes over jurisdiction. Hence, in many cases, carriers have sought to incorporate and enforce charterparty forum selection clauses against holders. As can be gleaned from the long history of US and English judicial decisions on this matter, the holders have frequently attempted to circumvent the chosen forum by alleging that forum selection clauses run counter to the non-derogation provision of the applicable Convention. Chapter 5 illustrated that such arguments do not in principle succeed under US law following the leading decision in *The Sky Reefer*, while English courts may invalidate a forum selection clause by reason of Article III(8) of the Hague-Visby Rules in very limited circumstances.

Perhaps due to the practical significance of forum selection clauses, bold steps are being taken to create uniform rules regulating their enforcement. The Rotterdam Rules have recently introduced a number of comprehensive provisions for this purpose. Nonetheless, it is unlikely that these attempts will receive the desired support, given that the Rotterdam Rules substantially curb carriers' rights to invoke forum selection clauses in bills of lading against the holders. With the Recast Regulation now appearing on the horizon, the effectiveness of forum selection clauses will no doubt be enhanced within the European Union. Given this recent trend in favour of forum selection clauses, the bill of lading holders must now be even more prepared to litigate or arbitrate pursuant to the carrier's forum selection clauses.

INDEX

Lightning Source UK Ltd.
Milton Keynes UK
UKOW05f0204190117
292343UK00001B/18/P